Conversations With

the Dead

The Grateful Dead Interview Book

DAVID GANS

CITADEL UN DERGROUND

A Citadel Press Book
Published by Carol Publishing Group

CITADEL UN | | DERGROUND

Carol Publishing Group Edition, 1995

A Citadel Press Book
Published by Carol Publishing Group
Citadel Press is a registered trademark of Carol Communications, Inc.

Editorial Offices: 600 Madison Avenue, New York, NY 10022
Sales & Distribution Offices: 120 Enterprise Avenue, Secaucus, NJ 07094
In Canada: Canadian Manda Group, One Atlantic Avenue, Suite 105
Toronto, Ontario, M6K 3E7

Queries regarding rights and permissions should be addressed to:
Carol Publishing Group, 600 Madison Avenue, New York, NY 10022

Manufactured in the United States of America
10 9 8 7 6 5 4 3

Carol Publishing Group books are available at special discounts
for bulk purchases, sales promotions, fund raising, or
educational purposes. Special editions can also be created to
specifications. For details contact: Special Sales Department,
Carol Publishing Group, 120 Enterprise Ave., Secaucus, NJ 07094

Library of Congress Cataloging-in-Publication Data

    Gans, David.
    Conversations with the Dead : the Grateful Dead interview book /
by David Gans.
        p.   cm.
    "A Citadel Press book."
    ISBN 0-8065-1223-7
    1. Grateful Dead (musical group)—Interviews. 2. Rock musicians–
United States—Interviews. I. Grateful Dead (Musical group)
II. Title.
ML421.G72G28   1991
782.42166'092'2—dc20
    [B]   91-22914
                                                              CIP
                                                              MN

Contents

Acknowledgments

This book would not exist were it not for Dan Levy's inspiration. It was Dan who created the Citadel Underground series and decided that *Conversations With the Dead* was an appropriate addition to the line. And he wouldn't have made that decision if he hadn't seen the full transcript of the 1981 Jerry Garcia interview; we have John Leopold to thank for that.

I am grateful to Blair Jackson not just for his permission to include the Garcia interview but for including me on that expedition in the first place, and for plenty of "help on the way."

The Grateful Dead publicists arranged for the interviews: the late Zohn Artman, Julie Milburn, Ren Grevatt, Rock Scully, and Dennis McNally. Eileen Law and Alan Trist of the Grateful Dead staff have been extremely supportive over the years, as have Annette Flowers, Nancy Mallonee, Maruska Nelson, Patricia Harris, Cassidy Law, Diane Geoppo, Frankie Accardi, John Cutler, Hal Kant (Legally Dead), and Steve Marcus. Thanks also to Dick Latvala for his generosity and his personal sacrifices.

For practical and philosophical assistance, I am thankful to Mary Eisenhart, Goldie Rush, Susan Weiner, Susan Dobra, Carolyn Jones, Marsha Dunbar, Bonnie Simmons, Joel Bernstein, Alan Mande, Fred Lieberman, Herbie Greene, Rebecca Adams, Regan McMahon, and Naomi Pearce. Much appreciation to the authors of *DeadBase:* Stu Nixon, John W. Scott and Miek Dolgushkin. Thanks also to Wavy Gravy, Bill Graham, Ken Kesey, David Crosby, Ned Lagin, and Carolyn Garcia—the one that got away—for interviews and insights.

I've learned a lot about Grateful Dead music through my adventures with my fellow musicians, especially Bob Nakamine, Tom Yacoe, Mike

Shaw, Alan Feldstein, Steve Horowitz, Gary Lambert, Henry Kaiser, Mark Crawford, Tom Constanten, and the Once a Year Band.

And, of course, the ones who did the talking (and the playing and singing and writing): Bob Weir, Jerry Garcia, John Barlow, Robert Hunter, Mickey Hart, Steve Parish, Dan Healy, Bear, Ram Rod, Bill Kreutzmann, the late Brent Mydland, Jill Johnson Lesh, and especially Phil Lesh. It's a privilege to work with you.

Foreword

I know they mean well most of the time. The "straight press," that is.

Here's how it works: The Grateful Dead are coming to town. The editor of the local paper's "Lifestyles" section sees kids wearing tie-dyes wandering around the downtown area, and notices dilapidated, bizarrely painted school buses taking up three and four metered parking spaces near his office.

"What's going on around here?" the editor asks at his department's regular Monday morning meeting. "Didn't this stuff die out in 1968? How come I can't find a parking space?"

"They're Deadheads," one reporter offers. "The Grateful Dead will be here in a couple of days."

"What? Are they still around? Didn't they die in a plane crash or something?"

"No, that was Lynyrd Skynryd. This could be a great story, chief. You know—sixties gypsies surviving in the nineties. The last vestiges of psychedelia. Flower children in the Age of Greed."

"Hmmm. Maybe you're on to something. OK, Shepherd, give me two thousand words. Schuster, get your camera and get me some pix of these weirdos. The stranger the better. We're talking page one of the Sunday section!"

Come Sunday, it's all there in black and white. Shepherd has interviewed an aging hippie named Moonstone, who's been following the Dead for twenty-three years. There are a few quotes from some inarticulate local high schoolers, and the obligatory comment from the head of security at the arena where the Dead played. "Sure, they look funny, but they seem to be pretty good kids by and large," he says. "We had more problems when AC/DC was in town." The photographer contributed a nice portrait of the young hippie family selling veggie burritos in the parking lot and a concert shot that ran with the accompanying review of the concert. "Graying guru Jerry Garcia: Grateful to still be playing," the caption read. The review itself, by a woman who two nights earlier had written about Whitney Houston's show in the same basketball arena, mentioned the ecstatic dancers gyrating to the Dead's mellow grooves, singled out the two Dylan covers she recognized, and complained for a whole paragraph about "aimless noodling" in the second half of the show.

Meanwhile, in the *next* city on the Dead's tour, an outraged editor shouts at no one in particular, "What's with those damn buses outside? What the *hell* is going on around this city?"

● ● ●

This is the view of the Grateful Dead that most of the world sees. Year in, year out, the scenario above is repeated in cities around the country. When the Dead went to Europe in the fall of 1990, we got to read the Swedish, German, French, and English versions of it all. Maybe it's coming soon to a newspaper near you. Except for rare occasions, even the rock press treats the story the same way—when they deign to write about the band at all.

It wasn't always like this. Throughout most of the seventies, almost nobody wrote about the Dead *at all*! The band's following wasn't as large and visible as it is today, of course, so there was no hook for mainstream newspaper editors. And most rock critics wrote the Dead off after *American Beauty* in 1970. The Dead were, after all, "a sixties band," the typically misinformed thinking went. On to the next trend!

Hey, I was willing to check out the new trends as much as the next guy—Oh, okay, this month it's twenty-five minute synthesizer solos?—but I never gave up on the Dead; rather, my interest in the band increased the more I saw them. And as I attended more concerts by other bands, the specialness of the Dead became even more apparent to me. I loved it all— the eclecticism of the music, the depth and mystery of the lyrics, the rapture of *the event*—and I loved the weird chemistry of the members of the Dead. I'd read some pretty hip profiles of the group in magazines like *Rolling Stone* and *Crawdaddy* during the late sixties and early seventies, and those articles reinforced my thinking that somehow these guys were tuned in to a wavelength I could *dig.*

By 1976, I was involved in rock journalism myself—in the Dead's own San Francisco Bay Area, no less—and I was determined to give the Dead the attention I thought they were due in the pages of *BAM*, a regional music rag where I was an editor. By the end of that year, I'd met a writer whose interest in the band matched my own, and whose knowledge of their music far exceeded mine. David Gans was a singer/songwriter type who wanted to break into journalism. The Grateful Dead was his favorite band; in fact, he was an accomplished guitarist who had studied both Jerry Garcia and Bob Weir while searching for a style of his own. You might say the Grateful Dead had infused his muse.

We became fast friends, and it wasn't long before David started working the Grateful Dead beat for *BAM*. We even had a regular column called "Dead Ahead" that was filled with news about the band. But it was when he landed superb interviews with Bob Weir and Robert Hunter in 1977 that it became clear that David really did bring a unique perspective to his writings on the Dead: Here was a thoroughly knowledgeable Deadhead who could *intelligently* discuss the Dead's music and lyrics with the band members. This was extremely rare then—and now, for that matter; the sociology of the Dead scene is still topic A with most interviewers, But there's *so much more* to it all.

I still have great fondness for the interviews David and I did with Garcia in the spring of 1981, which are printed in their most complete form ever in this book. There's no question that David's deep understanding of the mechanics of the Dead's music is what took Garcia on so many interesting paths in our discussions. It's nuts and bolts with *soul.*

In the years since then, David and I have traveled on parallel tracks through Grateful Dead country, working for similar ends in different media. Through his excellent book, *Playing in the Band*, and his long-standing syndicated radio show, The Grateful Dead Hour, David has continued to peer into hitherto unexplored regions of the Dead world with a weird combination of scholarly intensity, a fan's inquisitiveness, and great humor. My own appreciation of the band—as both musicians and people—has been greatly enhanced by reading and listening to David's conversations with the Dead.

This volume contains a megadose of some of David's finest interviews with members of the Dead, as well as with a couple of nonmembers whose interviews are extraordinarily illuminating in unpredictable ways;

road crew member Steve Parish offers a literally backstage view of life with the Dead; and Owsley Stanley ("Bear"), in his first major published interview *anywhere*, speaks with tremendous feeling and eloquence about the Dead's formative years and early acid scene.

There are anecdotes, trivia, and GD *obscuriana* galore in these pages, but what I come away with most is the pulse of *humanity* David extracts so beautifully from his subjects. Ultimately, this is a book about artists and their vision. And truly communicating about those subjects is an art in itself.

BLAIR JACKSON
March 1991

Blair Jackson is publisher and editor of *The Golden Road*. An anthology of writing from the magazine's pages will be published by Harmony Books in 1992.

Introduction

The One Thing We Need Is a Left-hand Monkey Wrench

I was a musician before I was a Deadhead, and I was a Deadhead before I was a journalist. I started writing for music magazines in 1976 in hopes of meeting the songwriters, performers, and producers I admired, and over the years I acquired a priceless education by getting to the sources of the information and inspiration. I've interviewed dozens of big stars and undersung heroes, watched promising artists get eaten alive by a merciless industry, encountered surprising pockets of warm humanity near its heart, and learned quite a bit about what it takes to thrive in that world.

Nothing I've encountered in the music industry has captured and held my interest like the Grateful Dead. Seeing the Dead for the first time changed forever my understanding of what music was about and what music could do. I should say my first Dead encounter (March 5, 1972, at Winterland in San Francisco) *began* the process of reshaping my understanding, because it took me a few years to get a handle on what was going on. Coming from the singer-songwriter school, and with no exposure to jazz or other improvisational forms—and not being terribly interested at the time in dancing and the extended grooves that accompanied it—I wasn't too keen on the Dead's lengthy jams at first.

The '72 Grateful Dead was a songwriter's band, perhaps more so than in any other period. The band that started as the Warlocks in 1965 and

1

then became the Grateful Dead was an amalgam of folk and R&B influences drawing material from a variety of sources; the *Anthem of the Sun–Live Dead*-era Dead dealt with larger forms and collective composition as well as spontaneous creation. Robert Hunter was the lyricist, guitarist Jerry Garcia and bassist Phil Lesh were the composers, and the band was their magnificent instrument. When I got on the bus, guitarist Bob Weir was just stepping forward with an LP's worth of tunes from *Ace*, Hunter and Garcia had developed a one-on-one collaboration that was bearing rich and plentiful fruit, and with vocalist Ron "Pigpen" McKernan sidelined by the illness that killed him a year later, what the band lacked in showstoppers they more than made up for in the quantity and quality of songs. This was also the time when pianist Keith Godchaux was becoming a member of the ensemble; by 1973 Godchaux's jazz was infusing the jams and all those songs were beginning to flow together. Everybody was getting better at their axes, too.

Rather than composing their songs and presenting them in a consistent and precise fashion to a carefully cultivated audience, the Grateful Dead paradigm has emphasized spontaneity, candor, and the inseparability of music and band and audience. In sixties parlance, the medium is the message—if you care to see it that way. These days it's also pretty engaging music if you just come for the show.

It is, to use a now-unfashionable word, a matter of coevolution. My outlook on Grateful Dead music is a product of who I was and who they were when we first crossed paths, and my own growth as a musician and as a person has been greatly informed by my continuing relationship with the continually evolving music and culture of the Grateful Dead.

I was—and am—interested in all kinds of music, but when I hooked up with *BAM* magazine in 1976 I put extra energy into fishing for Grateful Dead–related assignments. I had some competition higher in the ranks—including Blair Jackson, who later became managing editor and very generously invited me to join him on the Garcia interview in 1981—but I landed interviews with Bob Weir and Robert Hunter in 1977, and I was on my way. I wrote *BAM*'s "Dead Ahead" column for a while, and I worked at getting free-lance assignments on my favorite subject. In 1981 I managed to corral the elusive Phil Lesh, with the help of the late Zohn Artman, and that interview was the start of a friendship and professional relationship that continues to this day (I am the producer and engineer for "Rex Radio," a monthly new-and-unusual music show on KPFA hosted by Lesh and Gary Lambert).

From 1980 until 1986 I worked for Mix Publications, ultimately serving as music editor of *Mix: The Recording Industry Magazine*, which gave me an opportunity to explore the technical side of the music business, in the studio and on the road. I got to poke my nose into the Grateful Dead's studio and I met John Meyer, who has advanced the art and science of loudspeaker design from ideas born in the Grateful Dead's backyard. Meyer is mentioned repeatedly in the interviews with Dan Healy and Bear.

Concurrent with my tenure at Mix I worked for a *Rolling Stone* spin-off, *Record*, from 1981 until its untimely demise in 1985, and after much lobbying on the twenty-third floor I persuaded *RS* music editor Jim Henke to give me a shot at the Grateful Dead profile that had been on the back burner for years, with countless writers having had the assignment without completing it. When I got the assignment, Bob Weir decided the magazine should send me with the band to the Jamaica World Music Festival, held in Montego Bay over the Thanksgiving weekend on 1982. The 1983 interviews in this book were gathered for that piece, but I never turned it in for a number of reasons having to do with the band's and my distrust of the magazine's intentions (*Rolling Stone* didn't feature the Dead until Mikal Gilmore's excellent cover story in July 1987). On that trip to Jamaica I met the photographer Peter Simon and his editor, Bob Miller of St. Martin's Press, who were planning a book on the Grateful Dead. That connection eventually resulted in my collaboration with Peter on *Playing in the Band: An Oral and Visual Portrait of the Grateful Dead.*

I wandered into the radio business in 1985, when *Playing in the Band* came out and I appeared on a local station's Grateful Dead show to plug the book and play some tapes. I had a lot of fun and immediately had more ideas for the program, and within a year I was doing that to the detriment of my work as a writer and editor. I wrote a book about Talking Heads right after I finished the Dead book, but working directly with the music of the Grateful Dead was a siren song I could not resist and before long I was blissfully free of magazine deadlines, slaving over a hot splicing block.

The radio show is one of the reasons why there are few new interviews from recent years. The medium demands very short bits of talk, so instead of long, leisurely rap sessions I could boil down in a word processor I found myself collecting very short interviews on very specific, often ephemeral subjects. I also found that the more closely I worked with the music itself, the more firmly I believed that the best thing that can be said for the Grateful Dead is that which is said by the music itself. But from the time I started listening to the Grateful Dead I wondered what sort of people I'd find behind these intriguing musical personae. This book presents the best of what I found there, and while it makes no attempt to cover the entire terrain it does go into great depth in certain areas.

Portions of these interviews were used in *Playing in the Band*; that book's collective narrative was constructed from literally hundreds of sources, including interviews from magazines and other media. My interviews appeared, in edited form, in various consumer and trade magazines, including *Record, Musician, BAM, Mix, Recording Engineer/ Producer,* and others. It always seemed a little sad to me that a magazine article had a life span of one month, and given the importance (to me, anyway) of these particular interviews I was grateful when an opportunity came up to gather them together in a more permanent form.

These interviews were redacted for music magazines, but it wasn't only for music magazines that I asked the questions. What struck me about the interviews with, reports on, and even reviews of the Grateful Dead that I'd read over the years was the relative lack of attention paid to the music itself and to the act of collective creativity, the group-mind experience demonstrated by the Grateful Dead. What was it like to be part of a band with a mind of its own?

I was also interested in the mystique that elevated the musicians unrealistically in the eyes of their followers and at the same time diminished them in the esteem of the industry and the mainstream culture. There is a *stigma* in being a Deadhead, because twenty-five years down the line the Grateful Dead have become—in some people's eyes— an icon of a bygone era. Never mind that that brief wrinkle in the social fabric, the Summer of Love, was more a creation of the media than of its participants and that its preservation is of interest to very few people other than those who profit from the sales of memorabilia. The Grateful Dead touched down in the sixties but it's been forward motion ever since. Fortunately, they got in the habit of recording their concerts so there are plenty of remains to analyze. What interests me about the Grateful Dead's past is the light it casts on the development of a unique musical form that bespeaks a unique social form.

One chief characteristic of the Grateful Dead scene is that it has invented itself on almost every level—musically, technically, and culturally—and it grew and remained strong enough to hold its separate definition even as most of the rest of the counterculture withered or reassimilated. The music took a separate path from "commercial" music, because the Dead's audience rewarded diversity even as the radio-driven mainstream compartmentalized and narrowed the stylistic reach of entertainers who depended on airplay to generate record sales. Radio fostered recording practices that emphasized precision over spontaneity, but the Dead were able to avoid those necessities and remain squarely in the realm of improvisation long after the rest of their peers surrendered to fixity. It seems as though the Allman Brothers Band was the only other rock group that emphasized improvisation, and that road came to an end with the deaths of Duane Allman and Berry Oakley in the early 1970s. Of course, the Grateful Dead aren't the only band who jams, but they seem to be the only band who earn their keep by performing live and whose audience has not become conditioned to demand "perfection" in the form of precise performances and computerized lighting cues.

I encountered the opposite end of that continuum when I interviewed Don Felder of the Eagles. I saw that band in concert and was so amazed by their note-perfect performances of their records that I went back the next night to see if they could do it again—and they did. And they made it look as fresh as if they were creating it before our eyes. When I interviewed Felder a few years later I told him how impressed I was by their perfect performances, and he explained that a fan would be disappointed if he came to the concert and didn't hear his favorite guitar lick in "Hotel California."

Well, that's obviously a very successful mode of presentation: it's the state of the art, in fact, and on most major concert tours the sound and light people have their cues planned out to the second, from start to finish.

In the Grateful Dead, the idea is to regard each performance as a unique opportunity. Each player's relationship to the other musicians and to the music itself has evolved steadily over the years. Each one has his periods of affection and estrangement, as Garcia observed in 1981. And so do the listeners, many of whom have attended hundreds of performances over the last twenty-five years. And I must also note that as my understanding and my agenda evolved over the years, my opinions—and my questions—evolved commensurately. Phil Lesh complained of the "ossifying" of the Grateful Dead concert form that took place in the period when I was becoming a Deadhead—the development of the "warm-up set" and the reduction in the number of opportunities to take the music "outside"—but I'm not sure he would use the same word today; he is a different person now. I would characterize the change as a natural result of the proliferation of material—some of the Dead's sets in '73 and '74 contained as many as thirty songs, *and* nonsong jams of prodigious length—but I have no idea what was going on in and among the minds of the musicians, and Phil would acknowledge that his view of events is his alone, valid only from his unique perspective.

There is very little unanimity on any subject in the band, the organization, or the Deadhead community—and that, too, is a key point. Community is not about agreement, it's about acceptance and diversity. John Barlow, former cattle rancher from Wyoming and longtime Grateful Dead songwriting partner, started teaching me about that when we met in Jamaica in November 1982. "I came from a place where even my enemies would help me out if I were in certain kinds of trouble," he told me in 1986. "America...is erasing the whole idea of community, and people need that desperately.... [Deadheads] realized that you don't have to do it in one place...they take it on the road."

Before I came to understand that cooperation in the Grateful Dead isn't necessarily a function of agreement, I asked a lot of inappropriate questions—by which I mean I asked the wrong guy. I got some generous and sometimes humorous responses—e.g., Garcia's reaction to my comments about Bob Weir's having learned slide guitar onstage in front of the multitudes—but I also got a lot of "How the hell should I know? Ask him!" and/or "That's not something I feel qualified to talk about." And at one point I was chastised for having asked gossipy questions, questions that to my mind were the product of informed curiosity. There are a lot of naïve questions in this book, and reading these interviews now I can see my own development as a Deadhead and a journalist and a musician. I had my own mythologized picture of the Dead when I started, and I'll confess to some discomfort at reliving the naïveté of some of my interrogations. But that sort of thing changes every day, almost, because there is no center to the character of the Grateful Dead. No one person— not Jerry Garcia or anybody else—embodies the personality of the Grateful Dead. Each person who works and plays there manifests the Grateful Dead as he or she sees fit, and that is what makes the musical and extramusical environment so rich. And that is why you will find in these pages an interview with a member of the road crew.

I was not a part of the Grateful Dead when I wrote *Playing in the Band*, but I am part of it now because I have a license from the band to play their music on the radio every week and I earn my living doing it. Like most of the people who work in the Grateful Dead world, I operate without a clearly defined job description and without appreciable supervision. There are some restrictions on what I'm allowed to play on the Grateful Dead Hour, but for the most part I am free to do what makes sense to me; I define the Grateful Dead by the editorial choices I make in my weekly radio program, and in the way I interact with the people who listen to it.

Conversations with the Dead is missing several key players, because I have not interviewed all the members of the Grateful Dead. My ongoing relationships with Bob Weir and Phil Lesh got me plenty of in-depth, on-the-record talk, and it is not hard to get a great interview from Jerry Garcia, so those three men contribute the bulk of the material in this book.

DAVID GANS
Oakland California
April 1, 1991

Bob Weir

August 9, 1977
Los Angeles, California

My first Grateful Dead interview. Terrapin Station *had just been released, and "rhythm guitarist" Weir was working with producer Keith Olsen on his second solo album,* Heaven Help the Fool. *Photographer Ed Perlstein and I flew to Los Angeles and met with Weir in his hotel room for the interview, then drove to Sound City in Burbank to take some pictures and listen to some tracks.*

*What was it like doing it with [*Terrapin Station *producer Keith] Olsen and the Grateful Dead, and how did that lead to your individual project?*

With the reintroduction of Mickey [Hart], the band reached critical mass for all intents and purposes as far as the number of ideas and opinions expressed at any given time—most vocally expressed at that. And so we just had too many horses pulling in too many different directions. We were faced with the prospect of going into the studio and taking years to make a record, or trying out a producer—which we hadn't done in twelve, thirteen years, something like that, ever since we got started.

At that point, looking at the situation that lay before us, we all figured that maybe it was time to at least look over a few producers. We contacted Keith, and he came up. We talked with him, and then a few of us came

8

down and saw his studio. It seemed like it was fairly compatible, so we thought we'd give it a try.

What was it about Olsen?

Number one, availability. Number two, his choice of equipment: he uses all Studer equipment, and a Neve console, which is indicative of the fact that he uses the same sort of approach, electronically, that we do.

Mickey stated that "Terrapin" is a whole new musical direction for the group. He saw it as a taking-off point, like "The Other One," or "St. Stephen"—

That whole "Terrapin" sequence can become endless. We can just string it out further and further and further. I guess the rules are set that you have a few thematic lines here and there. Maybe with each new approach to it we might introduce one new thematic line, and try to work that into variations of the older themes. That would be one approach. Like Mickey says, it's a jumping-off point. We can go from anywhere to anywhere—within or without it, for that matter. We can tie other songs into it. Eventually, we might get it long enough that we can start off the evening with it and end the evening with it, and work in most anything anybody would want to hear.

"One More Saturday Night" has taken on a brand-new vitality. Did that come out of any particular place?

Probably a sound check: "We've got to go over 'Saturday Night' because it seems stale—either come up with something new or put it to rest for a while." We generally only play that on Saturday nights these days.

How did a song like "Brokedown Palace" get brought out again? Did someone say, "Let's see if we remember that one"?

We have a book of all the songs that we've done, or at least an honest attempt at collecting them. Every now and then, we'll just look through the book and say, "There's an old chestnut, why don't we pull that one back out?" as opposed to trying to learn something new. It's often nice to go back and visit with some of those old friends.

Why did Phil [Lesh] stop singing?

He blew his voice with improper singing technique. There, but for fortune... He just wasn't singing properly, and he abused his throat. You can only do that so long before you have no range left.

I'm at least aware of it, and boy, I don't want to lose my voice. Phil could get it back with an operation, but it's an expensive operation, and after that you can't talk, whisper, or anything for six weeks, and then you come back very slowly.

...Singing is the most fun I know.

More fun than playing?

Yeah, basically. Playing is a great get-off, but the only thing I know that tops it is singing.

What's your favorite song to sing?

Oh, it depends on the song and the evening and the moment. That's an impossible question to answer.

About Kingfish: You didn't write a lot of songs with them.

No. I never really found just exactly what I was going to be doing with Kingfish. The problem was that I didn't spend enough time with them. I had the Grateful Dead's various projects, records, movies, and, in the end, touring. That left me very little time to devote to Kingfish, so I never really homed in on what my place was in that outfit and what that outfit was really up to. I was just beginning to get a handle on what Kingfish was all about, and then came a Grateful Dead tour, and a lot of movie work, and it just became impossible. I became a very run-down boy.

The live Kingfish album [Live 'n' Kickin', Jet JT-LA732, 1977] came out very strangely. I heard your guitar in the ambience, but your track was gone. It left a lot of holes in the vocals, too. Did they purposely mix you out of certain tracks?

Yeah, the point being that they wanted to establish themselves as Kingfish without me, and they only had a tape with me to work with. They couldn't erase me completely, because I was in the drum track. Otherwise, I think they would have, and covered by doing another guitar part in my register. If I was playing or singing a pivotal part, they left that in.

It was fun when it was happening. It just wasn't happening that much. It must have drove them all bonkers, sitting on their hands.

What are you looking for in solo recording that the Grateful Dead doesn't give you?

Actually, what I'm doing here is going fishing. With the Grateful Dead, when I do a song, I throw it up to them and it's subject to whatever interpretation it gets. I don't know anybody who has the energy to tell six other strong-willed musicians, "Play this, you play that"—you get a lot of, "Hey, eat my shorts. I'll play what I feel, man," and all that kind of stuff, so it's pointless to try to do that with the Grateful Dead.

But when I get into the studio with a bunch of musicians I can say, "I want this"—plus these musicians here are perceptive to the point where they know real well how to go for what you're looking for and then enlarge upon that.

With the Grateful Dead, I never get exactly what the song was supposed to have been to me. I never get exactly what I had imagined.

Can you give me an example?

Hmm. Not right now, but I can soon, I'll say. Because I'm going to take this record back up north with me before we go out on tour again, and let the band learn whatever tunes they want. I guarantee they won't sound much like the record.[1]

I wanted to ask you about "Estimated Prophet."

Essentially, the basis of it is this guy that I see at nearly every backstage door. Every time we play anywhere there's always some guy that's taken a lot of dope, and he's really bug-eyed, and he's having some kind of vision. Somehow I work into his vision, or the band works into his vision, or something like that. He's got some rave that he's got to deliver. So I just decided I was gonna beat him to the punch and do it myself. I've been in that space, and I know where he's coming from.

If there's a point to "Estimated Prophet," it is that no matter what you do, perhaps you shouldn't take it all that seriously. No matter what. I don't know how better to say that than with the song. It pretty much illustrates a point that's so nebulous as to defy description with prosaic words.

It's not that one doesn't appreciate the adulation, but some of the importance that people ascribe to what we're doing may be undue, it seems. I'm not entirely sure that a whole lot of good can come from that. It's music and poetry and it's art, and it can do what art can do.

I don't think there's anything wrong with being a devoted Grateful Dead fan, any more than there's anything wrong with being a devoted fan of Bach.

[1]None of the *Heaven Help the Fool* material was ever adopted by the Grateful Dead. The title song appeared as an instrumental during the acoustic sets the band played in San Francisco and New York City in the fall of 1980, played by Weir and keyboardist Brent Mydland. Other band members joined in sporadically, but it never received the attention of the ensemble.

I can see every point in the world in that. I'm a devoted fan of Stravinsky, of Coltrane—I could list my heroes. But when they start getting bug-eyed, I start worrying about them. As long as it's fun, taken in the spirit of lightheartedness.

You talk about the song in first person. How did you and Barlow write it?
It just sort of occurred to me, that line "My time comin' any day now." It occurred to me with the melody, and it took me a long time to reach into that one line and melodic phrase and pull the picture out of who that was that was talking. Finally it occurred to me that it was this guy that I've seen at the back door and on the street corner, or whatever, who's taken some dope and had a flash or two and is taking it a little too seriously. He seemed like the kind of guy that you might write a song about. I don't know why. It's a signpost, y'know? "There but for fortune"—like "Wharf Rat." That's a real guy, too: "I used to fly with Cap'n Eddie Rickenbacker," and once again, there but for fortune go you or I.

How long has it been since you've taken any acid?
It's not been that long, really, but then I don't know how I feel about that. Times aren't the same these days, and acid doesn't do the same thing anymore. Not that it was ever the same back then, either, but we seem to be laboring over a whole different zeitgeist these days. LSD was fun, and all that kind of stuff *is* fun or whatever, but [*pause*] I don't know where I stand on that, really.

I'm naturally pretty spaced out to begin with. I don't require dope to put that good old-fashioned wedge in my head—I was born with one. I also take less dope than most of my friends do, and always have, simply because I react to it more than most other people do—no matter what it is, it seems. To the point where I get up and go out running and by the time I come back in, I'm just ringy, and it takes me a while before I can make any good sense. Running is a mediation of sorts....

You...have written several songs in cycles of seven beats,[2] *a potentially awkward rhythm—*
I like it, because you can get the "best of three, best of four" if you play it right...three then four, four then three, two then two then three—whatever. Break it up however you like. It gives you a chance to get two

---

[2]In addition to "Estimated Prophet" (*Terrapin Station*, 1977), recorded examples include "Money Money" (*Mars Hotel*, 1974) and "Lazy Lightning" and "Supplication" (*Kingfish*, 1976).

different rhythmic feels happening at the same time, and you can play them against each other to interesting effect.

Did you set out to write in seven/four?

Yeah. I sat down with a little thing called a Trinome, a sort of metronome that counts out a signature. I just played it in my living room, and I got a snatch that way. It was a long time ago that I became fascinated with seven/four. I'd just come up with little vamps for seven/four. I think I'm going to lay off it for a while, though, because I think I might be overstating my case if I do it again in the near future.

● ● ●

I'm doing two covers [on *Heaven Help the Fool*]: an old Marvin Gaye tune, "I'll Be Doggone," and a Lowell George song called "Easy to Slip," from [Little Feat's] *Sailin' Shoes.*

Do you listen to Little Feat?

They're a good band. I don't listen to much rock and roll, but they're one of the bands that I do listen to.

What do you listen to?

Almost anything else.

Elton John listens to everything that comes out, I've been told, and he keeps up on it that way. I like to listen to, like, African music or classical music or jazz or North Indian classical music—anything that I might not normally run into. It just seems like my own little obsession with getting away from where I am right now.

It seems kind of pointless to listen to nothing but rock 'n' roll and then try to come up with an original approach to anything. That's kind of beside the point, because what you really need to get an original approach is that good old-fashioned flash of inspiration, no matter what your sources are. I like to bring other kinds of stuff into what I'm doing.

I've come up with a lot of stuff while listening to the Grateful Dead. Not copping licks from you guys...there seems to be some kind of soup in the air there, and I'll write down words, or draw a picture of a melody. You can come up with an idea while listening to a different kind of music, it just triggers something....

Oh, you bet. If something rings a chord, then you at least know that you and this other source, from whence comes the music, agree, and you have the possibility of a universal lick to draw from, something that can reach beyond just your own little world. I have things that occur to me that when I get them out and play them for somebody else, I realize that it's really just me that I'm talking to.

Oftentimes if I'm listening to something and it strikes a chord within me, then chances are there's a more universal language being spoken. At that point, it's good to develop that, because you'll reach more people with what you're trying to say.

How do you take a new song to the Grateful Dead?

I try to have it worked up so that I can sing it and play it at the same time. Sometimes I put it on tape. In the case of this record, I'll just give 'em a copy and say, "Here: you gotta love it, 'cause there it is. If there's anything that intrigues you, we'll work it up." I'll give them chord sheets and they can learn them.

And, of course, the Grateful Dead won't do any of the stuff anywhere near what I've got down in the studio. But then it'll be interesting to see what I do get. Sometimes you get better, and sometimes you get not quite what you're looking for. There's no real rule to it.

What happened to "Money Money"?[3]

A couple of the people in the band didn't like the little story, which, though tongue-in-cheek, was maybe a little too…I don't know….A couple of folks in the band didn't think it was as funny as I did. Didn't think it was all that funny at all, so we just put that one away.

Some critic credited Keith Olsen with the new arrangement of "Dancin' in the Street"—

He had a lot of influence on us, but that wasn't it.

Is that going to be the first single [from Terrapin Station*]?*

Well, [Arista Records president] Clive Davis seems to think so….I don't think that's the strongest possible statement on the record.

Musical statement, artistic statement, or possible commercial success?

Artistic statement, or possible commercial success. I think at this point they're almost identical, as long as it's short enough.

---

[3] From the 1974 studio album *Grateful Dead from the Mars Hotel*. The band performed "Money Money" (a.k.a. "Finance Blues") three times, in the Pacific Northwest in May 1974, and never again.

So what would you choose?

[*Laughs*] I don't know. The one that I think could actually make it would be "Estimated Prophet," but it's too long, and it can't be edited, so that's out.

"Samson and Delilah"...[4] It's a good tune. I'm not entirely sure that all those folks out there in those discos and stuff like that who are down into some heavy sinnin' want to hear a Bible story.

Where did you get that song?

Old Negro spiritual. The version I do is a lot closer to the Reverend Gary Davis's. I've always wanted to do it. I've always loved the story. There are a lot more verses, too. I might expand that song. It's a favorite of mine, always has been.

It's fun to sing. Once it gets rolling, it's just impossible to stop it. I find myself real sorry that it's as short as it is.

So let's hear some more verses.

If I do more verses, chances are I'll be blowing my voice more often. I don't know what to do about that, except try to get stronger, or take it easy singin' it, but I'm not entirely sure I can. [*Archly*] I don't know if I have that kind of self-control....

• • •

The first time I saw the Grateful Dead play I was locked into it. Do you have any feelings about that? I don't know what kind of feedback you get from fans and nonfans, people in the business.

I guess really where we get our most converts is from any of a number of good nights we have. It's pretty evident that what we're doing is going fishin', and sometimes we come up with catfish, and sometimes we come up with trout. On a good night, when somebody can see that we're going fishin' and we're actually doing something, yes it can be done...I don't know. That kind of stuff appeals to me, obviously, 'cause that's what I like to do.

Do you plan out those expeditions at all? There are times when songs just seem to come out of nowhere, and sometimes it seems very definitely planned, and you're forcing the change from one song to the other.

[4]The Reverend Gary Davis version is available on several releases, including *Gospel, Blues and Street Songs: Reverend Gary Davis and Pink Anderson*. Riverside Jazz Archives RLP-148, remastered in 1987 and released as OBC-524, distributed by Fantasy Records.

Yeah. We generally try to plot them as best we can, and leave them open for something. Oftentimes we'll say, "We'll do this, and we'll follow it with this and take it into this space, and see where it goes." That is pretty much the standard. It's not all that often that we plot out a set exactly, unless somebody has a real precise idea of what they want to do. And even then, it's anybody's guess as to whether it's gonna come out the way it was planned. Most often, we'll plan it up to a certain point.

There are certain ones that stick out in my mind, like the second day at the Oakland Stadium last year [October 10, 1976, splitting the bill with The Who]. During "Dancin' in the Street," three or four times during the jam, I thought you were going to go into this or that or the other thing, then BANG! out came "Wharf Rat," and then back to "Dancin' in the Street." That was just killer! One of the nicest surprises—

Surprised us, too.

The day before, we tried, "Well, there are all these kids out there, we'd better do a professional set, boys." [*Laughs*] And so we went out there and played a fairly slick, but kinda sleepy, set. Didn't work, didn't work, and it was Sunday and the hell with it. "What do you want to do?" "I don't know, haven't figured it out yet." "Well, we gotta start playing." "Something will occur to us." And something did. That's a neat way to do it.

● ● ●

Are you pleased with Terrapin Station?

Pretty much—we got a record out [*laughs*]. I learned so much working with [Olsen] that I've decided to do another project with him. Watching him, how he does stuff, is just amazing to me.

Is he drawing good performances out of you? Do you feel that he is a good producer for you, the musician?

Well, he certainly knows when to draw the line and keep it rolling. Given my own way, I would probably belabor some points far beyond any reasonable return, and let other things go that need more work. He has a more even view of things, I think, than any artists really can, coming from an extremely subjective space. Working with him, you start to gain his overview, where you get the idea that maybe it's more important to keep things rolling than to settle down on any one thing, or vice versa. Oftentimes it's a good idea to keep going into one particular thing, like a guitar part, beyond where you would have, just because you haven't really got it rolling yet. He's real good at that.

Did you do a lot of retakes, various things?

Some things yes, some things no.

One tune that took the longest to get was one that we didn't use, another of Phil's originals.[5] It was just too long, the song itself was too long to put on without crowding something else off the record. It was just very long and quite involved, and it was looking to require a good deal of work, and we only had so much time for what we could do on the record—you can only put about nineteen minutes per side on a record before you start losing fidelity. Phil's tune was six minutes long or so, and it would have put both sides well over that, so we decided to axe it and bring it back some other time. We got a great basic on it.

Did you have to shorten the "Terrapin" side at all? Would it naturally have gone a little longer?

I think that the "Terrapin" side pretty much came out to be—let me think…there was one piece that was shortened a little bit, but that was more for purposes of making it more succinct, really.

Was the master edited, or—was the basic live, or was it spliced together?

We did all the sections. We did the first section, up to the end of the first "Terrapin" chorus, live, right up to "Terrapin Transit."

What is that scraping noise?

I was not there that night. Mickey put a whole bunch of stuff in a box, and they miked it in stereo. Essentially what that scraping noise is is a dragon on roller skates, as far as I'm concerned. That's what it sounds like to me….

Did you then do "Terrapin Flyer" [The double-drum solo]?

Then we counted off "Terrapin Flyer"—wait a minute. That comes right out of—what's the name of that?

"At a Siding"? Where Garcia sings again?

Yeah. That's called "At a Siding," hey.

We did that separately; then we did the "Terrapin Flyer" section, then we took a snip of the original "Terrapin" refrain, or whatever it's called, and tacked that onto the end and put it all together, and then it was orchestrated.

[5]"Equinox," with Jerry Garcia singing lead, was never released. Rehearsals and/or "outtakes" have been floating around the taper circuit for years.

How did you feel the first time you heard that Mormon Tabernacle Choir?

Well, the first time I heard it, it was mixed way, way more prominently than it is now, and I was pissed off—or, not pissed off, but concerned that all the orchestration and choral stuff was going to be given too much prominence in comparison to the band. So we began the long negotiation, as it were, to put it in a more reasonable perspective. Keith was real stoked; he'd gone over to England and gotten these parts. They're kinda nifty parts, anything but 101 Strings—it's off in a peculiar direction, but I think it serves the song well. I think what it sounds like is English court music, but it serves the song well, that particular grandiose conception of how the orchestration would be done. I didn't mind the parts—there were a couple of lines that I would have spent more time with, but it's real expensive to do a sixty-piece orchestra.

That first violin line in "Terrapin Flyer" was a bit rushed. If Mickey had been over there (Mickey and Phil pretty much came up with that part), if we'd all had a chance to work with [arranger Paul] Buckmaster, Mickey would have found a way to make known to the players that the feeling that he wanted there was a little more mechanical. If you know Mickey, you know that he has a mechanical feel that he likes to lay into that kind of stuff. It's neat, it makes everything sort of busy and clocklike. Anyway, I could find fault here and there, but in general, I like the lines. There was just too much of it, and I thought it had to be backpedaled considerably.

Whose idea was Tom Scott [lyricon solo on "Estimated Prophet"]?

Keith said, "I'm going to bring Tom Scott in and see if he wants to do anything on this stuff." Being familiar with Tom Scott and his work, it sounded like a good idea to me. I didn't know what tunes he had in mind, really. I didn't know that there was going to be anything added on "Estimated Prophet." As it is, I'm kinda pleased overall with what he did on "Estimated Prophet"—it's not often I hear one of my tunes all dressed up like that. It sort of tickles me.

Looking back on recent Grateful Dead records, in the light of Terrapin Station, *are there some tunes that you'd like to do over again?*

Oh, a number of them. I don't know where I'd even begin. As far as I'm concerned, a great many of the tunes that we wrote and worked up and took directly into the studio without ever taking out on the road, I wish I had a second chance at the majority of those tunes, simply because they really blossomed on the road, oftentimes with just one tour, and they were nowhere near what they were in the studio. "Sugar Magnolia" is an example. We recorded it, and that was that.

Was "Sugar Magnolia" as big a flash to you when you recorded it as it has become?

No. Well, it was a flash to me, but we took it into the studio and recorded it, and I wasn't altogether pleased with what it came out like. It wasn't everything that it should be. I didn't know how to tell anybody that, but as soon as we took it out on the road, it immediately evolved into a whole lot more than what we'd just put down on vinyl, and became at that point exactly what I had envisioned it as being.

How much road testing did you do on "Estimated Prophet" and "Terrapin"?

Fortunately, those two tunes, we had a chance to play them three times onstage, and it made a huge difference. We tried doing basics on those tunes the first week we were down there, and got something that we decided that maybe we could live with, maybe we can't, we'll see. Then we played down here at San Bernardino, up in Santa Barbara, and up in San Francisco,[6] and then we came back and we knew what the songs were about. When you can do it for a whole roomful of kids and really get a feel for what the hits and misses are, play each line...Playing something onstage gives you a chance to get a feel for how to put it over, and it really helps to do that before you try to record it.

Do you do a lot of analyzing? Do you sit down and talk about stuff, dynamics...?

We've had to do a lot of conscious work on dynamics, simply because with the reintroduction of Mickey—he missed out on like years of tacit agreements and understandings that we came upon, and so we finally had to start talking about it, because otherwise he'd go banging and crashing through the quiet parts, or he wouldn't know when that sudden sucker punch is coming. We had to tell him, which means we had to be thinking about it, which means while we were thinking about it, we might as well be *thinking* about it.

[6]February 26, 1977, at the Swing Auditorium in San Bernardino; February 27 at the Robertson Gym, University of California at Santa Barbara; and March 18–20 at Winterland in San Francisco.

Can you talk a little bit about the mechanics of Mickey's reintroduction to the band? He said in an interview that he just brought his drums down to that last night at Winterland [October 20, 1974].... Was that it? He just trucked his stuff in and "I'm back"?

Essentially what happened was, that was the last night as far as we were all concerned, that was it. There was a chance that we might reconvene at some future date, but really, this was—we weren't looking towards that, we were just looking at the night as being the last night.[7]

Why?

Well, because it had become unmanageable...We had pretty much roped ourselves into an unworkable situation. We had this huge PA that we were carting around, we had a crew of—god knows—about forty people, and all that kind of stuff, and we had to work too hard and too much to support it all, to the point where every time we played somewhere we lost money, but we had to keep working just to pay everybody who was on salary. All the money that we'd make from records would go into supporting this whole organization, and it was still in the red. Millions and millions of dollars went into that. It wasn't any fun after a while, not having enough time to really get loose and get creative, having to stay on the road all the time. So we decided that we had to knock off.

Were you really prepared not to have the Grateful Dead...?

Yeah. It was the greatest likelihood of all, at that point, because everybody was getting involved in other stuff, and so Mickey came on down figuring, "This is the last night—I'd better get my drums down there." Essentially, he didn't want to miss out. When he got there, showed

---

[7]The October 1974 Winterland run was recorded and filmed, and although the band ceased touring they began work in Bob Weir's new home studio. They showed off their new material in four performances in 1975: March 23 at Kezar Stadium in San Francisco, a huge benefit for arts and athletics in the San Francisco schools ("SNACK" which also featured Bob Dylan, Neil Young, the Doobie Brothers, Joan Baez, Jefferson Starship, and others), with keyboardists Merl Saunders and Ned Lagin augmenting the seven-member Dead lineup; June 17 at Winterland, a benefit for the survivors of poster artist Bob Fried with "Jerry Garcia and Friends" plus Kingfish (with Bob Weir), Keith and Donna (Godchaux), and the Mirrors; August 13 at San Francisco's tiny Great American Music Hall, a record release party that was recorded on sixteen-track and released in its entirety as a two-CD set, *One from the Vault*, in 1991); and at a free concert in Golden Gate Park with the Jefferson Starship on September 28. A live album from the October '74 gigs, *Steal Your Face*, was released in 1976; the *Grateful Dead Movie*, edited by Garcia, was released in June 1977. The Dead returned to regular touring—with Mickey Hart back on board full-time—in June 1976.

up at the back door with his drums, "Oh, Mickey, that's right! Set 'em up!" And when we finally did convene after all, there was Mickey. It was like he'd been reintroduced that last night, and it was a different situation.

Was it like he'd never left?
    No, it wasn't like that at all.

Robert Hunter

A Rose Grows from the Shadows

The Grateful Dead's Lyricist Speaks About His Life and His Art

This interview appeared in the January 1978 issue of BAM: The
California Music Magazine. *There were two interview sessions, both in
November 1977; the first was at Hunter's house, the second at the Dead's
rehearsal/recording hangout in San Rafael.*

After posing with his fellows for the cover of the Grateful Dead's 1970
Workingman's Dead, (but not the individual portraits on the back),
Grateful Dead lyricist Robert Hunter, in his words, "rethought the matter
and decided to keep my face my own."

In 1976, Hunter emerged from the anonymity he had chosen for
himself. He got the feel of the stage under the name Lefty Banks for a
while, then revealed himself with Roadhog, an interesting but lamentably
sloppy country-rock band which included his friend Rodney Albin. After
Roadhog bit the dust a few months later, Hunter played a few local gigs
with Barry Melton (formerly of Country Joe and the Fish, later with the

Dinosaurs, with whom Hunter performed for a few years in the eighties), then retired from public view once more.

In the summer of 1977, Hunter once more came onto the San Francisco club scene, this time with Comfort, a more versatile and self-sufficient band with the range necessary to support Hunter's variety of songs.

Hunter's vantage point on the Grateful Dead is unique. Sometimes, he says, he has "felt like the Wizard of Oz, behind the curtain, pulling all those levers." In recent years he has retreated from his role as a principal with the Dead, working more extensively on his own writing and performance. His collaboration with Jerry Garcia thrives, and he works but sporadically with others.

"I'd really prefer not to get into tearing apart the symbology of my songs," he said, "and I'll tell you why: symbols are evocative, and if there were a more definite way to say things, you'd say them that way. A symbol, by its very nature, can pull in many, many shades of meaning, depending on the emotional tone with which you engage the piece.

"If you were to engage 'Terrapin' in a cynical fashion, the symbols would be very limp, and they wouldn't yield much. If you were to approach it with the feeling that there is something to be gotten, the symbols are solid enough to give you the impressions that I wanted to give—to evoke the feelings."

What was the first song you wrote for the Grateful Dead?

I moved out to New Mexico to be an artist about the time the Dead really started. I wrote "Alligator" and "China Cat Sunflower," and I knew they had a rock 'n' roll band, so I mailed them up. Then when I came back, the band was going to Rio Nido [a resort town on the Russian River, north of San Francisco] to play a gig, and Phil asked me if I wanted to come along.

I went up, and I wrote the first half of "Dark Star" that day. Garcia asked me how I'd like to be "lyricist in residence" for the Dead, and I thought I might like it fine. I had written lyrics on and off since I was seventeen, but I fancied myself a serious writer, and rock 'n' roll wasn't exactly what I had planned for myself. But things were changing at such an intense rate, and it seemed like it would be a nice thing to do. [*Laughs*] "A nice thing." I went right to work, fell right into it.

How did you write "China Cat Sunflower"?

I think the germ of it came in Mexico, on Lake Chapala. I don't think any of the words came, exactly—the rhythms came.

I had a cat sitting on my belly, and was in a rather hypersensitive state, and I followed this cat out to—I believe it was Neptune—and there were rainbows across Neptune, and cats marching across this rainbow. This cat took me in all these cat places; there's some essence of that in the song. Oh, I wrote part of it in Mexico and part of it on Neptune.

Did the song come out rhythmically the way you felt it when you wrote it?
Not at all. [*He runs downstairs and gets his guitar, then plays; it's a folksy, ballad rhythm, and the voice is likewise gentle and melodic. It's more fairy-tale than psychedelic in feel.*]

> Ever been ten thousand miles away from home, sweet Susie?
> Where a drummer drums the waves upon the shore
> Where the clatter and the tingle and the rush and the roar
> Light up the ocean from the surface to the floor?
>
> Ever been to see a comical collection of gears
> Grinding out galactical illusions of years?
> Golden-haired Madonna with a yellow silk ribbon
> Been waiting...been waiting for years
>
> Look for a while at the China Cat Sunflower
> Proud walking jingle in the midnight sun
> Copper-dome bodhi drip a silver kimono
> Like a crazy-quilt star gown through a dream night wind
>
> Krazy Kat peeking through a lace bandanna
> Like a one-eyed Cheshire, like a diamond eye jack
> A leaf of all colors plays a golden string fiddle
> To a double-e waterfall all over my back
>
> Comic book colors on a violin river
> Crying Leonardo words from out a silk trombone
> I rang a silent bell beneath a shower of pearls
> In the eagle wing palace of the Queen Chinee
>
> Eight-sided whispering hallelujah hatrack
> Seven paced marble-eyed transitory dream doll
> Six proud walkers on the jingle-bell rainbow
> Five men writing in fingers of gold

Four men tracking down the great white sperm whale
Three girls waiting in a foreign dominion
Riding in the whale-belly fade away a moonlight
Sink beneath the water to the coral sands below

*A lot of people will just let your songs wash over them and experience them
without judgment, and then there are people who analyze, looking for
everything that's in them. Do you expect that people will understand what
you're saying most of the time, or that they'll care to?*

I work on my own visions, my own internal relationships. Some songs
are trying to make sense, and others are just dreams.

"Terrapin" came in on a pure beam. I sat down at the typewriter with
my electric guitar plugged in, put in a piece of paper, and typed "Terrapin
Station." I started with an invocation to the muse, because if it wasn't
going to come from there, it was going to come from nowhere.

The invocation carried me all the way through. I must have written a
thousand words on it, eight twelve-inch pages—song after song after song.

That's the mark of a good song—the words just come. With "Terrapin,"
I was in a state of pure well-being for three days while I wrote. "Must
Have Been the Roses" was like that, too: straight transmission. I sat down
to write a song that would be perfect for Butch Waller's bluegrass band,
High Country.

*[Ana Kreitzer, the choreographer who, with two other dancers, had been
performing Hunter's "Alligator Moon" suite as a ballet at Comfort-Hunter
concerts, was present at this discussion of the ephemeral quality of
inspiration. "Sometimes I go into a rehearsal studio not having the slightest
idea what I'm going to do," she said. "I put on the music . . . and I have to do
something to open up.*

*"Sometimes I'm sitting there with the music on, saying, 'Okay, I know
you're there. Open up and fill me with your ideas.'" Hunter puts on an
impish grin and asks, "Ever feel like rebelling against them?"]*

What do your muses look like, Bob?

I have one set of muses which always comes in threes, very transparent,
very feminine, full of brilliance, and very loving and mischievous.

Then there's a rather solemn, overriding muse, that's definitely
overlooker of all the others. And I have some "son of a bitch" muses.
"Wharf Rat," basically, is a description of one of the low muses, and yet
the Wharf Rat evokes one of the other muses, which is pearly blue.

I've got this one spirit that's laying roses on me. Roses, roses, can't get enough of those bloody roses. [The spirit] gives me a lot of other good lines, too, but if I don't put the roses in, it goes away for a while. It's the most prominent image, as far as I'm concerned, in the human brain. Beauty, delicacy, short-livedness...

And thorniness?

Yes. There is no better allegory for—dare I say it?—life, than roses. It never fails. When you put a rose somewhere, it'll do what it's supposed to do. Same way with certain jewels—I like a diamond here, a ruby there, a rose, certain kinds of buildings, vehicles, gems. These things are all real, and the word evokes the thing. That's what we're working with, evocation.

So you finished "Terrapin"—

I called Jerry, and he came right over. Chord changes that he'd been working on fit perfectly into it. He got the first page and a half and the last page set. There are about seven pages in between that aren't set to music, and probably won't be.

A kid came up to me after a gig in Santa Barbara and said, "Could you tell me what the connection is between 'Lady with a Fan' [the first segment] and the rest of 'Terrapin Station'? I don't really see how they fit together." That was the first time I fully realized that without the further development and the tying in of symbols which occur later, there is no connection.

It's funny—at this point in my career, I felt rather separated from the Dead. I wasn't writing for the Dead; but when I finished it, there was no question in my mind that no one but the Dead *could* do it.

After all the years I've been listening to your lyrics, checking it all out, I sort of expected you to be passionately involved with what goes on with your words. I find your attitude—

Laissez-faire?

Perhaps from having dealt with those guys for so long, you're adjusted to the fact that it's going to be that way.

Yes, I am. This is very, very true.

I used to care passionately, and it never did a lot of good. I'll allow incisions and things like that now that I suppose six or seven years ago I wouldn't have allowed. It depends on the amount of ego involvement, to use an old phrase [*he turns it over in his mind, says it again: "ego…in-volvement"*], you have with your work. [*Laughs*] Hey, it's become so much more delightful to be alive and involved in the creative process since I've stopped caring about what happens with it after it leaves my typewriter. I put the best work I can into something, and I'm damned if I'm going to sit around and cry about it later, or hassle.

Now that you've come to this stage of enlightenment, perhaps you could start working with Weir again.

I do enjoy working with Weir once in a while, but he uses a lyricist like a whore, I gotta say. You can write incredible stuff for him, but he knows exactly what he wants. Often it's not where I want to be, but it ends there. I have a tendency not to want to write the sort of things he wants in songs.

When I'm working, I like to follow my own directions. The criticism I'll take is pretty much, "Could you improve the way you said that? It doesn't sing well," and I'll go back and find a different way to say what I said. Weir wants something more textural. He's not looking for the telling phrase, the apt combination of words to fire off a thought or an emotional process—he's looking more for a watercolor.

I think I haven't worked with him as much as I might, considering how much I respect his work—he puts together a damn good song. I've written some of the best Dead material with Weir, I think.

He'll give me a set of changes, and I'll come up with a set of lyrics. I'll give it to him, and if I forget to make a copy, that'll be the last I see of it. It'll go through the washing machine or get lost somewhere.

See, before you get into being a precious artist about these things, you have got to be a craftsman. Say you're a carpenter and somebody wants some shelves, and you come in with this beautiful door. There it is in a nutshell.

What about writing with Phil Lesh again?

We've agreed to do it, that I'd give him a set of lyrics and he'd give me some music. We might rip off two that way. I want him to give me music, because "Box of Rain" was an exceptionally quick song. I took the cassette home, and I started writing before I was through listening to it. The second listen, I neated the lyrics up, and that was that.

One of the reasons *Workingman's Dead* [1970] had such a nice, close sound to it is that we all met every day and worked on the material with acoustic guitars, just sat around and sang the songs. Phil would say, "Why don't we use a G minor there rather than a C?" that sort of thing, and a song would pop a little more into perspective. That's a good band way of working a song out.

Would you agree that that was your best writing?

The new songs on *Europe '72* are of a piece with *American Beauty* and *Workingman's Dead*. I'd love to see those released as a single album of tunes: "He's Gone," "Jack Straw," "Brown-Eyed Women," "Tennessee Jed," "Ramble On Rose."

I think "Ramble On Rose" is the closest to complete whimsy I've come up with. I just sat down and wrote numerous verses that tied around "Did you say your name was Ramblin' Rose? Ramble on, baby, heh, settle down easy."

What about "Tennessee Jack"?

It was Barcelona. Christie [Bourne, Hunter's girlfriend at the time] and I were out until all hours, drinking *vino tinto*. We were staggering back to our hotel, through this little alleyway between two church buildings, and it's cavernous—any sound you make just resonates and resonates. And there was this guy walking ahead of us, playing a Jew's harp. It was so out of place in Barcelona at 2:00 A.M., I just made the verses up and jotted them down when we got to the hotel: "Fell four flights and cracked my spine—[*imitating Jew's harp*] bwang tata bwang tata twang tata twang—Honey come quick with the eye-oh-dine." It was a good place to write a country song. That Jew's harp was so absurd in the context of Barcelona that it became realer than real.

You did an interview a while ago in which you talked about having created a character that represented the band, in songs like "Bertha," "Dire Wolf," and "Cumberland Blues." Then you said, "I think I might have mined·that particular vein clean. It seems that this character is well taken care of, and I can be free of him."

That's true. The character was dispensed with nicely in *Workingman's Dead*, then he popped up again in "Brown-Eyed Women." It's some composite relative of mine, part of my gestalt baggage. These things have as many layers of potential meaning to me when I've created them as they do to the listener, and I look for that.

My concept of symbols is that they represent something that you can't say straight out. You start manipulating concepts around symbolically in order to give the notion that you want. But if you could write it without symbols, then why not just write it without symbols?

People can take from a song what they will and give back to it what they can, but what is the responsibility of the writer to communicate? Are you just throwing some stuff out there and, "Here, come and pick through this pile of images and see what you can find"?

A song like "Row Jimmy"—

I like the little setups in that, the characters. I like "Julie catch a rabbit by his hair / come back step like to walk on air"—that's a whole song by itself. Then there's another song: "Here's a half a dollar if you dare / double twist when you hit the air."

From what? Hit the air from what?

From jumping down. Oh, I didn't make that clear. [*Mumbles lyrics to himself; eyebrows shoot up*] Oh. It has this image, I guess, of jumping from the levee. Actually, I guess I fancy a higher jump.

The main thrust of that is, do you dare jump in the air at all? And if you jump in the air, are you gonna have presence of mind enough to do a trick?

The title came from:

> How long, Jack, til we get to Singapore?
> How long, Joe, did we sign on for?
> Better keep bailing while the rain pours down
> The day crew's sleeping and the night crew's drowned[1]
> Row, Jimmy, Row
> Gonna get there I don't know…

Are my songs really that obtuse?

I could never get a handle on "Row Jimmy."

…Emotional impressions communicate through my symbols, which a person can relate to his own experience, and it isn't my business to detail the experiences that led up to them. Those impressions can relate to no one but myself, and the only way I can find out if I've communicated is through feedback. You're asking me these baffled questions about it, by which I judge that "Row Jimmy" didn't communicate on an intellectual

---

[1] See "Fair to Even Odds" in *A Box of Rain* (Viking, 1990), p. 76.

level, but you're concerned enough that it might have communicated on an emotional level.

Why did you stay out of sight all that time?

It's just common neurotic syndrome, that's all—isolationism, alienation, withdrawal. I am getting over it by the act of coming out, I think. It's not so weird out here. It's easy enough—you just have to work all the time, explain yourself. [*Laughs*]

I thought the Grateful Dead were so big that I'd have gotten mobbed. I didn't want to be unable to show my face, because I did a lot of walking, traveling; and being facially well known wouldn't have been a good trip at the time. Now it doesn't make any difference—I'm out performing, and that's what you do when you're performing....

Has it adversely affected the lives of your more recognizable friends?

Oh, it's very adversely affected them. They can't leave their hotel rooms in New York.

It's a little different here in Marin. Everybody's involved in rock and roll, or in law defending rock and roll bands against other rock and roll bands, or else they provide the corner grocery store where the rock 'n' roll bands shop. You see a little old lady on the street, you think "surely she's not involved with rock 'n' roll," but she turns out to be Phil Lesh's grandmother.

Jerry Garcia

Blair Jackson, David Gans
April 28, 1981
San Rafael, California

This interview, the first of two sessions for BAM *magazine, took place at Garcia's house. Blair Jackson, who was* BAM's *managing editor at the time (and later went on to publish the excellent Grateful Dead fanzine* The Golden Road*), invited me to join him as co-author, and our friend and fellow Deadhead Barbara Lewit, a member of* BAM's *administrative staff at the time, also came along.*

Gans: I just got a fresh copy of your yellow album, the John Kahn one.[1] "Russian Lullaby" is such a lovely song—

Garcia: It's one of the world's best songs. It's one of Irving Berlin's finest songs. It's a treat to play it, because compositionally it's so neat—it has nice chords, such a nice logic to it.

---

[1]Released on the Dead's own Round Records label, review copies of this LP had the words "Compliments of" stamped above the title *Garcia* on the cover. So the album was often referred to as *Compliments*, and when Grateful Dead Records rereleased it on compact disc in 1990 (GDCD40092) it was given the title *Compliments*.

Jackson: Do you listen to a lot of older stuff, looking for things like that?

Garcia: Not a lot. I listen to all kinds of stuff, and I don't really listen to look for things. I just listen to be listening, and every once in a while something jumps out and grabs me.

What happens to me is I get to be a fan of something. I listen to something for fun, and pretty soon it becomes something like an annoying commercial, almost. I just get hung up on it, so that pretty soon playing it or performing it is almost like the only way I can get rid of it. There's an element of the curse to it. Like anything, it sneaks up on you.

Most of those songs I didn't know, either, so I went in there like a studio vocalist, with the lyrics—most of them I'd only heard one or two times. That [album] was one of the few times when I didn't really go on a trip about the material. I let John [Kahn] do the material selecting, except for a few suggestions like "Russian Lullaby," which was one of mine. I wanted him to have something to do. I enjoy working with him, and it's one of those things that he can do, and it's one of those situations that doesn't happen to him much in the other parts of his musical life....John and I share such similarities of taste: something that I like, John is almost sure to like it. We're very like each other musically. That's one of the reasons I've been playing with him all this time.

Gans: Have you seen Group 87? Mark Isham, Peter Maunu, former Van Morrison guys. Like Weather Report, but they had a guitar instead of [saxophonist] Wayne Shorter. Like a young Weather Report...

Garcia: There are some real great those-kind-of-musicians. That's kind of like music-school music, state-of-the-art music-school music. Weather Report and the whole Chick Corea school of keyboard—an awful lot of it is like musicians' music. It's not really fun to listen to.

Gans: The feeling I get is that they are all playing on the same stage at the same time, but they aren't playing together. I'm used to the Grateful Dead, where there's incredible personal dynamics happening. With those guys, it was improvisations, but it was each guy on his own turf.

Garcia: I don't know why those guys, with their ability, don't have a concept that is sort of like ensemble improvisation. They're certainly capable of doing it but they don't, for some reason. They hint at it in their formal arrangements. There's like talk in their arrangements, nice things that happen between the bass and Wayne Shorter that are interesting, that they write formally. They are usually melodies and harmonies that would be fun to listen to them just play against each other in a more conversational style. I can hear it in my mind's ear, so to speak. But they don't do it, and I don't know why they don't.

That whole generation of players, all those guys—Weather Report, Return to Forever, and Al DiMeola—they all have that thing of real rigid solo structures. I don't know why they have chosen to tie themselves to that. I think it really limits the dynamism that's available to them in the music. They're like the first generation of really schooled musicians, like jazz musicians who have a good command of electric instruments—like as good as rock 'n' roll [musicians] have. It's like the first time that that technology has found its way into quote, serious, unquote, musicians.

Gans: There's this whole new generation of kids that woodshedded at home for years and never played with anybody. They have incredible licks—

Garcia: —but nothing to say. And they have difficulty working in a band context.

There's two or three classic life problems for musicians. It's not enough to just be good at your instrument—you also have to be able to get along with other musicians. You can't be entirely dogmatic, you can't become entirely self-serving.... You can't expect other musicians to play only your music.

Music stores are full of guys that play real great but don't have either the ability to get along well with other musicians or don't have a personal statement to make musically. It's like having a lot of technique and nowhere to go with it. Those are the curses of musicians—they always have been.

Gans: It turns up down the line in careers, too, when you see guys that end up with nothing to write about but the road.

Garcia: Right. That's another thing that's very annoying to me. That's why I've avoided writing that kind of song. It's a world that's so small—it really only relates to musicians, and it doesn't say that much to—

Jackson: Yeah, but if you spend 250 days on the road, what else are you going to write about?

Garcia: That's exactly true, that's the problem.

In reality, your life on the road is just like your regular life. The things that you go through on the road are just like the things that you go through anyway; it's a matter of finding something new to say about it. But that's like a trucker's viewpoint, which is a little bit hipper than a musician's point of view.

Jackson and Gans: Why?

Garcia: There's a little adventure involved in staying up all night behind the wheel of an eighteen-wheeler.

Gans: And there isn't in what you do?

Garcia: Naw. There isn't the kind of romance that I would decide would be something good to sing about. I'm not saying it's a bad trip. I'm just saying that of the things to write about, I would look for something more universal.

There are things that happen in that context that are universal, and I certainly can relate to lots of other things in life, apart from getting on and off airplanes, limousines, and backstage. Even though that's part of the furniture of my life, it's certainly not the events.

Gans: Thank god, because the songs that you write—

Garcia: Are few and far between!

I've got a whole bunch of them on the fire right now, but you won't hear them until, if I'm lucky, the autumn. If I'm not so lucky, January or February...I don't know when we'll be able to squeeze these in—it depends on when I get them done. If I get them done sufficiently before a tour, before one of these legs of our year's work, then we'll be able to learn some of them and start doing them before we record them.

Jackson: What prevents you from just sitting back for a few months and doing it?

Garcia: I'm not a forced writer.

Jackson: What I mean is, why do you have to go on the road all the time? Why can't the band just take a few months off—

Garcia: We don't make money except by going out and playing music. We don't get the kind of income from records—

Jackson: Last few records have sold pretty well, haven't they?

Garcia: But that money's already spent. You know, our overhead is immense. We're never that far ahead of ourselves—certainly not to the point of allowing us the luxury of two months to write songs.

Jackson: Do you think you'd be able to handle it if you did have the time?

Garcia: I wouldn't want to. I'd rather be playing. If I'm going to be creative, there's plenty of time in my day. It doesn't depend on the amount of time—if I had two months, it's possible that I wouldn't write anything. What'll happen is that those four or five songs that I'm working on, *working on* working on, will pop up the weekend after we go back on the road, and they'll all tumble out one after the other. It isn't something that—

Gans: I have songs that have taken years—

Garcia: That's right, and that's the way it is with songs. Some of them are real slow-growing, some of them are moments of inspiration. I can't make them happen. Every once in a while one pops out, all of a sudden it's there.

Gans: Can you name an example?

Garcia: Yeah, I can name several. There's a whole big part of "Terrapin" which was instantaneous. "Wharf Rat" was almost completely instantaneous.

Gans: Were the words already in existence?

Garcia: No, they weren't, but both of those things fell on incredible coincidences...just about the time I had those musical ideas worked out and showed them to Hunter, he happened to have lyrics that with a little alteration, a little fooling around, fit perfectly.

"Terrapin" was like bam-bam, it was right there. The "Lady with a Fan" part and the song behind it are both songs that I sat down at Hunter's house with the lyrics that he had and constructed the two with the thing of doing a lot of editing with his structures. I did a lot of editing. Then the whole thing [*hums the "Terrapin" instrumental theme*] and all the voicings, the instruments and everything, that whole thing came as a completely orchestrated idea. I got that idea driving my car. I drove home real fast and sat down with the guitar and worked it all out real quick so I wouldn't forget it, because it was all there. I had it completely envisioned, the whole way it would work. The next day, I showed it to the band, and I showed everybody their part, more or less, and then left them to construct more elaborations or variations if they wanted, all the things that they do which are their own additions to it. But basically, it's an orchestrated idea.

Jackson: How much intraband collaboration is there at this point? How far do you have the arrangements—

Garcia: The arrangements are almost nil. The intraband collaboration is almost total, insofar as that what a song is in the Grateful Dead is a melody, lyrics, and chord changes, and that's it, really. Apart from that, it's what everybody finds to say.

Gans: That speaks volumes about the development of your arrangements. I've observed Weir writing his songs day by day. Your conceptions seem to be a little more complete when you take them to the band, or you're a little more casual about how you present them.

Garcia: Yeah. Well, I make an effort to leave them—he goes for more highly evolved...but what happens to him is that he constructs everything but the melody. The melody is the last thing to get composed.. It's backwards from the way I do it, and you can tell, because a lot of times they're melody-weak. They're arrangement-strong and melody-weak. Every once in a while he gets real good ones, where the whole thing is real graceful, like "Estimated Prophet." I thought that was a well-conceived, well-written song.

The sung melody is where people have the hardest time getting access to Weir, especially his solo stuff. They don't have the kind of sung melody you find running through your head, a happy marriage of lyric and melody. And Weir knows about it; we've discussed it lots of times.

Gans: Do you write on the guitar?

Garcia: I write on keyboards more often than I do guitar. I sit down with a piano and sing. If I'm working off of lyrics that are already there, then what I'll do is like play a chord or a couple of chords and just let them ring, and see what saying the lyrics does. Sometimes I like to just start from what rhythmically the phrasing suggests to me, or what the meter suggests, and then I go from there sometimes.

Jackson: Do you play piano well enough that it doesn't limit you at all?

Garcia: No, I don't. A lot of times I have to figure out what I'm doing, but in a way that's liberating.

Jackson: I would think that would be confining.

Garcia: No, it's not. It puts you in a situation of seeing relationships in kind of a fresh way, since I don't spend a lot of time looking at a keyboard....I only started to [get into the keyboard] about the time I did my first solo album [recorded in 1971]. That group of songs I started writing using the keyboard. "To Lay Me Down" is probably my first keyboard song.

Jackson: Those songs seem to have worn very well.

Garcia: Really—I still do almost all of them.
  "The Wheel" is one of the songs that happened in the studio as a complete accident, almost.

Gans: Do you miss playing the steel guitar?

Garcia: No. Really, it's a hard instrument to play. I would love to play the pedal steel if I had another lifetime in which to play it. If I had a situation where I only had to play steel.
  It's really a weird instrument. Your first thought is to try and think of it in terms of a guitar. You have to erase that entirely from your thinking or you won't get anything out of it.

Jackson: David Lindley...says his whole key to success in playing fiddle, pedal steel, lap steel, etc., is to think of them basically as an extension of the same instrument.

Garcia: That might work for him, but it doesn't work for me. The pedal steel has its own logic. Does David Lindley play pedal steel? He plays lap steel—well, that you can think of as being a mutated guitar. But the [pedal] steel is an arpeggiated instrument. It has a different sense to it. The guitar has a certain sense based on the intervallic relationships in the tuning. The pedal steel's intervals are not designed so much for a vertical, harmonic approach to music, like a chorded approach—its layout is more like the white keys on a piano.

Gans: They're all there for you—

Garcia: Yeah. Fundamentally, what you have is a whole collection of triads that are separated various ways. Major triads are like a string apart. All the melodies are laid across those, like there are three or four keys superimposed. When you change the pedal settings, basically you're changing the triads and the tuning.

I just don't like to change tunings, and I don't like to change guitars on stage.

Gans: Did it embarrass you as much as it embarrassed us that Weir learned to play slide on the road for two or three years?

Garcia: It still embarrasses me, but luckily it doesn't embarrass him.

Gans: I got the feeling that you dropped "Stagger Lee" because you were sick of hearing what he did on it.

Garcia: Yeah, in a way. I'm into letting Weir do what he wants to do, and sometimes I like his slide playing. It's so nasty and outrageously raunchy, you know? Sometimes that's neat, when he hits it.

Jackson: I think there's something to be said for the garage band ethos. Why not learn onstage?

Garcia: Yeah. That's as good a place as any to learn.

Jackson: The only people who are going to be offended are the tapers who listen to it later, and who cares what they think?

Gans: I'm offended there, because a sour note's a sour note.

Garcia: That's the way I feel about it. Weir does them and sometimes isn't even aware of them. He was amazed to hear how outrageously out of tune some of his slide playing was.

Gans: You guys are forgiven a lot—

Garcia: [*Laughs*] Tell me about it. To me, it's totally amazing that we even have an audience, much less—

Gans: Greil Marcus sums it up: "It's like life—they'll bore you to tears in between the fabulously exciting moments."

Jackson: Recently, he said he won't even write about the Dead anymore.

Garcia: I can understand that.

Gans: As a musician…when I go to a show, sometimes there's a battle between leaving the guitar fingers at home and enjoying, and—I'm too analytical, paying too much attention to the musical things.

Garcia: That's the curse of being a musician. You can't turn your back on that part of yourself.

I'm that sort of listener, too. What you're after is what we're all after. What I'm after is a real great musical experience—and that means that it's in tune, that certain niceties are observed. That's what I want to have happen, and when that doesn't happen it's disappointing for me…being a member of the audience going to hear someone else play, if they perform poorly I'm disappointed. I want it to be great. Going onstage is no exception: I really do want it to be great, and I am terribly disappointed if it's not. That means every aspect of it.

But when you're working in a band, you have to try to let everybody have his own voice the way he best sees it. There are always going to be things that create friction. It's part of what's interesting between [Weir] and I. He's always going to make decisions musically that I'm not going to agree with fully, but I'll go along with them anyway….

The way it is with Weir is that he's continually making discoveries that are like old discoveries for some others of us. But on the other hand, there are ideas that Weir has that I would never have had, that in fact maybe only he has. That's his unique value—he's an extraordinarily original player in a world full of people who sound like each other. He's got a style that's totally unique as far as I know. I don't know anybody else who plays the guitar the way he does, with the kind of approach that he has to it. That in itself is, I think, really a score, considering how derivative almost all electric guitar playing is.

I hear my influences, to some extent, in myself. With Weir, I have a real hard time recognizing any influences in his playing that I could put my finger on and say, "that's something that Weir got from X and such," even though I've been along for almost all of his musical development. I've been playing with him since he was sixteen or so.

Gans: Does he hide it well?

Garcia: I just don't know where he gets it. He keeps up with other stuff more than anybody in the band, probably. He does an awful lot of listening, but he doesn't do much stealing. His ideas are—

Jackson: He's cagey.

Garcia: Yeah, he is cagey. He's an interesting player to play with. He and I have discussed our guitaristic relationship together so much that there's a lot of our playing together that ends up having a complementary quality to it, because we're both so different from each other. It's neat—it makes it fun.

• • •

Garcia: I keep saying in interviews and stuff—people say, "Aren't you surprised you've been together sixteen years?" and I keep saying it's like we're just getting started. There's so much that we haven't even done with the band in its present incarnation, places that we've already touched·into in other forms imperfectly—in our past incarnations we've had imperfect versions of things we were trying to do, which we'll be able to do so much nicer with the band the way it presently is constituted.

Gans: Are you really happy with Brent, then?[2]

[2]Keyboardist Brent Mydland had been playing in the band for two years at the time of this interview.

Garcia: Oh, yeah. I think he's an excellent musician, and a great choice for the band. But like I say, you're not going to hear how this band goes— it's down the road a piece. I would say that it's a couple of years in the future.

Gans: I'm so glad you got a guy with a synthesizer—

Garcia: That's what we wanted. What we always wanted was somebody that would produce color. The thing of having another percussion instrument in an all-percussion band was really too much of the same thing. The effect the piano had on the ensemble was something we could accomplish with guitars, so what we were really looking for was that sustain—you know, we were all hungry for color. Real hungry.

Gans: There was a time in the early seventies, between keyboardists— some of the best "Dark Stars."

Garcia: Yeah, because we were real free.

Gans: How come you gave up [Gibson] Les Paul [guitars]?

Garcia: I got bored with them. I felt that I really didn't have any place else to go on them.

Gans: So you switched to a Strat [Fender Stratocaster]?

Garcia: Yeah. It was more of a challenge. It wasn't that I wanted to lose the SG[3] part of my playing, but my reasoning was something along the lines of, "I think that no matter what guitar I play I won't have any trouble getting a sweet sound," even though the most difficult thing to produce on a Strat is a sweet sound. What I really wanted was to be able to get some of the metallic clang that Strats have. I like that first position, the clanki- ness—

Gans: You can finger-pick Fenders better too.

---

[3]The Gibson SG is a solid-body variant of the Les Paul which Garcia played for a few years.

Garcia: Yeah. They have better string-to-string separation...they don't mush up on you the way Gibsons do, and it was that clarity that I was looking for, too—that crispness that you associate with country-and-western guitar players. I was wanting to have something in between those two worlds.

Gans: My first extended Dead experience was at Berkeley [Community Theatre] in [August] '72, and Bobby was playing his [Gibson ES-] 355 and you were on the Strat—it was a great blend....

Garcia: Weir's whole trip with his guitar development has come closer and closer to the stuff that I've been into for a long time. Now his guitar sort of surrounds my sound.

Gans: He's got a lot more high end than he used to—

Garcia: Yeah. So now I go after a more hornlike sound, with less overtones.

Gans: Your idea of wiring an effects loop into your guitar—

Garcia: One of the best ideas I ever had.

Gans: You thought of it yourself?

Garcia: That's my own idea. It's really easy. The modifications are nil—all you have to do is put a jack in there.

Not every guitar is set up so you can do that. Fender logic is just really tailor-made for that, because everything comes before the tone and volume pots—switching...you can come right off the pickups, and you automatically pick up the selector switch, then you go straight to the gadgets full tilt, then come back. It's a straight-ahead wiring interruption. Other guitars, the logic is set up such that you can't do that—they have a more circuitous way of connecting the switch, and the order in which the tone controls follow the switch...if there's an independent volume and tone for each pickup, as on a Gibson, it doesn't work too good. My trip evolved from Stratocaster wiring, and it worked out so stunningly great that it knocked me out. The answer to the instability problem of gadgets onstage. The fact that they're all input sensitive—

If I don't plug in the stereo jack, it's just a regular guitar. And there's a switch so I can cut the circuit in and out.

I wanted to use those things, but I wanted them to be stable, and there's no way to make them stable after the volume control. It's the best way I've run into to make those things make sense. And it depends on your philosophy. My philosophy is one of predictability—basically, I want my guitar to do the same things every time I plug it in. That's been my approach to things like strings and picks and everything, because when you're on the road, if you're using something specialized and peculiar and you don't have it with you and you can't get it in a music store, you're fucked.

• • •

Jackson: I'd like to ask a question about production: You've worked with three different producers in the studio on three albums, and I'm wondering what you think you've gotten out of those three producers comparatively, and where it will take you on your next studio album. Certainly [Keith] Olsen [*Terrapin Station,* 1977], Lowell [George] [*Shakedown Street,* 1978], and [Gary] Lyons [*Go to Heaven,* 1979] have different styles—

Garcia: They're very good, and very different from each other. For me, it was interesting to see how other people deal with the Grateful Dead. I think that part of it alone was worthwhile, even if there was nothing else to it but just the way they went about working with it.

Jackson: Do you think that was their approach? "Let's see what we can do with the Grateful Dead?"—sort of like a bizarre challenge?

Garcia: Yeah, along those lines. They all had different relative levels of consciousness about it. None of them were as self-conscious about that idea as I would be, or I am. Insofar as a producer has to make an effort to understand what it is you're doing musically, we were lucky in that each of those guys, as far as I was concerned, paid some dues to understand where Grateful Dead music is at and what we were trying to accomplish with the material we were working with. They spent time with us while we were rehearsing the tunes. They made the effort—they would ask musical questions that had some sense to them—what's happening during these eight bars or this twelve bars of the tune. They all had their different ways of dealing with that level of understanding, which was nice. And there were just lots of little things, that just in terms of your growing encyclopedia, my vocabulary of little things, production licks, really—I picked up some stuff from all of those guys that are useful little things. I can't talk about them because they're not big hunks of generalized knowledge—they're numerous little specific things. There's always something to be learned from working with other people. Whether or not those records, or working with producers, has been in any way helpful for us as a recording band is maybe doubtful.

Jackson: How would you judge that?

Garcia: Well, one way you could judge it would be by sales. The sales on those were about steady, just like our other records. It didn't create any change.

Gans: Did you choose Keith Olsen, for example, with the hope that he would make a more commercial record?

Garcia: In a certain sense we did. When we went with Arista, we went with a spirit of cooperation, thinking, well, we've tried things our way; we've had our own record company, we've produced ourselves—we've done it a lot, in fact—and it'd be interesting to try somebody else's approach totally, and see where it takes us, because of the fact that our records—as records—have always been neither here nor there. They haven't been relevant. We wanted some fresh ears—that was part of why that idea didn't seem outrageous to us. People who were Grateful Dead purists said, "Why did you get another producer? Why didn't you produce yourselves, or why didn't you have Dan Healy produce you?" The reason is that we're very conscious of how easy it is to get into your own trip so much that you just don't have any sense of it, no objectivity at all. It's easy to do.

Gans: But neither approach has worked.

Garcia: By the standards of whether records sell a lot or not.

Gans: That's not the standard I was even thinkin' of. I don't feel like your records satisfy you guys very much, either.

Garcia: No. They never have. But I've had some good, successful, satisfying solo records.

Jackson: Is that because not as many compromises?

Garcia: No. I don't feel that compromises are made on Grateful Dead records. *Cats Under the Stars* [Arista AB-4160, 1978] is my favorite one. That's the one that I'm happiest with, from every point of view in which I operate on that record. We did all those tunes on tour right after the album came out, with John [Kahn] and Maria [Muldaur], Keith and Donna [Godchaux], and I think Ronnie Tutt was still playing drums with us on those first few tours.

Jackson: What is it about the structure of your solo band that doesn't allow you to go quite as far in different directions musically?

Garcia: Because it is my band, and because I myself as a musical personality am more limited than the Grateful Dead.

Gans: Is it more your guitarist band, where you indulge yourself as a guitarist?

Garcia: In a way—and also as a singer, and a performer. I indulge myself.

Jackson: It never breaks down and goes into other directions like it does with the Dead.

Garcia: That's probably because I don't open it up that often. And also part of it is that I've kept having new versions of my band that I wasn't quite satisfied with, and it's not until I'm really happy with the way a band is going that I start to throw in things that start to open up. I've got to feel real comfortable with it—I've done it with John Kahn, and some versions of our band we have opened up and let it blow.

Gans: There was a time you were doing "Don't Let Go" and it got real spacy.

Garcia: That's right. My band was good during that period of time. I was really comfortable with the way that band was going. We were doing all kinds of things—we had some Beatles tunes, some Rolling Stones tunes— all kinds of sort of daring things. We did "Moonlight Mile" with three-part harmony—that was really beautiful. We had some real beautiful things going, nice things. Me and Donna used to sing McCartney's "Let Me Roll It," and it was real nice. I'm just waiting for the band to evolve to the place where I can take it in those directions again. I may get some singers in the band.

Gans: You seem to have gotten back into your voice—

Garcia: I'm starting to learn how to sing, is what's happening.

Gans: Along about New Year's you started really sounding inspired.

Garcia: Well, it's one of those things—I got warmed up. As a tour rolls on I start to remember things I'd forgotten. It's a learning process, and again, if I'm really comfortable with the music and everything else is invisible, that's when I can really start to sing. For me it's real delicate: any little thing will disturb my singing. If the band doesn't sound just right, and if things aren't going just right, boy—

Gans: Is the batting average a little higher these days?

Garcia: Yeah, much higher. It's heading toward places it's never been. I think you'd have to be in the band to really know that level of it, but we've had so many instances of suggesting these spaces that are more wonderful in the suggestion than in the realization, and we haven't gotten around to the realization of certain ideas that we've instituted…just the ideas themselves have so much power that they continue to be legendary in spite of the fact that we haven't performed them for a long time, or they haven't found their way into our music the way it's presently constituted. That's the thing about the Grateful Dead: there's this amazing richness of stuff. It just takes a long time to get it to where everybody knows all of it. A lot of it is complicated, and it requires time. Nothing else will do but time, and I don't feel that what's there is going to be exposed for another couple of years.

Jackson: It's more an intuitive thing than something concrete?

Garcia: It's really both. What we would have to do is go through a bunch of Grateful Dead records, tapes of live shows, and I would point things out to you and say, "Listen to that passage there," "Remember how this worked," stuff like that. We used to spend a lot of time rehearsing, a lot of time. When we were working on odd time-signature things like "The Eleven," we spent a lot of time rehearsing, and as a result we worked out some tremendously intricate things.

Jackson: Some of the best jams came out of that stuff, too.

Garcia: That's true, because your best strength comes from having a secure knowledge about what's going on, having a real solid foundation and knowing where you are. With the Grateful Dead, those of us who have been with the band for a long time have put in those hours, but whenever we get a new member, that member has to go through a similar number of hours, in their own terms, and we have to turn them on to those discoveries, and that actual work that we did.

It takes a long time to get the band up to date in the sense of just us exploring our own past, our own good ideas which we have either decided not to do—well, the reason we don't do everything that we've ever done is because basically we have to relearn it. It really has to do with time, and that's the thing that's hardest to come by. Damn...

Jackson: Are you ever conscious of borrowing from specific parts of your repertoire? It sometimes seems to me that entire periods are totally left out. Is that just random?

Garcia: It's random. It has to do with—just that we don't flash on it. When we get in a place where we're purely rehearsing, like if we had a two-month period set aside in which we aren't obliged to deliver anything, any product, or to prepare for a road gig—then you start remembering things.

For example, all of that acoustic stuff that we did on that acoustic double set[4] was the result of about three afternoons of rehearsal. That means the harmonies, the arrangements, everything. We spent such a small amount of time preparing for that, and it yielded an enormous amount of results. I don't know whether that's illustrative, but what I'm trying to point out is that rehearsal time for the Grateful Dead at this point is the thing that we need most to be able to mine our own wealth, to get at the things that we're capable of.

[4]*Reckoning*, Arista A2L-8604, 1981. Recorded in San Francisco and New York in the fall of 1980, the same series of performances that yielded the electric double-LP *Dead Set*.

Jackson: What are the sort of things that would lead to a radical transformation of a song like, for example, "Friend of the Devil," from a zippy up-tempo thing to a very slow—

Garcia: It's the thing of flashing on a song from a different point of view. What happened with that one was that I heard a tape of Kenny Loggins doing the tune. Loggins and Messina used to do it as a solo acoustic tune, and he did it as a slow ballad. I heard a tape of that, and it stuck in my head and I thought, "Wow, that's a nice way for that song to go. It is a nice ballad." It was somebody else's version of the song which exposed a character thing to it that I had never noticed before.

Any tunes that we do from the past have to be rearranged, the vocals reworked. It's all lying there in rehearsal time—that's what the Grateful Dead wants.

Gans: The shows seem to be increasingly set in concrete, [although in] the places in the second set where it opens up, it is really opening up wide.

Garcia: One gives you the other: the more rigid the form, the greater your sense of exhilaration at the freedom at the other end of it—the light at the other end of the tunnel. But all those capabilities can be improved upon. It's really a matter of time; that's the only thing that's keeping us from moving in all the directions we can. It's an interesting problem. In a way, we're burdened by the amount of good potential we have. It takes a little while to crack the egg.

Grateful Dead rehearsals aren't strictly rehearsals in the sense of going and working a piece of material out totally. It's a matter of like throwing out half a dozen tunes and working on them all at once in little bits, getting them halfway presentable. That whole process pulls in little bits and pieces of other things, and other ideas start flying together. It doesn't yield results in the sense of a real slick show. What happens is that all of a sudden there's bunch of new tunes here and there, or tunes you haven't heard for a long time, and they may be kind of rickety or the early performances may be kinda rusty, or there'll be a lot of forgotten lyrics. But during the course of a tour or a working period, this whole change will happen.

The way the Grateful Dead works is kind of nonlinear. Any kind of effort in a creative sense yields results on all different levels. That's the payoff of having been together for a long time: it gets you oiled.

Jackson: Are there songs you have that for whatever reason you just will not do because they don't mean the same thing?

Garcia: Yeah. Like all those *Aoxomoxoa* songs. A lot of them are cumbersome to perform, overwritten. "China Cat Sunflower" is marginal. But a lot of tunes on there are just packed with lyrics, or packed with musical changes that aren't worth it for what happens finally with the song. There isn't a graceful way to perform them and have them have what they originally had.

"Cosmic Charlie" was really a recording song, and even when we did perform it it always had its weaknesses. The weaknesses were part of what's musically clever about the songs, but part of what's cumbersome about performing them. "Cosmic Charlie" has some really complex chord voicings in the bridges. Being able to pull off the changes and do the vocals—last time we worked it out was with Donna [in 1976], and it was pretty effective, sort of. But we still had a hell of a time getting through those bridges, and the fact that it didn't stick as a piece of material tells something about what was flawed about the construction. It's not quite performable.

Gans: The group instinct and the individual instincts at work are perhaps even more powerful than the intellects at work.

Garcia: That's our strong point, if there is one: our intuitive sense. Compositionally, there are things about those songs that are embarrassing to me now, but at the time I wasn't writing songs for the band to play, I was writing songs to be writing songs. Those were the first songs me and Hunter did together, and we didn't have the craft of songwriting down. We did things that in retrospect turned out to be unwise, just from the point of view of playing songs that people enjoy—it's important that the musicians in the band enjoy playing the tune. You should try to take that into account when you write a song—it should be fun to play. When you write a song that's a chore to play, the performances never sound anything but strained. Even if the song has something great going for it, if the musicians you're playing with don't enjoy the song it'll never work. If the song requires more of you than you can comfortably come up with onstage...songs like "Cosmic Charlie," there's technically too much happening there for me to be able to come up with a comfortable version of it that I can sing and play on stage. I never would have thought about that when I started writing songs. I didn't realize that you had to think about that stuff, or that I would eventually have to think about that stuff.

Jackson: Why do you think there aren't more bands that play heavily improvisational rock?

Garcia: Couldn't tell ya. I just don't know. We do it because it's our basic drive, an inescapable part of what we do musically.

Jackson: At one point there were tons of people who did it, and then they dropped off one by one by one by one, and now there's the Grateful Dead.

Garcia: Well, one of the reasons is that all the pop music trends have been for songs and, you know, catchy shit. It's all been song/formula-oriented. You can't say that improvisational rock 'n' roll is a leading trend. It isn't exactly in the forefront of what's going on in music.

Jackson: Yet people coming up would see in your stuff a constant growth in terms of audience. In '71 you were playing the Fillmore East, and now you're playing Madison Square Garden. It's not like it's anticommercial music.

Garcia: No, but we don't get that kind of exposure, and when we do get exposure on the radio, it's not our improvisational stuff. There is no place for that to happen. I guess that's partly the reason that a lot of young musicians that are happening now and getting their first exposure, the framework in which they see themselves playing is like three-minute songs, a snappy show. It seems that things go in fits and starts, and maybe even big waves and patterns—maybe there are and maybe there aren't— where what happens is that that style of playing, that approach to music, will be rediscovered pretty quick here in one of these flashes....
    There's a very, very recent new psychedelic music, postpunk, which may find itself going in that direction, but I don't see that direction ever really being prominent. It really depends on whether the players see their music as being able to support inprovisation.

Gans: There's got to be thousands of guys like me that cut our teeth on your music, and yet hope to succeed.

Jackson: Yeah, but you guys are getting into your thirties now, and it's going farther away from the idea of music as a vocation, I think.

Gans: But it seems like there must be younger Deadheads, and there's nothing more fun than playing—

Garcia: If there are younger players who enjoy playing, and their playing is interesting enough that their audience enjoys it as well, then they will be encouraged to do that the way we've been encouraged to do it. We do it partly because it's who we are—we even did it when we were playing in bars, five sets a night—and they *hated* us for it.

It's really difficult to extrapolate from the Grateful Dead to the music business or the music scene—we're really not quite in that whole world as it's presently constructed. We're like the exception to every rule. We're in some kind of nonformula, nonlinear developmental path which is definitely growing. We are experiencing growth in terms of our audience—it's not like we're just dragging along the same audience, we're actually getting new people. I don't know why that's happening—least of all me, really.

Jackson: I always thought it would have been interesting to see what would have happened with the Allman Brothers in that respect if Duane had lived.

Garcia: That's the direction they were trying to go in. They were definitely in that space. All you can do is wonder what they would have done.

Jackson: Are there any groups that you feel any particular affinity to? I would have guessed Weather Report, but from what you said earlier, you don't feel that.

Garcia: Not really. I don't really feel any affinity toward any group, really.

Gans: There's an emotional tone about the Grateful Dead that's unique. I've often likened it more to theater than to music, because I get the same mental relationship to the stage with you guys that I get at a really hot theatrical performance.

Garcia: It's the same kind of chemistry.

Gans: There's much more trust happening at a Grateful Dead concert than is ever required at a James Taylor show.

Garcia: That's right. The whole thing is this mutual agreement that allows the whole thing to happen. I'm conscious of that. It's definitely that for me. Being in the Grateful Dead is taxing in a way that nothing else is. When it's hard, it's the hardest thing there is, and when it's easy, it's magic.

Gans: When is it hard?

Garcia: It's hard when it's hard. It's not quite black-and-white. If things aren't happening really perfect, then the Grateful Dead is really hard work. If things are happening, in some kind of special way, then it's the easiest thing in the world—it's reflexive, almost. You don't think about anything, you don't plan anything, and it's no sweat. There's not much effort involved.

It's either one or the other—when it's not that then it's this hard, kind of taxing—there's no middle ground.

Gans: Like a six-person marriage?

Garcia: That's sort of what it's like. And for reasons that we don't know, sometimes it's all there, and other times no amount of effort can make it there.

If I tell somebody from the audience, "Tonight was really hard work, and it seemed impossible to get anything together," I always get these reports back that it was great. I'm not able to tell whether or not what happens to us emotionally or physically has any kind of relevance to the way everybody else experiences it. One of the things that's amazing about it is that everybody experiences it on their own terms, but from the point of view of being a player it's this thing that you can't make happen, but when it's happening, you can't stop it from happening. That's the closest I can come to really explaining it. I've tried to analyze it on every level that I can gather together, and all the intellectual exercise in the world doesn't do a fucking thing—doesn't help a bit, doesn't explain it one way or another to any degree of satisfaction. The Grateful Dead has some kind of intuitive thing—I don't know what it is or how it works, but I recognize it phenomenologically. I know it because it's reported to me hugely from the audience, and it's something that we know because we've compared notes among ourselves in the band. We talk about it, but all those things are by way of agreeing that we'll continue to keep trying to do this thing, whatever it is, and that our best attitude to it is sort of this stewardship, in which we are the custodians of this thing.

Gans: One time I came home from a concert and wrote, "The Grateful Dead is immortal, but these men who play in the band are not."

Garcia: That's exactly right, and that's the way we feel. It takes the responsibility out of our hands, which is comfortable. It's scary if you feel like you're responsible for it—that's a lot of energy to be responsible for. I've had to pay those dues in the psychedelic world.

Gans: You know how much power is ascribed to you—to the band as a whole, but to you as the focus.

Garcia: Yeah, I know, and luckily I've already been able to disqualify myself from it. I know it's not me. They make the association, but that isn't the case—well, it doesn't really matter what they believe, I've already tested it. People can believe whatever they want—I know from personal subjective testing that that is not the case.
 Everybody has their own version, and that's good. That's one of the things about music that makes it a special thing. It can be experienced that way—it's so close to being perfect fascism.

Gans: What does that mean?

Garcia: Well, it's so close to being perfectly manipulative. It borders on that, and people who use formula things on the audience are basically manipulating them in the same sense that fascism manipulates people.

Gans: You mean show-biz tricks?

Garcia: Sure. That's just what they are, show-biz tricks.

Jackson: There's a certain amount of that involved, though, with what you do.

Garcia: Oh, yeah, a certain amount of it, but our trip is to learn the tricks and then not use them. For us, we've discovered them—"Oh, far out, when we do this, look what happens to the audience." "Yeah, let's not do that." We want for the Grateful Dead to be something that isn't the result of tricks, and we don't trust ourselves with it. We certainly don't trust anybody else with it.

Jackson: It's always struck me that in the second set, where theoretically things are very open-ended and loose, there always seems to be a time where you're in the middle of "Stella Blue," and all of a sudden it's "Sugar Magnolia," which is like the most manipulative thing you can do. It says to everyone, "This is the end of the show," no matter what mood you're in. "Get into your party mood, 'cause this is it." It's really no different.

Garcia: We end up closing the door just like we open up the door. In that sense, we create that framework. It has its ups and downs.

Jackson: So in a sense, you are conscious of it as a show.

Garcia: The contour of it...

Jackson: I've always thought it would be very interesting if you ended on a down note, if suddenly the end was "Stella Blue."

Garcia: We've done it. We used to end with real dire things in the old days—we used to end with "Death Don't Have No Mercy," and things like that. I like to end it gently sometimes. I really feel like I'd like for it to taper down.

Jackson: It seems very manufactured sometimes.

Garcia: Sometimes it is.

● ● ●

Jackson: Are you pretty comfortable now in places the size of Madison Square Garden?

Garcia: The Garden used to be tremendously frightening and intimidating, and we'd always heard the worst things about it. But playing there has been nothing but fun for us, so far. Every time we've played there it's been good. You never can tell about a place. I don't know whether it's the energy of the New York crowd, or whether it's just the place itself, but for some reason, we play well in there and we enjoy playing there. That is really something good, a real good score, because it's tough to play in New York City.

...We play with greater sensitivity and clarity here [in California] than we do on the East Coast. We play with greater energy there.

Gans: More rock and roll there and more space here?

Garcia: Well, that's a simplistic way of looking at it, but you could put it that way. The ones around New York City have their own flavor.

Jackson: It struck me that the whole fifteenth anniversary thing was sort of foisted upon you—

Garcia: It was, man. I don't know whose idea it was. Actually, it was somebody's observation. Somebody noticed it.

Jackson: Fifteenth anniversary from what?

Garcia: From when the band was formed, or when we played our first gigs, or something. Actually, Phil remembered—he's got an uncanny memory for things of that sort, like numbers, dates, days, that kind of stuff. He remembers that kind of stuff, and I never do. He was able to come closest to sort of pinpointing it. He may have called it. I would never have noticed it, really.

Jackson: Is it inaccurate to think that his role in the band has diminished in the last couple of years?

Garcia: Well, he doesn't sing—

Jackson: But even live, he doesn't seem to have the same kind of presence.

Garcia: It's possible, He's a different kind of guy than he used to be— he's definitely changed a lot. You'd have to ask him. I can't tell you, because he's a hard guy to know, and it's also one of those things where I can't characterize him in a way that I think is fair to him. To get insight into his personality you'd have to talk to him about it and see where he thinks of himself as being. Phil has a much tighter sine wave to who he is. He goes through his changes much more frequently and much more intensely than I think of myself as doing. This is really coffee-table psychoanalysis at its cheapest, I don't mind telling you. Phil is an incredibly complex and brilliant guy. He does things for reasons of his own that are, just like his music, not easy for me to understand. I don't know why he is the way he is, or why he does what he does, or what kind of thoughts he thinks on and off, but I do know that his periods of being enthusiastic and estrangement, which we all have about the Grateful Dead—we're all ambivalent about the Grateful Dead, it gets to be a love-hate thing after a while—that he goes through those changes with greater frequency. Sometimes during the course of a gig, he'll go through two or three great big changes. He's much harder on himself than anybody is on him. He punishes himself in his own mental being, his own artistic space or whatever it is. But he's a tremendously brilliant guy, and I think he has a huge role. He's like one of the fulcrumatic personalities in the band. If Phil is happening, the band's happening.

Gans: If Brent was on the rag, would it affect you as much?

Garcia: Not as much. Nor me, or [Bill] Kreutzmann, or Weir. Phil has more power individually than any of the rest of us has. He really is super-important, and...

The way our relationships are in the band is that we can see each other clearly and we can't see ourselves. That's the position that we're in, relationshipwise. It's very difficult to see how you yourself fit in, and it's easy for you to see how others have power, but it's not easy for you to communicate to them the amount of power that they have. You can tell somebody, but that doesn't mean they can know. We try to report to each other to some extent what it's like and what we think is happening. We have frameworks through which to talk about it—we have our own metaphors, our own ways of discussing what's happening in the Grateful Dead that make the most sense to us, but ultimately you can't tip off anybody—the Grateful Dead has this weird quality, and everybody feels this, people in the audience feel it regularly, that "if I could just get everybody to do what I wanted them to do, or do it the way they did it that night, it would just be perfect." You know? It has this fixable quality.

Gans: And it never happens.

Garcia: Right. You can't do it just by knowing the symptoms. You'd think that you would be able to make corrections in music just by saying what it is you think is deficient.

Gans: I get the feeling that certain guys in the band, or different guys at different times, would automatically do the opposite if you ever asked them to do something.

Garcia: Oh, yeah. There is that degree of perversity.

Barbara Lewit: One time I asked you to play "Cold Rain and Snow," and you said, "Well, we were gonna play it last night, but Mickey wanted to do it."

Garcia: You know, if we can't fuck with each other, who can we fuck with?

Lewit: Who's the moodiest in the band?

Garcia: Everybody is pretty moody. I couldn't assign that to anybody, because everybody has their moments of tremendous reasonableness that stretch on for years at a time sometimes, then go through years of craziness, intractable weirdness. Everybody's weird, everybody's bent in the Grateful Dead. Nobody is that "clean," you know what I mean?

Gans: It seems to me that the crew, especially the sound men, are almost like full members of the band.

Garcia: Damn near. They're there when we have our business meetings. We're dragging them through life; shouldn't they have some say about it? We're all working on the same thing—why should we treat each other any differently?

Gans: How lucky you guys are to have the freedom you have. I know of no other human beings that are able to walk out on stage—the economics of it notwithstanding—you guys can do what you do every night—

Garcia: Yeah, you're right. We're insanely lucky! I appreciate it like crazy.

I don't think there's a good excuse for being unhappy. I'm not particularly unhappy, but I know what pain is. I think that life is characterized by pain, partly. Part of the way you can tell you're alive is by how much pain you're experiencing, or how little.... You get your ups and your downs. I've always assumed that something like the laws of karma prevail. Something good happens, something bad's going to happen of equal volume. I haven't spent my time measuring and collecting data on it—I just have a suspicion that things are sort of that way.

You don't gain an improved position just by virtue of being in the Grateful Dead, for example. We're frequently seen as being privileged somehow, but being in the Grateful Dead is in no way privilege. It doesn't exempt you from anything particularly, and the reward is a fleeting, existential kind of reality, where really the most important thing is the gig that just happened. Everything that we've done is culminated in the last note that we played. If it was a bad gig, it's like there's nothing but suicide, that the only reasonable thing to do is end it all. But the hope that there'll be a better one is an ever-present possibility. Luckily they change for the better often enough so that it isn't complete darkness. But the nature of the experience is such that it's just balanced, really, on the most recent experience. No matter how good it's ever been, if the last gig was a bum one, god, you're stuck.

Jackson: Do you get suspicious if you have a streak?

Garcia: Yeah, then I start worrying. "What's gonna go wrong?"

Jackson: You say, "Maybe I'd better fuck this up"—

Garcia: Sure, that's exactly right! I've gone through so many of those things, all the way up to and including perversely trying to make it be as miserable as I can. But I wouldn't want it to have less range than that. If it had less range than that, we would be cutting it off somewhere short of its full capacity as an experience.

Seeing as how we're living our life through this medium "Grateful Deadness," whatever that is, we definitely want it to have as much room as it can possibly have, and that means it should be able to incorporate all the shading and all the changes that you can possibly put yourself through. It should have that much room—otherwise we would be making it too small, and it wouldn't fit.

Gans: By all the rules by which other musical aggregations play, you guys are failures. But you've survived outside of those definitions, and it's a privilege in that respect.

Garcia: That is true, but I don't believe we're doing anything extraordinary. My feeling is that if any person felt there was something they were involved with that they could put as much energy as they wanted to, and did so, that their life would give them the kind of freedom that we seem to have as well. In other words, we're just doing what can be done.

Gans: But you're involving thousands of people in it—

Garcia: And hopefully, someone will see—and a lot of them do—see it as a model. In fact, some of my ideas about it come from the input that I've gotten from other people. Other people have seen tremendous amounts of stuff in it, stuff that I never would have imagined, really. For me it's been a learning process.

Somebody actually pointed out to me that there is like vertical range in the Grateful Dead experience that turned them on to how they could do what they're doing with greater freedom. It represented a real learning increment, like learning a lesson. There's a lesson to be learned—if you're able to enjoy something, to devote your life to it or a reasonable amount of time and energy, it will work out for you. It will work. I don't believe we're the only people illustrating that, but I think it really has something to do with whether or not you have sufficient faith in the vehicle. In some ways the whole thing is an act of faith, but for us it's like somewhere along the line, we agreed to stick it out past what would normally have been discouraging experiences. It's turned out for us in such a way that it's had enough encouraging input to nurture it, or to at least let us suspect that we can have faith in it. It's very marginal, because we're really skeptical. There's been just enough, but there hasn't been more than enough.

Gans: Have there been a lot of times when it felt like time to break it up and do something else?

Garcia: No, not really, just because the nature of it has been about right. It always has been an improvement over the state of things.

Gans: Is it still so?

Garcia: Yeah, for me it is. It's really a very personal thing, and for me it's a thing that changes from day to day. After our next gig I might not feel this way—I might feel like, "Naw, it sucks, when am I gonna get to retire?" I change as well. I'm subject to an emotional thing about it, but I've spent enough time in this position where I'm forced to confront aspects of it, partly through things like interviews—where people ask me questions I wouldn't ask myself—then all of a sudden I go, "Oh, wow, I never thought of that. Maybe it does or maybe it doesn't," and a door opens and I'm compelled to look at it in some new light, because somebody else is saying, "I see it this way." I can't say with any certainty that the way somebody else sees it isn't the truth of it. I can't believe that my point of view is the only correct one.

Gans: Do you feel an obligation to it?

Garcia: In a kind of a large sense, yeah I do sort of feel an obligation to it. But I don't know the nature of the obligation.

Jackson: Is it in the sense that so many people would be let down if you didn't do what you're doing?

Garcia: No, it isn't that kind of obligation.

Gans: As a human experience, on a par with religious cults and small political things—it's a minor movement in the history of mankind, but definitely one that deserves its place in history.

Garcia: Yeah, we're in there somewhere.

Jackson: You're more than a footnote.

Garcia: Oh…jeez, that's a relief. I thought I was going to have to go and shoot a politician.

Jerry Garcia

June 11, 1981
San Rafael, California
Blair Jackson, David Gans

This is the second of two sessions for the two-part interview for BAM *magazine. Like the first one, it took place at Garcia's house. Photographer Dennis Callahan arrived near the end of the session and took pictures for the* BAM *cover.*

Jackson: ...We're doing an issue [of *BAM* magazine] on the Doors—

Garcia: I never liked the Doors. I found them terribly offensive...when we played with them. It was back when [Jim] Morrison was just a pure Mick Jagger copy. That was his whole shot, that he was a Mick Jagger imitation. Not vocally, but his moves, his whole physical appearance, were totally stolen from right around Mick Jagger's 1965 tour of the States. He used to move around a lot, before he started to earn a reputation as a poet, which I thought was really not deserved. Rimbaud was great at eighteen, nineteen, and Verlaine. Those guys were great. Fuckin' Jim Morrison wasn't great, I'm sorry.

I could never see what it was about the Doors. They had a very brittle sound live, a three-piece band with no bass—the organ player [Ray

Manzarek] used to do it. That and that kinda raga-rock guiter style was strange. It sounded very brittle and sharp-edged to me, not something I enjoyed listening to.

I kind of appreciated some of the stuff that they did later, and I appreciated a certain amount of Morrison's sheer craziness, just because that's always a nice trait in rock and roll. No, I never knew him, but Richard Loren, who works for us, was his agent and had to babysit him through his most drunken scenes and all the times he got busted and all that crap. He's got lots of stories to tell about Morrison.

I was never attracted to their music at all, so I couldn't really find anything to like about them. When we played with them, I think I watched the first tune of two, then I went upstairs and fooled with my guitar. There was nothing there that I wanted to know about. He was so patently an imitation of Mick Jagger that it was offensive. To me, when the Doors played in San Francisco they typified Los Angeles coming to San Francisco, which I equated with having the look right, but zero substance. This is way before that hit song "Light My Fire." Probably at that time in their development it was too early for anybody to make a decent judgment of them, but I've always looked for something else in music, and whatever it was they didn't have it. They didn't have anything of blues, for example, in their sound or feel.

Jackson: Did you sense the negativity?

Garcia: No, not really. All I sensed was sham. As far as I was concerned, it was just surface and no substance.

Then we played with them after the "Light My Fire" thing, when they were headliners. We opened for them in Santa Barbara some years later, when they were a little more powerful. Their sound had gotten better—they'd gotten more effectively amplified, so Manzarek's bass lines and stuff like that had a little more throb, but their sound was still thin. It wasn't a successful version of a three-piece band, like the Who or Jimi Hendrix or Cream, or any of the other guitar power-trio-type three-piece bands. It's an interesting concept—a three-piece band that's keyboard, guitar, and drums—but it was missing some element that I felt was vital. I couldn't say exactly what it was, but it was not satisfying for me to listen to them. When they were the headliners, it was sort of embarrassing for us to open for them, 'cause we sort of blew them off the stand just with sheer power. What we had with double drums and Phil's bass playing—it got somewhere, and when they played there was an anticlimax kind of feeling to it, even with their hits.

In the part of my life when I was impressionable along that androgynous input, for me the people that were happening were James Dean and Elvis. Early rock 'n' roll—I'm like first-generation rock 'n' roll influence. For me, James Dean was a real important figure. He was the romantic fulfillment of that vision.

Jackson: I was always interested in that concept, of someone being rock 'n' roll without playing music.

Garcia: All the confusion and energy of adolescence. That was the model that was happening for me. When that was happening in the sixties, I was already like twenty-four, twenty-five, twenty-six, and that part of my life was long gone.

Jackson: You didn't want to hear about the leather pants—

Garcia: No, I didn't give a fuck about that. Besides, as far as androgynous, we had Weir, who for the longest time people mistook for a girl. I thought he was a more effective androgyne.... He and Mickey were in this weird makeup bag for a long time, where they wore this weird silver samurai makeup that blanked their eyebrows. When you see the black-and-white pictures, you can't tell what the fuck's wrong with them, but there's something very wrong.

• • •

Jackson: Do you ever deal with [Arista Records president] Clive Davis directly?

Garcia: ...Every once in a whle he talks about lyrics. He complained about Brent's lyrics—thought they weren't "Grateful Dead enough." I don't know what the fuck he meant.

Gans: Brent said Clive made him change the lyrics [of "Easy to Love You," on *Go to Heaven*]—

Garcia: If I had been Brent I wouldn't have done it, and I didn't know that Brent was going to take it that seriously. He never should have done that—what the hell does Clive Davis know?

Jackson: I could see being the new guy in the band and being intimidated by Clive Davis.

Gans: And from a critical standpoint, I think the song was improved by the changes, but Brent didn't think so—

Garcia: I didn't think so either. I thought the song had a real natural quality before, and then it took on a sort of forced thing.

Brent is a talented guy. I hope he gets a chance to get his stuff going. He's a good writer, he writes nice songs. He needs to relax, and to get a non-interference relationship going with Weir. Weir is like a great interferer in other people's work. [*Laughs*]

Gans: Brent has picked up a lot of speech patterns and phrases from Weir.

Garcia: It goes around, because Weir steals from Brent, too. Weir steals from everybody. He's a shameless thief.

Gans: Last time we talked here, you said he hides his thievery very well—

Garcia: He does. He's good at it. On guitar, he's copped to having been influenced by people, but I can't hear it in his playing. I know that he thinks it's true, but I swear to god I can't hear it. He says he's been influenced a lot by Pete Townshend, and I can't hear it. And a couple of other people, too. You'd have to be Weir to understand what he meant, or to have followed the evolutionary path that he's followed.

Gans: It could be some really angular aspect of Townshend's playing, not some particular lick. . . . In his own context it's invisible to anybody but the architect.

Garcia: That's right. I've been influenced by people, too, where I haven't been influenced by the notes they played but by the attitude, the gesture—the other part of it. The substance rather than the form.

Jackson: Give us an example?

Garcia: Oh, like Coltrane. I've been influenced a lot by Coltrane, but I never copped his licks or sat down, listened to records and tried to play his stuff. I've been impressed with that thing of flow, and of making statements that to my ears sound like paragraphs—he'll play along stylistically with a certain kind of tone, in a certain kind of syntax, for X amount of time, then he'll like change the subject, then play along with this other personality coming out, which really impresses me. It's like other personalities stepping out, or else his personality is changing, or his attitude's changing. But it changes in a holistic way, where the tone of his axe and everything changes.

Perceptually, an idea that's been very important to me in playing has been the whole "odyssey" idea—journeys, voyages, you know? And adventures along the way. That whole idea has been really important to me. Golden Gate Park is another example of the kind of work that works that way—

Gans: You can step over a hill and be in another world—

Garcia: Yeah. All of a sudden you're in one of those places where everything is that weird prehistoric-looking shit, huge ferns—and it changes seamlessly from one thing to another. It's just a beautiful work: to walk from one end of Golden Gate Park to another, you go through all these different worlds. And they really are different—their whole texture and everything. Walking through there stoned on acid…It's the work of an artist.

Jackson: In that case it's probably a conscious construction, whereas with Coltrane it would be more instinctual—

Garcia: Right, but maybe not. Coltrane was a smart guy. He knew what he was doing; he spent a lot of time studying music.

Gans: Do you always know?

Garcia: What I'm doing? In what sense?

Gans: Like in a long solo passage where you play those paragraphs, and you'll maybe change something in your signal processing and start a new thing—or sometimes it won't even be a gross change like that, but you'll change modes or scales—

Garcia: Sometimes I do and sometimes I don't. It used to be more rambling than it is now. Somewhere through the seventies, it's been my goal to be more in charge, to know what I'm doing. So now, pretty much, if you stopped me somewhere I'd be able to tell you what it is I'm trying to do. I've got that kind of a handle on it, but it's also one of those things where when things are going really well, I know automatically—certain lengths start to be apparent. I automatically know how long eight bars is, sixteen bars, and where the *one* [downbeat] is going to be. I can turn it around all different kinds of ways. I like to be able to know where it is, but I also like to be able to forget about it entirely.

Gans: So it becomes an ongoing, subconscious kind of thing that's there when you need it—

Garcia: That's right. In the Grateful Dead, there's a certain philosophy about that. Rhythmically, our policy is that the *one* is where you think it is. It's kind of a Zen concept, but it really works well for us. It makes it possible to get into a phrase where I can change into little phrase spurts, spitting out little groups of notes that are attached fives—five in the space of four, or five in the space of two, is more common for me—and then turn that into a new pulse, where those fives become like a sixteenth-note pulse. Then I'm inside of a whole irregularly rotating tempo in relation to what the rest of the band is playing, when they're playing, say, the original common time. It produces this ambiguity, but all I have to do is make a statement that says, "end of paragraph, *and* one," and they all know where it is.

We all have that kind of privilege—it's partly something we've allowed each other, and partly something we've gained the confidence to be able to do just by spending a lot of time playing together. When we started working on "The Eleven" back in the late sixties, we'd spend hours and hours and hours every day just playing groups of eleven, to get used to that phrase, when we started working out things in seven, and from seven we started working out things that were like two bars of seven, three bars of seven, four bars of seven—patterns, phrases, and licks that were those lengths, and play them over and over and over again.

Jackson: In an almost academic way?

Garcia: Oh, yeah, a real academic way. We had to do it! You can't play confidently and fluidly in those times without really knowing what you're doing.

You can't play the way the Grateful Dead plays without working at it. It's not something that just happened to us.

It didn't happen overnight, either. There was a long, slow process that brought that into being. It really started when Mickey first met Alla Rakha. It was the first time he'd ever heard Eastern players. He was so impressed with the level of technical ability, and the odd times got to be a big thing, because with Mickey, technique was no problem—he was a champion drummer. His background was fundamentals, which is more the military trip and less band music. But for him, the idea of that kind of discipline, what Indian music seems to have—the combination of tremendous freedom and also tremendous discipline—that really impressed Mickey, so he started right away studying with Alla Rakha. That influence got the rest of us starting to fool with ideas that were in certain lengths. The challenge with us was, "How do you take these lengths and make them translatable to Western body knowledge?" Westerners' body knowledge is basically twos and threes and fours, smaller increments. It's harder for Western ears to hear the large divisions, the long meters.

Gans: Dancing to "The Eleven"—well, dancing to the Grateful Dead doesn't look like people dancing to most other music—

Garcia: No, it isn't, but it's rooted in gravity, you know, and human body design, like all dancing is. Dancing is a function of gravity acting on the body, and the body is basically a gravity-designed thing. Its evolution, the backbone—those things are functions of this gravity on this specific planet. Dancing has to do with, like, you jump up in the air, and gravity pulls you down at a certain rate. That's the reason why the march is always 110 [beats per minute], and when you march there's always a certain meter, which is marching meter—it has to do with the average stride length of a human—

Gans: How much thought have you put into this?

Garcia: A lot. I haven't thought about it in some kind of methodical "now I'm gonna make music that makes people dance" way, but just in terms of "Why do these things work? Why do some things work and some things not work?"

Why, in some grooves, do you look for some slower division of the meter? If something's going terribly fast, you look for a slower part of it, the half time or whatever—something to get comfortable with, where your body knowledge works for you. The thing that I see—for me, where I can rock back and forth or tap my toe—it's gravity. It's that simple, it's like the test for me. It's part of what makes music so compelling. Music is like echoing, and talking about, physical laws—at least logically, physical laws in this universe, on this planet. It's part of what makes it really interesting.

Also, other people, in other kinds of music, think about music that deeply. In Indian music, they have organized it to the point where, in any one of those ragas, each interval has a definite emotional connotation. It probably has to do with some kind of real, nervous-system recognition. The nervous system has some rate, which you can describe as pitch.

In Eastern music, there's a raga for each time of day, and so forth. There's ragas for particular activities, and then within each raga, each of the intervallic relationships all have some definite, specific emotional sense. That's the way the music is structured—it's part of the learning process.

It's fascinating as hell, especially since it's an oral tradition. You know that drummer talk—they teach you to sing it. Every Indian musician, no matter what instrument he plays, starts by learning how to sing each of those figures. It's fantastic. That's how they do arrangements—they talk them to each other. They're as tight at that as any Western musicians are at sight-reading. They have phenomenal ability to remember long, long things, phrases that last the equivalent of sixty, eighty bars. One guy can sing it to another guy one time, and the other guy's got it.

Gans: I wonder how that maps into the organization of the nervous system? There must be some—

Garcia: That's what's interesting about these Inayat Khan books: he does talk about that. He's Ali Akbar Khan's grandfather. There are four or five books on classical Indian music, and they're all far out. It'll blow your mind how highly organized the music is.

I have an interesting treatise by this Dutch guy about medieval church music, from before Bach, before baroque music. It's a study of this kind of music called *tactus*. This music is written in an early kind of notation that doesn't give any indication of the time. It's before they had rhythmic notation, but there are note values. These are like four-part vocal things, contemporary with Gregorian but four-part instead of unison. They were written to be performed by these little groups of monks in Gothic cathedrals. This guy ran a complicated analysis of all the intervallic relationships in these works, which are commonly very short. They look like they're about eight bars long, in four-part vocal—harmony, you could say—early counterpoint. This guy made an effort to study all the relationships, and also to see if he could deduce what it was that they used for the time values. There's no bar lines or anything. There's this incredible readout of all these relationships, which the guy then applies to all the alchemical and Masonic magical numerological traditions, the significance of all these—really complex things but also, it would take a monk twenty years to write one of these things, and they wondered what the heck would take 'em so long, with these things that look like simple pieces of music. It turns out that they're really super-complex, highly coded, sort of magical stuff designed for specific architectural spaces, to be sung in a specific place in a Gothic cathedral, and they reflect all of the same relationships that you find in a Gothic cathedral.

Gans: Taking into account reverberation times, standing waves—

Garcia: It basically has all that kind of physics in it, but the way they—in those days they had it all in octaves, remember, and the divisions of twelve for the twelve apostles, and the Trinity runs all through it because of the magical significance of all those numbers. It's a huge body of complex knowledge that's codified that way.

It turns out that the way this music was sung, this guy's deduction is—there's a little wood engravings and stuff like that on the illuminations that this music was written on, pictures that show the group of monks, which is usually twelve or fourteen, and they have their hands on each other's throats. His deduction is that they got the tempo and the time relationships from the heartbeat, from the pulse of each other. So the implications are very far out.

Gans: Would that imply that eventually their pulses became synchronized?

Garcia: Right. When they sang this music, they would get tremendously high in the church. In those days, the whole thing had power to make changes—the idea of music as drugs.

Gans: Did you have formal religious upbringing?

Garcia: No, not really. I come from a Catholic background, but nobody in my family was very serious about it. I was forced to go to church, but only until I was about ten or eleven. I was never confirmed.

Gans: Do you have any relationship with the Western God, then?

Garcia: Mmmmm, I wouldn't say so.

Gans: This whole thing brings to mind the book *Altered States.*[1]

Garcia: I haven't read the book, but I saw the movie.

Gans: The book was much more involved than the movie in the union of theology and science. It raises the possibility that there is much information about our history encoded in our genes.

Garcia: That's one of the things I'm interested in.

Gans: Chayefsky raised similar questions to those neurological connections. Essentially, the ape that runs around in *Altered States* is the "missing link," the bridge between the apes and man. By combining the isolation-tank experiments, intensifying the effects of the drugs that he found in Mexico, he—

Garcia: The keynote is that that tribe in Mexico all have the same experience with the drug. There's a lot of interesting work that's been done on that subject.

There's been an interesting book by Michael Murphy, the Esalen guy. *Jacob Atabet* has to do with...you know how yogis are reputed to have control over their nervous system? That idea is expanded to where you have control over your whole physical shape, and that is the next moment in evolution, or whatever: that consciousness wants to be able to freely make decisions about your body. It's interesting.

[1] By Paddy Chayefsky. Harper & Row, 1978.

I read an interesting book[2] by these two hard-science guys that are heavily medicine men. They went to the upper Amazon basin, because they'd heard about this psychedelic there, a tryptamine, one of the *cubensis* family. It may be a mushroom, or one of those barks, I'm not sure which. They heard about this one specific one that supposedly created a mutation in your mouth and larynx and face muscles that made it so that you could produce visible sound waves. A very far-out idea, and they also had this further idea that the high-pitched humming and buzzing that you hear whenever you take tryptamines is what they call electron spin resonance—the pair-bonding of donor molecules that are at the top of the psychedelic, on the input side, bonding to the bottom of the DNA molecules that have two receptor molecules at the bottom. They put the DNA and RNA into spin, furling and unfurling—it's a great image—and that pitch is basically the rate of the DNA/RNA unfolding and folding.

Gans: In which cells?

Garcia: In all cells.

Gans: Your body just gets electric!

Garcia: Yeah, and you hear it.

Jackson: That's a little spooky.

Garcia: Yeah, but not unlikely. Anyway, they imagined that by taking this psychedelic that produces visible sound waves, and singing along with this electron spin resonance, they would produce a holograph, exterior to themselves, of an idea.

They went down there and set up this experiment, and both of them flipped out totally, and spent like thirty or forty days, or a couple of months, in this complex, shared hallucination in which they felt that they

[2]*The Invisible Landscape: Mind, Hallucinogens and the I Ching*, by Terence and Dennis McKenna, first published in 1977 by Seabury Press, New York, and to be reissued in 1992 by HarperCollins, San Francisco. *The Invisible Landscape* is a record of the discoveries the McKenna brothers made on a legendary trip to the Amazon in 1971, in which they explored the furthest reaches of the psychedelic experience while on a hunt for hallucinogenic plants used by the local shamans. A more accessible introduction to the ideas of Terence McKenna, who has been called "the culture's foremost spokesperson for the psychedelic experience," is his recent book *The Archaic Revival: Speculations on Psychedelic Mushrooms, the Amazon, Virtual Reality, Lewis Carroll, UFOs, Evolution, Shamanism, the I Ching, the Rebirth of the Goddess and the End of History*, also published by HarperCollins.

were in the presence of what they described as a futuristic, insectile entity that was like an anthropologist from the future. It's just one of the most mind-boggling books I've ever read.

That's how far-out some of this stuff is getting.

Gans: [*Reading from* BAM *article on the Ghostriders, a local band*] "For Dan Stickler, the new musical direction made total sense to him after he had an experience on LSD at a 1977 Grateful Dead concert.... 'I was watching them play, really getting into it, when I saw the stage disintegrate in front of me. A Buddha face appeared above the stage, and everything seemed to be very harmonious and together. It was the first time I'd been touched by a cosmic messenger.' At another Dead show, Dan says, 'A bright arc shot between my third eye and Jerry Garcia's third eye, and it was like I could hear him telling me, "Dan, you've got to carry on this tradition. Don't let me down."'"

Garcia: Right on. Don't let me down, Dan. I say, *yeah*, go for it.

People have reported to us so many times that experience: "You looked at me and I knew what you were going to play," or "I knew what you were going to play before you played it," or "I was making you play"—all those variations. It's like flying saucer reports. Thousands of 'em, so much so that I can't pretend it doesn't happen. I have to admit that there's some validity to that experience, even though it's not something that I know about. There's something to it, that's all I can say. It doesn't matter to me what mechanisms are involved—it's just that I'm very, very interested in it.

Gans: There are times I've felt like the music plays the band, or that we're all definitely linked.

Garcia: We know that's the case.

Gans: And there are times when I'm playing that I've lost willful control. It's such a good feeling

Garcia: It's wonderful. It means that you're no longer responsible. That's the stuff, the pure gold of the experience.

Gans: How often do you get that?

Garcia: Not very often. For me, it's the kind of experience where I am so distrustful of anything that's invisible or occult or that can't be measured, tasted, or touched.

Gans: Do you seek it, though?

Garcia: Oh, yeah. I seek it, but I don't seek it in a directional way—the way I seek it is to follow my nose. I don't have an *approach*.

Gans: You'd be open to some miraculous proof of these things?

Garcia: Definitely. That's partly why I keep doing it, and partly what keeps the Grateful Dead such an interesting thing to keep doing. It keeps it fresh. It's definitely, truly and authentically, a new experience very time, and that's not bullshit. And because of that, it can't be duplicated. There is no way to make that happen, to will that experience into being, no matter what kind of good vibes you have. We've had it happen to us in every kind of way, every kind of way. We know it for what it *isn't*—we know everything that *isn't* it, but we can't make any real direct statements about it. We're in the same position as Deadheads are, really, fundamentally, about that phenomenon, the magic side of it. Just the kind of person I am, I'm not trustful about stuff like that. I'm the first one to worry about it— "Maybe we're opening the door for some demons from the ninth dimension," or something.

Jackson: *Raiders of the Lost Ark* is sort of about that...
   It's apparently based on some truth, that Hitler was really into collecting sacred objects.

Garcia: He was. Did you ever read *The Spear of Destiny*? It's by a guy named Trevor Ravenscroft—a fantastic name for an English writer. It's the spear of the Roman centurion who pierced Christ's heart at the moment of his death. In Christian symbolism, that's the heavy moment, the moment of decision, because the rap is that Christ's blood was spilled to wipe out the sins of all people. That's what spilled the blood, so that's a tool of great power. All kinds of people had it—Charlemagne, and the first Christian emperor of Rome—what was his name? Constantine—and then a whole bunch of Germanic kings and princes. It was in the Vienna Museum, and when Hitler flashed on it—the book is essentially about Hitler's occult side, the guys who turned Hitler on to mescaline. His first mescaline trip, he saw the spear and decided he had to have it, because it said that whoever has this thing has the power of absolute good or absolute evil or whatever. It's true that when he took Austria, the first thing he did was go to that museum and get it. It's back in Vienna now, I think. It's very powerful.

• • •

Jackson: There's a band in Los Angeles called Paradigm Shift, based on this notion that the paradigms of each age shift in a certain way and that we're undergoing a paradigm shift right now of our basic values, etc. It's a five-person group—synthesizer; reeds played through a synthesizer; a Stick, and they also have two visual accompanists. One is essentially a computer colorist, and the other runs some kind of synthesizer, and she colors what he plays on the synthesizer. He's not playing audibly, but he's creating whatever waves are involved, and then she colors those waves and they use terminals and a big video screen.

Gans: In the *Ace* version of "Playing in the Band," I always used to see this little guy like the Dutch Boy paint kid squeezing out colors in the sky, the sound of your guitar.

Garcia: I aim notes for the room that I'm in. Notes for me have shape and form and everything, color.

And for me, that would be the way to have music come out of a computer—to first tell it what the music looks like. Give it color versus timbre, size versus pitch, shape versus attack, envelope…It's a real natural for computers.

Jackson: That's not ridiculously far from what Walt Disney was trying to do with *Fantasia*.

Garcia: He just did it the hard way!

Jackson: These Paradigm Shift people are heavy Deadheads, too. But their music doesn't sound anything like the Dead—

Garcia: That's nice. The way we influence people doesn't have to be one of those things where they copy note for note. It's more an idea, the approach, which is one of those things that can be used in any form, really. I've had my eyes opened to the Grateful Dead on some interesting levels by graphic artists.

One graphic artist turned me on to a whole level of what the Grateful

Dead does that I wasn't even cognizant of until this guy sat me down and showed me his version of the Grateful Dead, what it meant to him in terms of influence. He showed me this whole bunch of prints that he'd made, and he hipped me to the idea of full range, which was an exciting concept to me at the time. His name is Sätty, Wilfred Sätty.[3]

He took me over to his house after a Grateful Dead show one night and really turned me on. He was one of the first of the environmental artists of the early sixties. He showed me all these prints that were made by assembling bits and pieces of prints. He's a lithographer, sort of. He showed me these, and each one was slightly different from the others, but each one was a print all in itself. They were each like others, but it was the graduation, the overall effect, that he showed me. He told me about what it was like to see the Grateful Dead when he was stoned on acid, what it meant to him visually. Sometimes he would just be terribly sick and brought down and it would make him cry, and sometimes it was beautiful and joyous, sometimes it was ugly and revolting—

Gans: I feel really left out! I have never had heavy visual experiences when I was tripping. It was always very internal and intellectual and speed-of-thought stuff, but I never had visual images.

Garcia: In what sense weren't they visual?

Gans: I always heard stories of hearing colors and seeing sounds, and having things dissolve in front of your face—hallucinations.

Garcia: I've never had things like that happen, but I've had whole other universes dissolve and reappear. I've had things that were visual, but they were hypervisual, they were extravisual—they were more than visual, I would have to say.

One time I had this experience when we were living up in Olompali, one of the times I completely blew myself out. We all took a big hit of acid and a hit of mescaline at the same time, and I lay down and closed my eyes—but I could see, it was like my eyes were still open. What happened was, you know where your vision ends, the periphery? All of a sudden that started to open like an old-time coffee can with a key, that metal band, and my vision opened out until I had 360-degree vision. There was this pattern—that dark place back here opened out into vision, revealing... I

---

[3]Coincidentally, *The Archaic Revival* has illustrations by Sätty.

kept seeing this part of a pattern, like if I could only get enough distance on it I could read it, I could see it. This pattern finally opened up to 360 degrees with this winding process, amazing—a beautiful-looking process. It revealed the word *all*. It was a totally cosmic experience. Somehow the fabric of the lettering contained in its whole design, the way it was put together, every kind of thought form somehow. It was just an amazing experience, really, and it was beyond visual. It was effectively opened out into some kind of totally "otherly" dimension beyond time and beyond physical reality. It was just amazing.

During that day, more happened to me than would happen to me in a thousand lifetimes. I'm still mulling over that day, you know? There was so much information that was revealed to me, like DNA or whatever. It was like infinite lifetimes. But I can revisit it, and it had the same effect on me as any experience I've ever experienced in this life, certainly.

Gans: Was it totally outside of real life?

Garcia: As far as my subjective reality, yeah, definitely. Things happened that I've never recovered from. It was definitely one of those "before and after" experiences.

What would we do without psychedelics? How gray life would be without psychedelics. How limited.

Gans: I stopped for seven years, after I lost an argument to you and a hot dog on the same day at Kezar Stadium [San Francisco, May 26, 1973]. I was walking around the rim of Kezar Stadium going, "Why is Jerry mad at me?!"

Garcia: Oh, I'm sorry, man. I didn't mean to bum you out.

Gans: Then one night at the Warfield, I decided I was in control enough to try again. I loved it. Now I can come back to it feeling whole enough that it won't defeat me.

Garcia: Yeah, me too. I scare myself bad, too.

Gans: ...you say something stupid, then you add another layer of stupidity trying to explain...

Garcia: Right. Language is so small and ridiculously cumbersome and stupid. You can't even make yourself understood on any level. You're just going through changes a gazillion miles a minute, and language can't possibly hold it. You can't possibly hope to communicate with anybody about it, so you have to jump to another level.

For me, with psychedelics, I've scared myself real good where it was real hard to just get high and forget about it. It's still a difficult thing for me to do.

Gans: I always sort of needed to get some work done, some mental work. I've never been able to just sit back and enjoy the trip—

Garcia: For me, the idea of taking drugs always was to enjoy it first, to have something happen that was fundamentally enjoyable. Then if there was more, maybe I would know it and maybe I wouldn't, but I never had made those kind of judgments.

My first psychedelic experiences were all kind of running through the woods, gaily tripping out on things, but later on they took on a curious sort of purposefulness, like there was something making an effort to communicate with me, and really had a teacherly attitude toward me.

Gans: Were you under [Ken] Kesey's tutelage?

Garcia: Not really. I was getting high with these guys, but it wasn't coming from them—it was coming from "it," whatever "it" is. I never have known whether I should trust it or not, but a lot of it came in the form of a big voice saying, "Now do you get it?" Or going through that lesson, you know, where you go, "I see. Now I get it"...You get moments of that, "Oh yeah, right," where everything settles down and you realize you're doing just exactly what you were supposed to be doing, everything's the way it's supposed to be, and all that.

...The mind has such an enormous amount of stuff in it that you didn't get in this lifetime. I know those ideas and those concepts and that wisdom, and the incredible ingeniousness with which it's put together— for me, the bum-trip side of my mind, the scary side, the part of me that freaks out, has that thing of knowing your worst fears, that flash of taking you to that place where your worst fears are horribly true, with this kind of hollow, mocking laughter in the background—where you're the butt of the cosmic joke. There's something about the coherence of that persona, whatever it is, that's so much more than the me which is this sort of cringing, ineffectual, completely powerless dumbshit—yeah, a human. I don't know whether it's global or not, but it had such resonance to me, that stuff, that I assume that every mind is equally well organized.

Gans: There has to be some purpose for us jamming our minds full of so much information. If we're just going to die and it will dissipate—it can't be.

Garcia: I can't see it either—

Gans: There needs to be something that will continue, right?

Garcia: Why would the universe go through the trouble of evolving consciousness? If it wanted life that would succeed, just to create the most effective living things, it could have stopped at bacteria. Or it could have stopped at vertebrates, or sharks, or it could have stopped at tigers—there's all kinds of things that survive great. But consciousness goes a quantum step further than just life, you know? I think consciousness has a place in the cosmic game, the atoms-and-universes game, the big game. I can't imagine that it's mindless—there's too much organization, and the organization is too incredible. It has that huge, vast wisdom—

Gans: But yet it's random—

Garcia: Is it? When you take psychedelics, the way your mind spins information to you, does it have that thing of synchronicity, and all that sort of miraculous quality?

Gans: Sometimes.

Garcia: Wouldn't you say that that suggests organization of an extremely sophisticated nature, somehow?

Gans: Implying some neurological process going on, running through the memory banks—

Garcia: At the very least, it's doing something like that, yeah.

Gans: I had to tell myself that the little green and pink balls I was seeing had something to do with my retina, right? I couldn't ever go, "god, I'm seeing things!"

Garcia: Well, maybe you were and maybe you weren't. I don't know how high you've gotten, and I also don't know what kind of steps you've gone through.

Gans: How can you quantify a trip?

Garcia: You can't—I'm just assuming that every mind is at least as heavy as mine is.

Gans: Is that borne out in your daily life?

Garcia: No, but day-to-day life doesn't have anything to do with it. In our day-to-day life we're just like other animals on this planet, neither more nor less. We're fuckin' around is all, basically [*laughs*]....My idea is basically that the operating system is more wise than what we are able to stick into our consciousness.

Gans: There are people who have great spatial memory—somebody said, "Jerry doesn't remember dates," but when tickled properly you do remember specific events very well. Somebody says, "Phil remembers things much more linearly"—people have spatial memory, associative memories—

Garcia: Yeah. People's minds are organized along different lines, definitely. I guess it's right- and left-hemisphere accessing, somehow.
...We're trying to figure out how the mind works. It obviously works well enough. I think consciousness is really far-out stuff, myself. It might be that consciousness is the whole reason there is a universe. There might not be a universe apart from consciousness. It's not provable, except in a kind of a very weird, small—the problem of existence is that it's this weird, small point of view that is just the now, in time, and there's nothing else—and that you have to prove everything that you can prove about what the universe is from this little perspective of consciousness. It's tantalizing in some peculiar way.

Gans: But there are so many shared assumptions that become invalid when you step into a different country...

Garcia: That's why reality may be this thing that's locally constructed by consciousness itself, and it might be possible for any small number of people to hypothesize successfully this more full reality that is more like, say, what we would want it to be. Instead of being victims of reality, reality is our own invention, which we have total access to in the most creative, direct, one-to-one sense. Local realities change enough, locally, that those

Hindu guys can walk through huge, blazing fires and not get burned. The fact, to me, that that is a measurable and demonstrable phenomenon is just incredible. Why would it be that flesh would burn in one part of the world and not in another? It's got to be that consciousness modulates reality.

Gans: It's unfortunate that differently wired Protestants are able to wreak such havoc on the lives of the differently wired Indians. We are going to be able to wipe out everyone else in the name of our way of doing it.

Garcia: That's what all that born-again Christianity is about—it's an organized way to make the miraculous happen. The drag about it is that it has that exclusivity clause.

One of my hobbies lately has been to watch TV preachers. Some of it— you ever see "The 700 Club"? "The 700 Club" is like the *Christian Science Monitor* of the air. It's intelligent—Pat Robertson is like a Yale Law School or Business School graduate—he's a bright guy, not a dumb fuckin' country preacher. They go into things in great depth there— more, in some cases, than the regular newspeople. And they're very topical—but what's really interesting is that they regularly have this stuff on there which is the weirdest shit on TV, all these healings and this miraculous stuff, after-death visions. They're talking about what they call charismatic Christianity, and by that they mean "charismatic" in the Greek sense of the word, the gift of the gods. They're talking about the charismatic Christian keynote experience, of having a one-to-one relationship with Jesus is the way they describe it. It's this powerful, measurable experience—it's like flying saucers, experiences people have had—

Gans: He's been dead for thousands of years—

Garcia: It doesn't matter, man. These are people who will tell you that they've had that experience.

Gans: But you also know that if you want something bad enough you can talk yourself into seeing it—

Garcia: I'm not saying that I believe any of this shit, but you have to admit that there's something about it which is very, very powerful as far as humans are concerned, insofar as they believe it and they believe it so much that it can cure them of cancer and raise them from the dead and all that shit. Is that a real thing outside ourselves, or is it an indication of the power of consciousness to create full integrity?

Jackson: That's what I want to find out.

Garcia: Right! Well, if it's the power of consciousness, then we have the power to create a full-integrity reality on any terms.

Here's the thing: since there's a squabble over reality on earth—in other words, consciousness is fighting over reality insofar as there are Moslems and Hindus and Christians and so forth, and they're all striving to create the reality which contains their God and only their God, and that's the truth of the matter and everything else is wrong—they're copping to nail down reality. What I wondered is why those people are so afraid of everybody coming up with their own reality on their own terms, because they would mesh anyway. They have to come together somewhere out here in this common reality which we'll agree to experience together.

Jackson: Yeah, but part of their experience is that they're told that their experience is ultimate.

Garcia: I know, well who's the asshole that tells them that? Is it that there is an ultimate out here? If there were an ultimate—

Jackson: Maybe that's the ego getting in there—

Gans: There'll always be—the speed dealers came into the Haight and cleaned out that idealistic little world, and there will always be—

Garcia: You think there's always going to be spoilers? What a bum trip! I'd rather believe that the tendency in consciousness is to seek freedom, in a completely individual way—each organism and its consciousness has things exactly the way it wants them all the time.

Jackson: That's too scary for me.

Gans: If everybody respected each other's space, it would be a marvelous world—

Garcia: I see it as being very possible. Don't you?

Gans: No, I don't, just because of the sheer numbers...

Garcia: Have you ever been to New York City? When you go to New York City, you see a place that's basically not being governed, and it runs pretty well. It's amazing to me that there aren't a million murders on every block every day. When you're there, you have this feeling of out-of-controlness which is unreal, but it somehow works. All those people are able to exist as governments of one, and do business, play their games, whatever, on their own terms. It just seems to me that consciousness wants that to happen—that's where we're trying to get to, something along those lines. I just don't see what's wrong with it. I can't figure out where all that stuff came from....

• • •

Gans: One of the questions we didn't ask you back in April was, "How come there aren't any love songs, how come there isn't much sex in Grateful Dead material?" And all of a sudden, at the Warfield (the acoustic gig), I realized that if you listen to "To Lay Me Down" carefully—

Jackson: I really don't see that song like that....

Gans: See? For years, I didn't, either.

Garcia: It's a love song. How could anybody miss that?

Jackson: It has a sort of gospelly feel to it. It sounds almost religious to me. I would hate to impose this sexual—

Garcia: Really? Well, love is religious, I thought. [*Laughs*]
As far as I'm concerned, a song should have all that stuff. A song should have everything in it.

Jackson: It seems, though, that there is very little stuff about open sexuality. There's almost—

Garcia: I've never been attracted to songs of that sort, I guess. It's mostly because most of them have real dumb lyrics.

Jackson: "Loose Lucy" is about the only one that hints at a raunchy side.

Garcia: So is "Scarlet Begonias," in a way.

Jackson: I can see that.

Garcia: Let me see if there's any other ones that I think are that way.
I think maybe "It Must Have Been the Roses" is a weird sort of love song. There's others, too. I think "Candyman" is pretty blatant. Shit.

Jackson: ...I think the music is sort of androgynous (Grateful Dead in general). It's not all from a clearly defined male viewpoint.

Garcia: Really? I've had feminists tell me that it was much too male, much too masculine.

Jackson: But compared to most—

Garcia: Maybe not. I'm not prepared to argue—I've never thought about it one way or another, but I've had women-libbers, especially back in the seventies—nobody's told me that for a long time—say that the stuff was like men talking to men—

Jackson: They've given up—

Gans: I think you could see that in Hunter's writing a lot.

Garcia: Definitely. Hunter's very much on that trip, acting out—he's definitely more masculine a person.

Gans: There's so much more important to write about...but what sells is a good love song, and a good love song is universal.

Garcia: It seems to be. I've never been very comfortable with—except, I do a lot of love songs in my band. I just never think in terms of writing them. I write what Hunter gives me.

Gans: You've got an old-boy network that goes back a long time; how much does the collective attitude of you and your friends have to do with it? It obviously has everything to do with it in one respect, but what do you suppose is unique about the approach, the certain flavor of the Grateful Dead?

Garcia: Jeez, I don't know. I haven't really thought about it in quite those terms. You'd have to ask me the question coming from a different point of view, I think....

Gans: It seems that you've been insulated some from conventional, mainstream developments in media attitudes.

Garcia: I really don't know. We all come from a kind of weird place— like, for example, Pigpen's orientation used to be straight-ahead sex. He'd get really dirty a lot of times. He occupied that position—if there was balance in our point of view, then Pigpen used to represent it, musically, I would say. I've always been conscious of myself as a person with a very definite flavor and very definite biases, musically, and all that. I have a certain kind of musical personality which I think of more in terms of its limitations than its inclusions, frankly. I think of myself as being a one-dimensional artist, if I think of myself as an artist at all, which I rarely do, but that's what I think of myself as.

Gans: You've got every right to be extremely self-assured and feel like you're an original—

Garcia: No, I don't feel that way at all. But at the same time, I appreciate it when somebody does, when somebody says something effectively for all of us. That's what was great about Dylan's songs, and that's why I love to do his songs. They speak to us in some kind of universal persona which you can pretty clearly recognize. He hits a real good deep nail on the head in terms of writing songs about something.

Jackson: Do you have any trouble singing a song as bitter as "Positively Fourth Street"?

Garcia: No, not at all. It's easy for me to cop that asshole space, easy. I was that guy, too. There's a certain kind of pose that that goes along with—there always were those people, in a way.
   For me, it occupies the same space as "Ballad of a Thin Man." It tells that person who's lame that they're lame, why they're lame, which is a very satisfying thing to do. Certainly something everybody knows about.

Gans: He was good at that in that period.

Garcia: Yeah.

Jackson: And later. Listen to "Idiot Wind."

Garcia: Really. "Positively Fourth Street" has this way of doing it where it's beautiful, too. And "It's All Over Now, Baby Blue" is basically a putdown, too. It's one of those things like "you're losing bad—dig yourself."

Being able to say that and say it beautifully—it was the beautiful sound of "Positively Fourth Street" that got to me more than the bitterness of the lyric. The combination of the beauty and the bitterness, to me, is wonderful. It's like a combination of something being funny and horrible—it's a great combination of two odd ingredients in the human experience. Anybody who can pull it off that successfully is really a score. That's something that only Dylan has been able to pull off, in terms of modern songwriting, I think.

Jackson: I think Lennon did it in a couple of songs.

Garcia: Yeah.

Gans: You ever listen to John Prine?

Garcia: Yeah. He's got a couple of songs—

Gans: Marvelous melancholy.

Garcia: Yeah. I love that song he has about the junkie ["Sam Stone"]. Great song. I haven't heard him in a long time.

Jackson: He's sort of been rewriting the same melodies forever—

Garcia: That's one of the things that bothered me about him. Him and Jesse Winchester both are those kind of really limited guys, unfortunately, melodically.

Gans: Their first couple albums are great—

Garcia: Right, and they say everything they have to say, sort of. But they said it so nicely so beautifully, naturally—Jesus. The first two Jesse Winchester albums are so good. I love the songs on those, every one of them. Nice records.

Jackson: *Let the Rough Side Drag* is pretty good. As a ballad singer, he's about as close to Johnny Horton at his best as anybody—

Garcia: Yeah, Johnny Horton was a great ballad singer. There's a guy who had a wonderful voice. "North to Alaska" was his coolest idea. The way he sings that—he's got such a cool voice. His rock 'n' roll voice is just great.

Gans: Somebody told me that you got an accordion for your fifteenth birthday and traded it in for a guitar.

Garcia: That's exactly right.

Gans: What kind of guitar did you get?

Garcia: I got a Danelectro, a good old Danelectro guitar. I was so happy with it. It had a kind of coffin-shaped case. And I got a little teeny-weeny Fender amplifier.

Gans: What did you play?

Garcia: My stepfather tuned it to this weird bogus tuning, or maybe he tuned it right and I evolved the tuning wrong in some way, but I ended up tuning it to this open tuning and working out chords and stuff, and playing along with just what sounded good, with absolutely no directionality, for about a year. Then I met a guy in school who showed me the right way to tune it, and four chords, maybe five chords—the basic first-position chords and stuff. I had to unlearn somewhere between six months and a year's worth of self-teaching, but I really was a slow learner and basically I didn't get into really learning the guitar with any kind of depth at all until the Grateful Dead started. Even then, it took a long time. I'm a slow learner. I didn't work hard at it, and I didn't have any lessons or anything—I didn't have any guidance. The banjo was the first instrument I got into seriously.

Gans: Did you study that with somebody?

Garcia: No, but I made much more of an effort to penetrate it, and master it and get to be really good at it. That was the first instrument that I really made a dent in what it means to play an instrument.

Gans: So in a sense the guitar became your primary instrument in that band the way the bass became Phil's?

Garcia: That's right.

Gans: Amazing. You fuckers learn on the job all the way!

Garcia: Absolutely.

Jackson: With all due respect, I think you can hear it to a certain extent.

Garcia: Certainly. Of course you can.

Gans: There's a lot of time that gigs seem like rehearsals.

Garcia: They are!
   It's always that way, in a sense. It always feels like we're just getting into it, you know. I think that, truthfully, we're just starting to get somewhere.

Phil Lesh

July 30, 1981
San Rafael, California

This interview was for a magazine that went out of business before I could submit the piece. A year later I got an assignment to profile Lesh for Musician *magazine; the follow-up interview took place on June 30, 1982.*

What music was playing in your house when you were a kid?

My dad played the piano a little bit, when he felt like it. Popular songs, just by ear. His dad had played the clarinet in one of those Sunday-go-to-meetin' bands back in Ohio, and he played baritone horn in his own school days. So he had some natural musical ability, but he never made anything out of it.

My grandmother had always been into the opera and classical music; she'd taken my mom to the concerts and operas that came to Kansas City when my mom was a child. Sometimes on Saturday it'd be the opera, but every Sunday for sure would be the Philharmonic on the radio.

The door to my room had a little window in it so they could observe my misbehavior when I was very young....I was in my room one Sunday and the Philharmonic was playing on the radio. My grandmother discovered me sitting on the floor with my ear to the wall, listening to the music.

89

Being the kind of person she was, she didn't say a word at the time—she just went about her business.

Come next Sunday, a few minutes before the broadcast she came into my room and said, "Philip, would you like to come and listen to the nice music on the radio?"

I said, "Oh, yes," 'cause I adored her. Wonderful person.

The program was Brahms' First, conducted by Bruno Walter. The introduction comes on like the wrath of God, man. It knocked me against the wall, figuratively speaking. I've never been the same since. As soon as I heard that, I knew—I just knew.

All I did for the next four years was listen, until I was old enough to get an instrument. When I was in the third grade, my parents decided I was old enough, so I brought home a violin. [*Laughs*] My dad...you know how it is when you're learning the violin: it's worse than seventeen cats howling in unison. They were patient enough to let me persist with that, but it really wasn't my instrument—although I was able to play in symphony orchestras, second violin, for quite a while. At fourteen I took up the trumpet...but the point of this is that until I was about sixteen or seventeen, my entire musical input was classical music.

I have a sort of pet theory, that the earliest stuff you hear never leaves you.

I agree with that. The other thing that could possibly be relevant...I remember it used to drive them nuts that I'd sing the commercials from the radio. They weren't into listening to the big bands or anything like that, but the radio was a big trip. They'd listen to "The Shadow," stuff like that. I remember being real pissed one time because Harry Truman came on and gave a campaign speech when "The Lone Ranger" was supposed to be on. Oh, man, I was pissed.

Anyway, I used to sing the commercials. There wasn't any TV then—we got our first TV when I was nine. So ninety percent of my influence.was classical music.

I started playing the trumpet at age fourteen. I was in the marching bands at first, of course, but the concert band was the real trip. For some reason, I was somewhat of a prodigy on the trumpet. Within a year I was able to play concert band lead parts and stuff. This was around age fifteen. I was at El Cerrito High School—that was dogshit. Even though the music director there, Oberholtzer, was basically a good guy, he was kind of a combination of musical director and football coach: he believed in a certain kind of discipline, which he only enforced selectively.

By the time I finished my sophomore year I was in the second chair, and the system at that time was to challenge the person ahead of you. I wanted that solo chair, by God, because I knew I could cut it. The director wouldn't let me. He thought it'd be bad for my ego—which just made my ego even bigger. I knew I could.

Had you been at all arrogant in dealing with him?

Not with him, especially. I'll tell you how that happened: When I was in first or second grade, they gave all the kids intelligence tests, and it turned out I was the smartest kid in school. It all came out at a PTA meeting, and a day or week or a month later the parents'd say, "How come you're not as smart as Philip Lesh is?"

I started eating it from that day on, and I ate it all the way through until I got away from those people. By that time, arrogance had been formed. That was my only protection: "Fuck you! You can beat me up, but so what?"

For a while I truly, truly hated those kids. I would have done something awful to them if I could have. But I always had the fear of reprisal, and I guess basically I'm not that kind of person.

The main event of my high school life was the switch. My parents did me the greatest favor that anybody could have done: they moved to Berkeley so I could go to Berkeley High School, where they had harmony courses, theory courses—the shit that I really wanted.

But then I was a new kid in town, and I had to work my way all the way up in the band and the orchestra. But I had the ace trumpet teacher.

Did you learn a little bit of diplomacy in the shift of schools?

Mmm, no. In fact, I never learned any diplomacy at all until I started smoking pot.

So you knocked 'em off right and left to get to first chair?

Yeah, and…it was the end of my junior year or the beginning of my senior year before I got to challenge for first chair. It was almost unanimous.

By that time I was already playing first trumpet in symphony orchestras outside. I played in the Young People's Symphony Orchestra, and in the past I'd played second violin. Now I was the lead trumpet. In the Oakland Symphony, I sat second chair to my teacher. It was semipro then. In those days—and they probably still do—they had two players on each part, not necessarily to play all at the same time but to play alternately so that the flow keeps going and there's no breaks. It's easier on the players. He was the first first, and I was the first second.

That man, Bob Hansen, was the conductor of the band in the Golden Gate Park band shell while that lasted. The only guy who got paid [in the Oakland Symphony] was the concertmaster, probably. We played all kinds of good music—Sibelius, Tchaikovsky....I kept that up until the end of my junior college career, you might say.

Were you into rhythm and blues at all, anything else?

I wasn't into any kind of popular music at all until 1964. Well, jazz, but I considered that high art.

I got into popular music backwards: I came from classical through jazz, jazz leading to the blues, the blues leading to rock 'n' roll.

I got into jazz because of the big bands—the later big bands, late forties, early fifties. The big, nineteen-piece bands. I was into Stan Kenton heavy, and from there it was the small groups....I liked West Coast jazz at first, and at seventeen I went to a summer music camp and met a guy who was a bass player. He was into East Coast jazz. We went round and round about that. I remember the first time he played me Coltrane. I was incensed—"How dare the guy play like that?" But my friend made me listen again, and finally I got over whatever it was. Maybe it was the tone, 'cause Coltrane's tone in the late fifties was really abrasive. *Really* abrasive.

What characterized West Coast jazz?

It was kind of loosely swinging, less of a blues feel, and kind of pretty tones. Shorty Rogers, Lou Levy, Bill Perkins—is that right?—some of them sidemen out of the Kenton band. Shelly Manne was the drummer; he still plays. He's got his own jazz club in LA.

Then these guys turned me on to Miles [Davis], and I didn't like Miles at first either. His playing in the late fifties was lots of air, a breathy tone—not the kind of trumpet tone that I'd been taught was the hip thing.

So you were a little hidebound—

Yeah. It was hard to accept that there was more than one way to do anything, especially play an instrument. Don't forget, I'm still in high school here, or just out.

Various life scenarios intervened there....I finally got to junior college. I went to [College of] San Mateo, where they had a jazz band. That's why I went there. The campus was on Coyote Point. It was really mellow, man. That's when the first jets were happening. We'd sit on the rocks at Coyote Point and smoke and watch the new jets land. This was '58, '59.

A guy named Elmer "Bud" Young was effectively the driving force behind the whole music department. The theory teacher was a guy named Roehr...Fred Roehr. Name didn't fit him at all.

I was there, fighting for the first chair—I was still into that—but it wasn't so important, because just playing in a unit like that knocks your socks off. You've got five trumpets, five saxophones, five trombones, and four rhythm. When they're swinging together, it's really an experience. Not even a symphony orchestra is quite like it. It's just an ass-kickin' experience.

That was one of the first times I learned to submerge my craving to play the top part. That was a big flash, believe me. I don't remember actually saying to myself, "It's just as cool" to do this as to be the soloist or the first chair, but something like that went down in my head.

Eventually the only guy ahead of me left school, and I had to take over—and I didn't do as good a job as he did, and that taught me something, too. So I gave up the trumpet. [*Laughs*]

During that time I wrote some charts for the band, which was my first writing experience: two originals. My friend who had turned me on to Miles Davis and Coltrane was the bass player in that band, and he got on my case because I'd forgotten to write at the beginning of his part, "Tune your low string down a half step."

That was the first real flash that I had of having ideas and writing them down. By that time I'd had a modicum of training in harmony, texture, orchestration. I picked up orchestration pretty much by myself, because you sit in a symphony orchestra or a band and you get a very good idea of what it's all about.

Had you been encouraged at all to create?

Yeah, by myself. Ever since then, nobody was going to do it but me. Nobody was going to write my music for me, live my life for me. I was going to be doing it, and that was part of my arrogance—and still is.

Does it get frustrating, then, when you have to depend on other people?

That's when you're involved in direct creation: composition, laying it down on paper. If you write a song, say, a rock 'n' roll song, you have to depend on the people in your band to play it. That's a whole different bag; you can't afford the luxury of that kind of arrogance, because it won't work—especially in our band. That's one of the reasons I don't write for the Grateful Dead—I can't get what I want, and I don't want to lean on these guys because I know it'll be counterproductive. Most people will say everybody contributes something, but it's never quite what you imagined when you wrote the song....

At that period in my life, that's what I was doing. I wrote those things, and I was studying.... The band played them in concert and everything— it was a great trip....

Was it avant-garde?

No, it was more or less mainstream at that time. I just wanted to see what would happen if I wrote it down and they played it. I wasn't interested in being avant-garde until later on. I was, but not in the jazz band.

Still hadn't figured out how to go outside?

No, I hadn't. But I sort of knew that in the jazz band those guys were all just like the rock 'n' rollers: you can't push them too far.

In one of those charts, there weren't any solos—no improvised solos. After that I quit trumpet.

By this time I'd been turned on [to marijuana]. You know how it is, your parents give you the scare tactic, and the first people who offered to turn me on were not the kind of people I wanted to get high with. Instinctively, I knew that, so I refused. Later on, after the right people had turned me on, I did get high with those people and it was suspicions confirmed. They were not the right kind.

The guy who did turn me on was Robert Petersen.[1] I met him in school, but we spent most of our time hanging out and raving, reading Henry Miller aloud to each other. That was really fun. There was no future....

As a poet, Petersen was into [Jack] Kerouac and those guys more than I was, but I loved [Allen] Ginsberg. Kerouac was okay, but I expected more, somehow, from *On the Road* than I got out of it when I first read it. Rereading it, I got more out of it, because I finally met Neal [Cassady]— who is the guy.[2]

I loved [Ginsberg's] *Howl* so much I started to set it to music.

---

[1] Petersen wrote a few lyrics for the Grateful Dead—"New Potato Caboose" (*Anthem of the Sun,* 1968), "Pride of Cucamonga" and "Unbroken Chain" (*Mars Hotel,* 1974). Petersen died in 1987, and a posthumous collection, *Alleys of the Heart,* was published by Hulogos'i in 1988.

[2] Neal Cassady was the model for the character Dean Moriarty in Kerouac's *On the Road.*

Does any of that survive?

No. But I could do it today if I wanted to. I got into it, but my life was falling apart. I had to leave school after the semester was finished. There was no money, and I didn't have a job for that summer. My parents were living in Napa. I persuaded them to let me try a pretty wild thing for a twenty-year-old in those days: hitchhiking to Calgary to try and find work in the oil fields. That's what we were trying to do...got as far as Spokane. My buddy's uncle in Spokane was supposed to have connections in the oil fields, but didn't.

That led to one of the great experiences of my life, which was riding the rails—a boxcar, from Spokane back to Seattle. What an experience! That was one of the great experiences of my life...you can't get away with that any more. The trains are fucked up....It only took like thirty-six hours, maybe less. I remember sneaking on in the early hours of the morning and...coming out of Spokane on a railroad....Spokane is on a big bluff, and there's this river at the bottom. The train goes across the river on the other side from Spokane, and there you are looking at this incredible panorama. I'm sure it's changed since they had a World's Fair. (We played there once, but it wasn't the same. We flew in....I spent one night there in 1960, and another night last year when we played a gig.) That experience was the tits, man.

Then everything went downhill from there. I got hung up with some friends of my parents in Seattle; they had to loan me the money to get home. I rode the Greyhound to San Francisco, then to Vallejo, and my parents picked me up—and boy, did I catch the shit then!

They made me get a job in a bank, and I worked there just long enough for school to be starting again in San Mateo.

...Both of my parents had gone to college. My dad graduated from Oregon State with a degree in pharmacy, and then he went into office machine repair. Strange dude—I never got to know him as well as I wanted to. He died when I was thirty.

My mom had completed all but her last year of college, and then her father died and she had to come home and take care of family business. But my parents were not uneducated.

What did they want you to do?

Be a doctor, or a lawyer...they wanted me to have a profession. Most importantly—and my mother still raps this shit—they wanted me to have something to fall back on in case music disappeared from the earth. It was so uncertain. They'd all heard about the Gene Krupa story, all that shit. It probably is still thought of in some circles as a shady profession, kind of like actors in the Middle Ages and early Renaissance. They were second-class citizens....

The second year at CSM [College of San Mateo] was better than the first—that's when I wrote those charts, got the first chair, and learned just about everything that I could have under those circumstances.

That whole thing I was just describing happened after my second year. My first summer I got a job at a resort run by a couple of Nazis from Argentina. I lasted a week; I happened to drop a tray of glasses right in front of the woman—it was a husband-and-wife team—and she fired me on the spot.

I was still under my parents' control when I was twenty. I conned them into allowing me to go back to school, on the condition that I'd get a job and take the right courses and get the grades to get me into UC Berkeley, which is where they'd always wanted me to go. I said, "Cool. You got it." And I did it.

So that school year—'60–'61—I got a place to live and got a job, and I reconnected with Petersen. That was the most important part [*Laughs*]. He turned me on—taught me everything I knew, practically....

Petersen had lived. He's four years older than me. Through his experience and his native ability, he was into writing, into literature. He turned me on to so much that you can't encompass it.

I got a job as board marker at the Dean Witter office, before they had computerized boards. I had to be there at five-thirty in the morning, and my job was to keep the brokers up to date. I read the ticker tape and wrote [the transactions] down. I did that for the whole school year....

What were you doing musically?

Not a thing. I made my first stabs at orchestral composition, because that's what I really was interested in.

Still no interest in electric instruments, or folk music?

I was interested in electronic music. One of the first jobs I had at CSM was in the library, listening to all the new records that came in and making sure there weren't any pops or scratches on them. [*Laughs*] I couldn't believe it—me, of all people, getting this job!

I was always into libraries as repositories of knowledge. As soon as I was old enough to read and understand how libraries work, I spent more time in the library than I did in the classroom.

I was takin' biology, getting the grades. I'd been reading about electronic music, but there were no recordings of it—none. It was being done mostly in Europe—Stockhausen.... Mills College was a year later. From '58, I had been interested in it, because there was a journal called the *Musical Quarterly*, put out by Schirmer in New York. The library, of course, had everything. If you wanted to know what was going on currently in the world of music, there was a section called "Current Chronicle" that laid out all the events that were happening in the world of classical music—mostly new stuff.

That was where I first heard of electronic music. I'd never even imagined it. What I read told me that music could be made out of its most minute components and stored on tape and controlled exactly by the composer without having to go through a performer. That intrigued me as the arrogant—

—solipsistic—

Exactly! That's who Stockhausen was at that time. Some of the first actual electronic music ever was made by Stockhausen in Cologne in '52 and '53. He studied with Messaien in Paris around 1950, and later on...he might have had something to do with *musique concrète*, that guy Pierre Schaffer. I'd have to do some research to check that.

This was all described in this journal. I stole the idea for the piece that I later wrote from Stockhausen, because in '55, '56, he wrote a piece for three orchestras called "Gruppen for Three Orchestras." It was what they call postserial. "Serial" means that everything in the structure of the piece is controlled by series—that is, proportions that are laid out in front. It hasn't anything to do with keys.

That itself derives from the twelve-tone series of Schoenberg, which derives from the total chromaticism of Mahler....

No key signatures?

Nothing. No melody, no key signatures. Nothing but sound, pure sound. It's amazing.

To give all these guys some credit in terms of melody—numbers versus not numbers—it was never a question of numbers, really. With Stockhausen, at least. For Boulez, yeah—he's the most cerebral of them all, and his music is less interesting to me than Stockhausen. Stockhausen has a heart; there's humor, all kinds of great stuff.

Then I was ready to go to Berkeley. I had more or less formed what my interests were—graduated from symphony orchestras and from bands and playing instruments. I wanted to be a composer, with a capital *C*—or maybe a capital *K* [*Laughs*]. At that time my hero was Charlie Ives,[3] who was anything but a *Komponist*. I'm referring with that term to guys like Beethoven, who was my first musical hero. Anybody who has classical music background probably has Beethoven as one of his heroes, as much as you have heroes at all in music.

Anyway, my hero was Charlie Ives—even though I'd never heard his greatest music, because it wasn't recorded. Neither was Stockhausen, nor Boulez, nor Berio. It was just written about—it was in no way commercial enough to be recorded, and at that time stereo was pretty new. Imported recordings were almost impossible—you had to go to New York City, probably, to find imported recordings.

Did you have your library job at this point?

No. That had been the whole first year, '58–'59. I kept up with it, though, at the library at CSM. Since it wasn't happening. I just contented myself, marking time, thinking about what I wanted to do and experimenting—trying to write stuff. Mostly really derivative, of course—what else could it be at that stage?

Finally I get to Berkeley. And guess what? It's dogshit. The music department at Berkeley is for musicologists, people who study about music. They have an orchestra, and they have analysis—but they don't have composition. It's really difficult to teach composition....

I enrolled, went through all that bullshit of required courses: one language, one science...at that time I was naive enough to expect that I was actually going to get a degree and then compose. Ha-ha-ha. I had enough arrogance, or faith in my talent, or whatever, to believe that. This was 1961, fall semester.

Lots of good things were happening. I met TC [Tom Constanten], who later played in our band, when we were registering in the music department. We had to earn our place in the music department by taking dictation. I was really good at that. The last thing was a Chopin thing, and I wrote it down the way I heard it—not the way it was notated. They wanted everybody to write it down the way Chopin had notated it, not the way the guy had played it. Is that weird, or what? It was the only way they knew how to do it.

[3] Charles Ives, American composer (1874–1954).

I said to the lady, "I don't give a damn how Chopin wrote it—I wrote it the way he played it." She said, "Nonetheless, you're going to have to take ear training." And I said, "The hell I will."

I tell you, I've had perfect pitch since I can remember. To me, that was a big fuck.

That was the same day I met TC, 'cause I was trying to explain to some chick about serial music—Stockhausen and stuff. This guy comes up and says, "[mumble mumble mumble]," and I said, "[mumble mumble mumble]," and then I knew that here was somebody I could talk to!

He became my roommate, and we spent more time together than either one of us did in classes. The only class that was really interesting was musical analysis. After half a semester spent on one Bach fugue from "The Well-Tempered Clavichord"—*half a semester on one fugue*. There are only two or three different kinds of fugues, and the difference between them is in terms of tonality and the number of voices. It's all really basic, but they wanted to make it so complicated....

Sounds like they took the joy out of it.

They took everything out of it.

I had a lot of trouble with Bach after that, but it wasn't because I couldn't dig Bach—it was because I was more interested in other kinds of music at that time.

I quit school after the middle of the semester, the fall semester. I didn't tell my parents for weeks.

TC and I were raving on together, and I was trying to compose. I actually composed a short piece, which I still have the score to, for orchestra. TC was always interested in chamber music, and I was always interested in orchestra. We did have common loves, like Mahler. It's impossible to get his music—I think there's one symphony that's recorded, the Second.

We both loved Mahler, so that was one point of contact. We were like two sides of a coin—he was into Bach and more of the constructionist kind of thing, and I was more into the expressive area....I never actually composed melodic music—I composed serial music. I can't describe it.

It sounds more like an exercise in how to further confound the sensibilities of listeners than it is in how to entice them.

You're right in that it's not an effort to entice the listener....It's hard to hear, but once you realize that it has a flow—and it's particularly hard to do in the case of instrumental music of this nature. It's really hard to get the flow. The instrumentalists, at that time even, had a very hard time keeping the flow, because...one of the things that came out of Schoenberg and Webern was what they called *Klangfarbenmelodie*—"tone color melody." You take an ordinary twelve-tone melody, like the theme from Schoenberg's violin concerto.

Schoenberg was a paradox: he was a classically trained musician, most at home in the classical forms—variation, that sort of thing—using twelve-tone techniques. So he would write themes and theme groups and episodes and variation movements, all in the twelve-tone style. So you take the concept of *Klangfarbenmelodie*—take an ordinary twelve-tone melody, which might stretch over four or six bars, and spread it around. Instead of having the violins play the whole thing, spread it around among six or eight instruments.

Each taking a note or two...?

Or two or three, and trading off. This was the difficult part, and still is—for listeners and for the musician. It has to be really smooth—you have to be really careful about what you're playing. Dynamics have to be almost perfect. It's very hard to do.

The composers of that time whose music seemed musical—that had the same sense of flow that older music had—were Stockhausen and Berio. Berio, it turned out, came to Mills College in the spring semester of '62 to teach. TC went right over there with his pieces; I was chicken. This was graduate level, and neither one of us had had a full semester of college— well, I had forty-one units or something...

TC took his piano pieces over there, and Berio said, "Join the class." TC said, "My roommate composes, also. Can he bring some of his stuff along, too?" Berio said, "Sure."

Steve Reich was in this class, and John Chowning.[4] I was accepted—I wasn't surprised as much as absolutely ecstatic. Here was a guy whose music I'd heard...at that time I was working at KPFA, and they had that music flown over from Europe. So I was finally hearing Stockhausen...this was '61, '62. I was a volunteer. There's also the connection with meeting Garcia and his first appearance on the media.

---

[4] John Chowning is one of the founders of Stanford University's Center for Computer Research in Music and Acoustics (CCRMA). Steve Reich is a well-known "minimalist" composer.

Were you engineering?

Yeah. I was getting into the dials and knobs. I was engineer for "The Midnight Special," the folk music show. That's what connects with Garcia.

Through that, I was hearing the music—and here I was studying with a man whose music I respected immensely, and still do.

I had given up playing instruments completely in 1960. I didn't play anything—except with myself. [*Laughs*]

That five, six months was one of the most intense experiences. This guy didn't teach—he just did his thing, and it just radiated from him. Compared to a half a semester spent on one Bach fugue, we went through the second half of *The Rite of Spring* [Stravinsky] in one day. The guy was—still is—a magician. I love him.

The only real exercises we had to do, he told us at the beginning of the semester that by the end of the semester we were going to create a collective composition—everybody was going to contribute a portion, a segment.

By this time, John Cage was becoming better known, and things were opening up. In fact, Berio organized a performance of one of Cage's major piano pieces at Mills. He had ninety-two pianos all over the place—there were some even in other buildings where you couldn't possibly hear them [*laughter*].

How do you keep that together?

You don't. That's the point.... Boulez coined the word *aleatoric*—from the Latin meaning "chance," I believe. Some of his mannerisms are a little suspect. Boulez wrote a long, long article in one of the musical journals in Europe, titled simply "Alea"—"Chance." He composed his third piano sonata...but Stockhausen beat him to the punch: he composed a piece where the pianist could go from the end of one segment to the beginning of any other segment, depending on what he'd played before.

It was revolutionary—a short piece, but everybody threw up their hands and said, "This is music?"—that famous question they've been asking for centuries, maybe even millennia. "You can't call that music."

I loved it.

Did you love it from musical or experiential criteria?

I would say experiential, because once you can love something like that, then it doesn't matter how it's made.

Had you managed to pull yourself loose from the uptightness of the training?

I guess it was the jazz.

And marijuana, I'll bet.

Yeah, a hell of a lot had to do with marijuana, because listening to that shit stoned always gives you a fresh viewpoint. You can listen to it straight and it'll say one thing to you; listen to it stoned and it says another thing; listen to it stoned again, it says yet another thing. In my opinion, the more facets you can find in work of art, the greater the work of art is—and the more there is for you.

That period was so exciting. When I told my parents I had jumped from sophomore to graduate school, they didn't know what to think. I think they were pretty convinced by that time that they weren't going to be able to get me to go through any bullshit to find anything to fall back on....

They wanted me to declare a major, but by that time I was twenty-one years old and I'd do whatever I fuckin' pleased.

Were you listening to different musics yet?

Mostly still classical and jazz. I was slowly getting sucked into the blues, because of the blues content of a lot of jazz.

Not bluegrass or jug bands or anything like that yet?

Not yet. At the end of the semester—I could spend an hour telling you what went down in those five months. So many different things—my first experience with sound in space. One example is a Stockhausen piece called "Gesang der Jünglinge." The text is from the Book of Daniel—the fiery furnace, that portion. It's boys' voices electronically modified, and electronic sounds.

Melody?

You can't call it melody, but it's still musical.

That was the first piece of electronic music, as far as I know. That was in 1956, I think. Berio had the two-channel tape that Stockhausen made for performances. They were colleagues, peers. There was a performance at Mills, five channels. We only had four in the room, so we put one in the hall. I got to run the knobs. That fifth speaker was supposed to be *out there*, somewhere. This is an Ivesian technique, also. That was my first experience of sound in space, which I had read about and we'd discussed in class. I hate to call that "class," because it was really more like a seminar, a round table or whatever.

Anyway, I got to control the positions of all the music in space—which meant trying to learn this piece, just from hearing it. There was no score—just the tape. It's an electronic composition, which means it's on tape—at least that's what that meant then. That was a total mindfuck, hearing this music just flow around you, or start from the center and divide.

Later on, down at the Ojai Festival, where Berio was the guest of honor that year, I got to do the same thing with one of his pieces, "Differences."

So you're performing the piece, in a way.

In a way. I had intellectualized it before, but just to experience it and be able to do it myself—wow! Even though the boss was sort of keeping an eye on the proceedings. He wasn't actually in the booth, but I knew that if I did anything really fucked-up I'd hear about it.

At Ojai, it was even better, because it was an outdoor concert and there were speakers in the trees. At the same festival where we were doing "Differences," which is for viola, cello, flute, clarinet, and harp, I think— those instruments recorded on tape and other parts of the music are modified, and there's purely electronic sounds, so there's a complete spectrum between the actual acoustic instruments and electronic sound. It was all available...there were speakers on the stage and four speakers out...

The proportion of artificial and real was already on the tape, but I was moving it around the room. In this case, it was around the amphitheater. Ooooh, boy!

The night before we'd done this Berio concert, Lukas Foss had done the most marvelous performance of the great Mozart C Major piano concerto I've ever heard. If Mozart had been there, he would have been in tears—as it was, I was in tears. So there was a whole range of different kinds of music. The Grateful Dead later did something with Lukas Foss in Buffalo....[5]

[5] March 17, 1970, Kleinhans Music Hall, Buffalo, New York. *DeadBase* lists Dark Star->drums (with Lynn Harbold) and Lovelight, and notes, "The Dead jammed on stage with the Buffalo Philharmonic Orchestra."

So there was some respect accorded this music, but it was still pretty out there. What was your life like at that time?

I was living in an apartment with TC and Petersen and my girlfriend. I still had a job, doing the same thing I'd done in San Mateo. Twenty-one, twenty-two years old—apparently the lack of sleep didn't bother me too much. But every day, up early and down to the stockbroker's office. But that left me free from twelve-thirty on, 'cause that's when the market closes in New York. I was totally free to compose....I didn't start to compose anything serious while I was in class, because I was too busy soaking it in. All I did was to compose my little segment for the collective composition.

The whole thing turned out pretty well; my part didn't come off well in the performance, but I heard it performed brilliantly in rehearsal, and that's all that mattered to me. I just wanted to hear it played with some kind of similarity to the way I wrote it, and that happened, so I was satisfied. I only needed to hear it once.

After the class was over, I wanted more of that. That was the most stimulating thing I'd ever encountered in my life, until I took acid. Being around Berio and that whole world of music was the tits for me.

Berio was going back to Europe, to do the summer circuit. He invited Tom and myself to come along. How the fuck am I going to get to Europe? I can barely eat. By this time, Petersen had stolen my girlfriend. She had an apartment of her own to satisfy her parents, so they spent most of their time there. What could I say to Petersen? He was—and still is—my closest friend.

I was ready for a move, so TC and I hammered out what was between us a deal. He was from Las Vegas, of all places. His dad was captain of waiters at the Sands. The deal was, we'd go to Las Vegas and get jobs, work as waiters or busboys, and earn enough money to go to Europe in the fall and connect with Berio. What happened when we got there [Vegas] was, there weren't any jobs. TC's parents had enough money to send him, and they kicked me out of the house because I was a "bad influence."

He did go to Europe, and he kept me informed of what was going on. He got to see the premiere of Berio's opera *Passagio*, which is a masterpiece. I've seen the score. It's been performed only once in this country, in Santa Fe.

There I was in Las Vegas. Luckily he had a friend who was just like me and him, a guy named Bill Walker. Walker had some room in his house, so I took my suitcase and went to his house, and I got a job at the post office in Las Vegas. I'd even tried to go out to the atomic test center for a job. Mercury, Nevada—ever heard of that place? It was just after, I believe, they signed the test-ban treaty.

I stayed in Vegas ten months, working for the post office until the last two or three months, when I worked for the Horseshoe Club on Fremont Street as a keno marker. The graveyard shift. What a scene that was! I had no money to get out....

They finally laid me off at the Horseshoe, because the management wasn't doing so well. At least that's what they said; maybe I wasn't doing my job well. I don't know to this day; how do you do a bad job as a keno marker?

During that period I started to compose this piece for four orchestras, with the audience in the middle.

Where were you planning to perform this?
Nowhere, anywhere, everywhere.

Four key signatures?
No—let's not get locked into that! There were no key signatures, no melodies. You have to have time signatures—in some places. In other places you don't. But mostly in that piece I used time signatures.

In the next piece I started to write, which never was completed, I started working back into a polytonal kind of thing, where I'd write a chord that was in, say, four keys at once. The low B-flat of the contra bassoon, all the way up to the high E in the piccolo. I was into polymusic. Polyphony traditionally means many voices; but what I was into was many musics. I'd started to get into that with "Foci" [the piece for four orchestras]. The new one was going to be an extension of that...it was for five groups of instruments, each one of them playing essentially different music. That's another offshoot of Ives.

So there I was in Las Vegas, starting to compose. I got halfway through this piece and I got the call: it's time to get out of here. I knew I'd just go fuckin' nuts if I stayed in Vegas another month. Walker's mother, or aunt, or cousin owned the house so he didn't have to pay rent, wasn't asking me for any rent, so it was easy to survive....I packed my suitcase and manuscript, got on the bus, and went to Palo Alto. See, during this time I had met Garcia, Kesey, all these people, through Stanford—Perry Lane [Kesey's house], the Chateau. I got to Stanford through a guy named Mike Lamb, who I went to CSM with. He lived in Palo Alto, and he knew these people.

By that time I'd met Jerry, Pigpen, Willy Legate, and other folks. That was the only place I could figure to go. I went to Kepler's bookstore, which had a coffee shop and was the hangout. That's where we did all our raving in my pre-Las Vegas period. By that time, Jerry was into the banjo, playing bluegrass with David Nelson. I was so astounded by Jerry's playing—I've never yet heard anyone play the banjo like that. It was the most inventive, most musical kind of banjo playing you could ever imagine.

I forgot to mention a couple of details, like the fact that during my KPFA period...I was the engineer for "The Midnight Special." I went to a party in Palo Alto, and Jerry was there singing and playing his guitar. I just had this flash—"God, this guy sounds really good; he makes the music live." I had always been impressed by somebody that could sing and play, and Joan Baez was big-time. So that quickened my interest in that kind of music, and so I listened to it closer and found that there were things to enjoy in it, things to listen to that were not so much alien to classical music but just part of music as a whole—just like classical is part of music as a whole. I had also had my first exposure to North Indian music, sitar, Ravi Shankar. This was around '62, early, I think.

I was at the party and Jerry was playing and singing, and I just had this flash. I said, "Hey, Jerry, if we could make a tape of you playing and singing, would you mind if I took it to Gert Chiarito [host of "The Midnight Special"] and played it for her?"

He said, "Shit, no, man."

I said, "Let me go get the tape recorder, and I'll make a dumb demo with one microphone and take it to Gert. You play whatever you want...." He rode with me back to Berkeley to get the tape recorder—this was when we had *all the time in the universe*—and he sang and played, I don't know how many, five or six songs. I played the tape for Gert and said, "Do you think this guy's good enough to play on 'The Midnight Special'?" I didn't know how good he was—I just knew I liked him.

She said, "This guy could have a show all to himself." That was really cool. Petersen and his friend David came down from Sacramento, and there was a big party. Jerry rapped with Gert—he was always a good rapper, of course, but this was the first time I ever saw him—and he played and sang. It was called "Long Black Veil," because that was one of the songs he was doing at the time. They did an hour show of Garcia on KPFA, and after that he was almost a regular. Then he started to bring up his buddies from Palo Alto....

I remember the last "Midnight Special" I engineered, they all came up. There was a party somewhere, and I just announced the party over the radio, shut the thing down, and we all went.

So now Jerry and David were playing, and they went down to a folk festival in '63. I also made it to Jerry's wedding, which was a classic—especially the reception. I don't think I made it to the wedding, actually. It was priceless at the reception: all of her friends were at the booze; his friends were all at the food. I'd scored a beautiful girlfriend, out of nowhere, and I had a little room to compose in with a bed and a bathroom, almost in East Palo Alto. Jerry and David came down and we sat around in the parking lot—they picked and sang, and it was so loose, really fun.

I finished my piece, "Foci," went to San Francisco; TC joined me after he got back from Europe and we got a place together. I got a job at the post office.

I got involved with some people who were really weird, and I was trying to compose again and I couldn't. I'd composed myself into a corner. I couldn't get back to the state of mind I was in when I was beginning the next piece after "Foci."

I walked away from music as a participant, essentially. I've always been a really good listener. In fact, I sometimes think I'm a better listener than musician.

Good trait in a musician.

Something you can't be a musician without, that's for sure.

So at that point I was shooting Methedrine and driving a post office truck up Market Street at rush hour, pickin' up the mail. The Muni [bus drivers] *feared* me, man. They had new respect for the post office trucks. I was a very aggressive driver.

I was completely divorced from music as a participant, but I was listening to everything I could suck up. By that time I was open enough to accept Dylan. I didn't like his first couple of albums, except for some songs, but *Another Side of Bob Dylan* came out, and I really liked that one—the material and his presentation.

I was still working for the post office when *Bringing It All Back Home* came out. You weren't supposed to do this, but I took a little radio in the truck with me, tuned to KFRC. "Subterranean Homesick Blues" came on, and I said, "Fuck me, that's Bob Dylan! On the AM radio—I don't believe it!" I pulled over and stopped, and forgot about the route. I couldn't believe it, and apparently they couldn't believe it at KFRC either, because they played it about three times an hour that whole day.

This was after the Beatles had come out. I hated the Beatles at first, and then I went to see *A Hard Day's Night*. I was the only guy in a theater full of screamin' chicks. I said, "There's got to be something to this!"

Then I started to let my hair grow long. Some old-school businessman in San Francisco wrote a letter to the Postmaster General of the United States about my hair. They called me into the postmaster's office in San Francisco and said, "Cut your hair."

"Why?"

They showed me a copy of the letter. The guy called me an "unkempt monkey," which I'll treasure for the rest of my life. This was also after taking acid for the first time. The combination of all these things was opening me up even wider; I imagine it'd do the same thing to you.

For me, acid came at the perfect moment: I was old enough to handle it, I'd had enough experience with pot so it wasn't a freak-out. I don't know how it is for anyone else; I knew it was okay for me. I remember saying to Petersen, "Shit, any pothead can handle this."

So I cut my hair, because I wanted to keep the job for a little while. I went back and they said, "It's not short enough." I said, "Fuck you," and I quit. And the rest of that spring I spent sitting around letting my hair grow and taking acid, fuckin' off, having fun, and being supported by my girlfriend—who also bought me my first electric bass.

At that point I was living at 1130 Haight Street, at Baker. In those days, the Haight was truly beautiful. This was before anything—it was just a community of people who happened to live there. A whole bunch of the right people lived there. Petersen was living there with Jane and their infant son. Somebody came in with the news that Garcia had gotten himself a rock 'n' roll band.

This was after the Rolling Stones and the Beatles had hit, and it might even have been after the Stones made their first appearance in San Francisco, in '65. That was the one where the kids rushed the stage, the cops were trying to keep them off, and Jagger was doing his dance around the cops with his microphone cord and tripping them up. It was far out!

[Danny] Rifkin [later the Dead's manager] led the entire Haight community dancing through the aisles. This was before any of the flower shit. I met Rifkin when we were both working at the post office.

Anyway, somebody came in with the word that Garcia's band was playing such-and-such a night at Magoo's Pizza Parlor. About a week before that, me and my old lady went to a party in Palo Alto. Garcia was there. I'd been listening to the Rolling Stones, the Beatles, and stuff like that. Jerry and I were raving, and—you know, "Where's the pot, man?"

"It's on its way—my rhythm guitar player's going to get it." Bob [Weir] was at this party, and we sat in Garcia's car and smoked. At some point during this party I mentioned to Garcia that I might like to get into playing some instrument, some electric instrument. I said, "Maybe bass guitar," something like that. It was a stoned moment, and I didn't think anything more about it—this is the honest truth!

Then whenever it was that they were playing, we took acid and went down there—[Hank] Harrison, myself, Petersen, Jane, and my girlfriend. We came bopping in there, and it was really happening. Pigpen ate my mind with the harp, singing the blues. They wouldn't let you dance, but I did anyway—we were so fuckin' stoned!

During the set break, Jerry took me off to a table and said, "How'd you like to play bass in this band? Our bass player is not a musician, and we have to tell him what notes to play."

I said, "By god, I'll give it a try." After they split from Dana Morgan, who was the bass player and the son of the owner of the store where they had been rehearsing, they moved over to this place called Guitars Unlimited in Menlo Park. The guy there was real neat, and he just let me have a loaner to work with.

Later, my girlfriend bought me the bass. I hated the instrument—a single-pickup Gibson with a neck like a telephone pole—but it was the only one I could afford. That's how that got started. It was all just [*snaps fingers half a dozen times*] one door after another.

I consider myself a very lucky person, and I consider us lucky as a group, to have been in the right place at the right time.

It can almost be said that everybody learned their axes in the band.

This is absolutely true: we all learned how to play together, and that's why we play well together.

Now we each know how to play well enough that we can play with other people, but for a long time it wasn't true—except for Jerry, who had a head start on all of us, and Pigpen, who was the king. It just came runnin' out—couldn't stop it.

It seems to have changed constantly.

Yeah. That seems to be the nature of the beast. I prefer it that way, 'cause otherwise it wouldn't exist anymore. You have to change...sometimes the change is not necessarily positive; sometimes it's not necessarily growth. Whatever occurs gives one certain person, or some people, or everyone, a different perception—which leads, then, to something positive. Sooner or later; sometimes it takes a while. This is sixteen years now, and it's still challenging enough. Sometimes it's challenging in a negative way—"Okay, I'll show these fuckers"—or a positive way, like "Wow, did we really play that?" or "Let's try and do that again" or "Let's try and get *there* again."

It seems like when you try really hard, you don't get there.
   That's also the nature of the beast. That's Murphy; this is Murphy's world.

It's been my observation musically—and it's been somewhat borne out in recent encounters with band members—that there's a perversity to this particular crowd of people that keeps itself from ever getting any momentum in any one direction.
   And who knows whether that's good or bad? Any one particular direction, it would eventually narrow down. If anyone was really in charge—if Jerry was really the leader of the Grateful Dead, let's say, which he isn't, because it doesn't go his way. The Grateful Dead doesn't go his way, it doesn't go Bob's way, it doesn't go my way—it goes its own way, as long as it's running, performing as a unit.

Seems like an awesome responsibility to each of you as individuals.
   After this many years, man, there's nothing awesome about it all, except the moments. Those moments, when you're not even human anymore—you're not a musician, you're not even a person—you're just there. .

It seems like a real privilege as a human being to be able to be in this kind of creative situation.
   I think so. You sort of take it for granted, like maybe a long-term relationship with a woman, until something starts going wrong. Then you say, "What's going wrong?" But as I was saying, those moments—they're a state of grace, in a sense.

When "the music plays the band"?
  Yeah, that's it.

• • •

*I remember a guy telling me that he was white-water rafting someplace
and a train went by—I'm not sure whether it was a real train or a
metaphysical train—but there is was, and it was a message from you.*
  And what did it say?

*I don't recall that there was any particular message—it was like "Hello
from Phil and the Grateful Dead."*
  That's great, man, because you know what that does? Whether it adds
to the mystification or not, what it means to me is that people are open to
those kinds of experiences, and the more people are open to that kind of
thing the better kind of world we're going to have—one way or the other.
  ...Somewhere before the seventies, the carrier wave ceased having
content imposed upon it collectively by the audience and just became raw
power. All we ever got was raw power....I don't really expect it anymore,
because after ten years of not seeing it...maybe I've forgotten how to see
it, forgotten how to pursue it. It's possible.

*It's so subjective. You can walk out of the show with the people you were
sitting with and have ten different opinions, or be collectively into it with
those guys and run into another group who are tearing their hair out. And
I guess the six of you go home with different opinions each night, too.*
  [*Lesh whistles in agreement.*]

*The last substantive question I want to ask is about the fact that you did
not come to the bass as a guitarist, and as far as I know have never been
influenced much by guitar players except the ones you've been playing
with. You do a lot more melodic business than most bass players do.*
  What I did was come to the bass as a musician. Period. Jerry said, "Why
don't you try playing bass in this band?" I said, "Okay, I'll try." It was
obvious that there were certain fundamentals that had to be observed—
deal with the bass drum, play the root of certain chords—but after six
months of that it was obvious to me as a musician that a whole bunch of

that could be disposed of. In other words, I could play offbeat to the bass drum, put the seventh in the bass, or the ninth—which I have done, and do—and it would still make sense.

You felt no obligation to the bass guitar role in a rock 'n' roll band?
Absolutely not. Except when it's absolutely necessary.

Bob Weir

November 12, 1981
Mill Valley, California

First of two interviews for an article for Music Exchange *magazine titled "Bob Weir's Double Career." Bobby and the Midnites [Arista AL-9568, 1981] was just being released. This interview took place at Weir's house.*

Where did this band come from?

In some ways, this is the Ibanez All-Star band. About three years ago Jeff Hasselberger, who was at the time marketing director for Elger Corporation in Philadelphia and with whom I'd been designing guitars, got us together at a NAMM [National Association of Music Merchants] show.

Jeff invited me and a number of other guys—Alphonso [Johnson, bass], Billy [Cobham, drums], Bobby Cochran [guitar], and Steve Miller [guitar], all Ibanez or Tama endorsees—to play at a NAMM show in Anaheim, to promote Ibanez instruments. We all sort of did waltz-on cameos and had a lot of fun.

We sort of reassembled it—without Steve Miller, who was busy at the time—in Atlanta about six months later. At that point, I was starting to entertain notions of putting together a solo project that incorporated these folks, because they are so much fun to play with. And finally that happened, late last year. Tim Bogert came through Bobby Cochran, and that kind of worked out, but when we knocked off in the spring of this year, Tim started his own group. When I started looking to reassemble this group to take it into the studio, Tim was busy and Alphonso was free. So we grabbed him, because he was the guy I always wanted to have in the band.

And then Brent [Mydland] came from the old *Heaven Help the Fool* band.

I heard there was a pretty bizarre variety of tunes played at that first NAMM jam. The thought of Billy Cobham and Alphonso Johnson doing "El Paso" is pretty off-the-wall.

[*Laughs*] Yeah, well, it was all done in the spirit of good fun. We did old rock 'n' roll, and some outside stuff, too. All kinds of stuff. I don't remember what songs…a couple of tunes of Al's, a couple of Billy's, a couple Steve Miller tunes, and a few of mine.

How'd you decide on the name "Bobby and the Midnites"?

It came to me in a flash, along with the album cover. The infamous cat and the fiddle, the reincarnation of Midnite the Cat. Midnite the Cat was a fixture on a TV show called "Andy's Gang." I remember it from the very dawn of my memory; when I was a real little kid, that show was on TV. Just about all I really remember about the show was the cat. He had a little cigar-box podium and he played the fiddle. I guess he was some sort of puppet—had me fooled at the time…

That picture [on the *Bobby and the Midnites* album cover] more or less came to me. I drew a rough sketch and gave it to Vic Moscoso, and he made it just perfect. I don't think Cochran likes the name especially well, but he hasn't liked any name I've come up with especially well. Course, I've come up with some ones that were not as easy to like as this one.

You've established a pattern of going into the studio with the Grateful Dead and then keeping the producer for your own project. If they can handle the Dead, they can do anything?

[*Laughs*] It's true. Also, you know who you're working with, what sort of stuff to expect. I like to work with one producer for a while. I hope to do some more work with Gary [Lyons, who produced *Go to Heaven* for the Dead before *Bobby and the Midnites*]: on top of getting good sounds, he's a lot of fun to work with.

Why do you want to go through all the headache of trying to break a record?

So I can make a bunch of bucks so that I can build my studio so I can keep doing it.

What's wrong with the one you've got?

It needs constant updating, and right now I need to put in a real bona fide, no-kidding control room and all that kind of stuff. I have to do construction, and I'll probably have to get a new board, and a few other things. So you can see that it's going to get very expensive.

Besides that, once you make a record—and I'm kinda happy with the record; there's a lot of stuff that I think I could do better, like get the vocals further out front—I'd just as soon that it didn't go unnoticed. So I'm going to do a certain amount of promotion. I'm actually not going to do that much—

Why do it half-assed? Why not go on television and lip-synch?

I'm not going to lip-synch—I'm thoroughly opposed to lip-synching. I'm going to do some media stuff, visit a couple of radio stations—my favorite stuff to do.

Well, it's the flip side to the completely anticommercial way it is with the Grateful Dead.

Actually, the Grateful Dead do a fair amount of that. Generally it comes down to me doing it, too, because I'm the guy who doesn't know how to say no. I must confess, with the Grateful Dead I've slacked off. I haven't done any interviews lately. I was taking the brunt of the interviews for a long time, and you get talked out.

Jerry contradicted himself [in the 1981 BAM interview]. In part one he said, "Yeah, Weir's a shameless thief," and in part two he said, "He's an extraordinarily original player in a world full of people who sound like each other"—which is about the highest compliment I think you can pay a guitar player.

There's a clear contradiction there; I caught that myself. He's right on both accounts—I am a shameless thief, but by the time whatever I'm stealing gets translated through my unique style, limitations, and abilities, it generally comes out sounding—no matter how much I meant for it to sound like the original—it gets completely transformed in the translation. So I can afford to be a shameless thief.

An "assimilator."
  An "eclectic."

How much homework do you do for the Dead these days?
  Well, as of right now I'm heading into a couple of weeks of writing for the Grateful Dead. In all, I'll put in about a month of writing for the next Grateful Dead record, and try to get some of it so that we can take it on the road before we take it into the studio.

That does seem to work out better. Don't you think a song like "Estimated Prophet" was much better defined by the time you got it to the studio?
  That tune is the most graphic example of that particular theory. We didn't have it on the road originally, and we went into the studio and tried to put it down—we learned the song, basically, in the studio.
  Then we went and did one weekend in southern California and then came back into the studio and got it in three takes. It was completely cohesive, as opposed to a disheveled mess....I think we only played it twice; that much is all you really need. It's nice to have more, but it makes a world of difference presenting it to people as a piece. Once you present a song from on stage, that's pretty much where it comes together. That's what it's for, anyway.

I watched you write "Lost Sailor" and "Saint of Circumstance" on the stage over a period of a few months....
  Yeah. Also we did "Slipknot" that way, from *Blues for Allah*. We'd take it and play it onstage, then think about it for a while, make some adjustments. The more time you have, obviously, the more you're going to be able to chisel away and sculpt it just the way you want.

You weren't playing gigs in those days!
  Yeah, we did. We did a couple of surprise gigs.

Just one or two times like that...?
  It makes a huge difference. I wonder what the luxury of having something out on the road for a month, say, would afford a given song.

Haven't there been any like that?

Not in recent memory. We'd been playing "Samson and Delilah" and "Dancin' in the Streets" for a while before we took them in the studio.

How'd you feel about how those came out on the record?

A little weird. "Samson" I thought could have had a lot more life. It fairly roars and snarls on stage, and on the record it sounded a little stiff.

How about the live version [On Dead Set*]?*

That's closer. It's not the hottest rendition we've ever done, but what the hell...

• • •

There was a time when we used to come back from the gigs and listen to the tapes every night. We're actually starting to do that again every now and again.

A good way to catch those little nuggets—

Whip them up into songs. That's exactly what the doctor ordered. It's a great way to do it.

Can you cite an example of a spontaneous thing that grew into a song?

"Estimated Prophet," for instance. I had a whole bunch of shards of stuff in seven that I'd been playing with, and one time while we were rehearsing, that riff came to me and it tied together all these other shards, and I was able to come up with a complete song.

About half the songs I write have their basis in some jam somewhere, and the other half...I make 'em up.

Talk to me about the creative reasons for Bobby and the Midnites. The financial reasons are good, but not inspiring.

A steady diet of anything can get dull, and the Grateful Dead—as dynamic as we can be from time to time—is still the "good ol' Grateful Dead." We all know each other real well; they know how to shore up my weaknesses and play up my strengths. If I go and play with a completely new group of musicians, I have to deal with all those weaknesses and strengths again in a new light, and I have to work on my weaknesses—and I discover new strengths and fortes of mine. I get to develop more. Besides, it's different—it's a holiday, a hobby.

Is it less work?

It's a little less work, yeah. Grateful Dead is pushing a boulder uphill all the time, until it gets rolling. But it's not always rolling, and when it comes time to get it started again, it's a lot of work.

The whole thing with the Grateful Dead is a challenge to get something new happening, even when you don't feel like doing anything new, or don't feel anything new lurking around the corner...to find something new in either a given treatment of a particular song or some totally new unexplored territory in one of our jams or something. We actually try to go for that every night, and to be together enough and responsive enough to do that sort of stuff, you have to really keep your wits fairly sharp and your chops together. And the band has to be a working, functioning unit. You always have to work at that, like they say you always have to work at making a marriage work. It's a whole lot like being married.

In the Midnites I get to be a little bit more like the boss, though the Midnites are a fairly democratic organization as well. Comparatively, I get like two votes, and if there's something I want to do with the Grateful Dead and I get a good solid "Go fuck yourself," then I'll go and do it with Bobby and the Midnites...the Grateful Dead, by and large, are a bunch of perverse gunsels.

You seem to be the one who runs the show, slamming home into "Sugar Magnolia" when "Wharf Rat" could go on for another nine or ten minutes.

I'm the "Mr. Show-biz" in the group. I've developed the attitude over the years that by the time I start getting bored with a given number, it's a fair guess that a certain portion of the audience is getting bored, too. I could be completely mistaken, but I'm just going by that assumption.

Like everything else about the Dead, there's raging controversy on that question: one guy on one side of me'll go, "That asshole!" and the other guy'll go, "Oh, thank god!"

[Laughs] I've just found that "to thine own self be true." If I'm going to play at a hundred decibels, I'd rather not be sounding bored. When you're playing that loud and being that forward, if you feel the urge to move on and you don't move on, it's going to sound loud and boring.

Do you like it?

Oh, on a good night I love it. And the good nights come more often than the bad nights. I liked pretty much all of Berkeley [Greek Theatre,

Family gathering at Rancho Olompali, Novato, California, circa 1966. "During that day," Garcia recalled, "more happened to me than would happen to me in a thousand lifetimes ... Definitely one of those 'before and after' experiences." (Photo by Herb Greene)

Phil Lesh (left), Olompali, 1966. (Photo by Herb Greene)

Fashion photo for Mnasidika, a store in the Haight. Left to right: Phil Lesh, Bill Kreutzmann, Jerry Garcia, Bob Weir, Pigpen. (Photo by Herb Greene)

The Grateful Dead. (Photo by Herb Greene)

Massachusetts Institute of Technology, Kresge Plaza, May 6, 1970. Free concert on a national day of protest following the killing of four students at Kent State on May 4. (Photos by David Spitzer)

Bob Weir. (Photo by Herb Greene)

Ron "Pigpen" McKernan.
(Photos by Herb Greene)

Bob Weir, 1972. (Photo by Andy Leonard)

Lyricist John Barlow, 1972. (Photo by Andy Leonard)

Berkeley Community Theatre, August 1972. Bob Weir (left), Jerry Garcia. (Photo by David Gans)

University of Nevada, Reno, May 12, 1974. Bob Weir (left), Phil Lesh. (Photo by Bruce Polonsky)

Winterland, San Francisco, October 1974. Five "farewell" concerts were filmed for the *Grateful Dead Movie* (1976). (Photo by Bruce Polonsky)

Phil Lesh, Golden Gate Park, September 28, 1975. (Photo by Ed Perlstein)

Bob Weir atop his Corvette at Sound City during the recording of *Heaven Help the Fool*, August 1977. (Photo by Ed Perlstein)

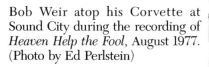

Lyricist Robert Hunter contemplating his next move, November 1977. (Photo by Ed Perlstein)

September 11–13, 1981], except for maybe the second set the first night—I ran completely out of gas. I'd been up the entire night before—

That was the zoniest part—

That was the zoniest part, but there was almost nothing left. On the other hand, if a musical idea came along, I didn't have the strength to resist it. I was completley will-o'-the-wisp that night.

The sound in [the Greek Theatre] is tremendous.

I think that's one of the best places around, period. I've wanted to play that place for so long, and I've encountered a lot of resistance. We played there a long time ago, and we didn't play so well, and so we blamed the place. I kept remembering it as not being that way—the place sounded OK, we just didn't have it in us that day. Sometimes the magic works, and sometimes it doesn't. It took us twelve years to get back around to playing there. Also, I was told that there was a security problem. Every time the idea of playing there came up for a few years our management would say, "No, we can't play there—it's impossible to make it secure."

Since when is a Grateful Dead crowd a security problem?

I don't know.

If there's any place in the world where a Deadhead crowd would just blend right in, it's Berkeley.

I would think, too. Well, that was quite apparently horseshit, but at the time we didn't know that. It's taken us twelve years to get around to the place, but I'm mighty glad we finally did. It's my favorite place around here by far.

• • •

How do you deal with fame? How responsible do you feel toward your audience with regard to your image as a cult figure?

How do I deal with fame...bite the bullet, I guess. Fame isn't all it's cracked up to be. Virtually everybody who's famous says it, and it's true: it can get to be a real drag.

The unconditional and undiscriminating love of all those people doesn't do that much for you?

Well, the undiscriminating and unconditional love and admiration and adulation of all those people doesn't do a whole lot for the music, I'll say.

We can do anything—we don't have a very critical audience. For instance, on a bad night, if the crowd goes wild after we just rendered a relatively dismal set, I feel horrible about that. I don't think they should clap at all. [*Laughs*] They should run us out of town on a rail, and they never do.

Have there ever been nights when you thought you guys were roaring good and the crowd missed it?
   Yeah. There have been those nights, too, though generally we're pretty well in tune with the crowd. But there have been nights—not so much recently as right before we knocked off in '74—we got so musically inbred that we were playing some fairly amazing stuff, but almost nobody could hear it or relate to it except for us. That's one of the reasons why we knocked off and went out and did solo projects. We were speaking a language known only to us, using a musical vocabulary that was really pretty damned esoteric at some points.

You don't think the crowd was picking up on it?
   A lot of them didn't—I know they didn't.

It's surprising that you comment that the crowd is at all out of touch, because I find that the Grateful Dead fans that I know listen more closely and care more about the music and render more judgments than most.
   Yeah, yeah. I'm speaking more or less about before we knocked off in '74. Still, we got fairly esoteric…there were the close-in core of fans, like yourself, probably, who could follow it. But your average kid who came to the show because it was the only thing happening on Friday night in town—"Go on down to the rock 'n' roll show. Who's playing? I think this band called the Grateful Dead, I think they're pretty good"—we lost them with pretty fair regularity. Since then, we've gotten more succinct. The space music, though it happens, generally doesn't go on for as long, and if it does go on for a while we generally get to the heart of what we're getting to a lot quicker.

Is that an improvement?
   Yeah, I think so. It's just a matter of cutting the fat, essentially. Getting to the heart of whatever it is we're trying to get at.

When the most self-indulgent band in the history of the world decides to acquire a little discipline…there are a lot of people who are conditioned to the other, and indulge you, and relish the indulgence of it. In '73, when you were doing three sets and there were three or four places where it opened up wide, those were the nights. I appreciate what it is now, but I sometimes miss when it spaced out more often and when it was less predictable.

I do, too. It's harder to do now, because with the reinclusion of Mickey in the group, it's one more person...when we were a quintet, it was a lot easier—particularly with the rhythm section—to be a lot looser. Now that you have another drummer, it's half again as cumbersome to turn a corner. Every single musician you add in a group like the Grateful Dead, in an ensemble that size, makes it a whole lot more difficult to be real open and real loose. And yet we can do it. It's just not as easy as it was back then to ramble from place to place, so we have to hone our instincts as to where to go and how to get there as quickly as possible.

We do read the crowd, all of us, and work with whatever spirit arises from that particular evening. It's a real-time experience, the way we approach it. Every time we do a song, it's different, because the mood of the evening is different. The crowd is only a part of that, but a fairly large part. The way everybody in the band's feeling, the way the place sounds— I guess those are the major ingredients in the moment.

If you feel that most of the crowd isn't discriminating...I guess that varies from venue to venue, too.

It really does. A San Francisco crowd, for instance, is probably the most discriminating. On the East Coast, they're the most voracious.

They'll eat anything?
[*Laughs, nods*]—and holler for more!

Is that where "Satisfaction" comes from?[1]

No, "Satisfaction" came up one night...[*laughs*] one of those little clouds of madness that drifted across the stage. I don't think we'll do "Gloria" that often, but we may do "Satisfaction" every now and again, because when I really feel like doing "Satisfaction" it's because I'm feeling pretty ringy. Oftentimes that means I'm going to come up with something to say in the end bit....We have never done that one remotely the same twice, and obviously we've never, ever rehearsed the song.

You're more telepathic than I thought.

---

[1]According to *DeadBase*, "Satisfaction" was part of the Warlocks' repertoire in the pizza-parlor days. The Grateful Dead played it as the encore at the Hollywood (Florida) Sportatorium in November 1980 and brought it out a couple of dozen times in the eighties, always as an encore or second-set closer.

There are a number of songs that we've never rehearsed, but that one's the prototypical song that rehearsal would ruin.

• • •

[On being a "Cult Figure"] There are a whole bunch of people who take me relatively seriously—perhaps a bit more seriously than I feel comfortable with, but what the hell.

I take everything with a grain of salt, really. But I feel a fair degree of responsibility to live up to their ideals and standards, because as I read them they're pretty reasonable: to strive for musical excellence. If there's anything beyond that, if there's a lifestyle or philosophy that's to be found in there, it's to be found in adherence to those principles: lean into the music, and be as consistently excellent as one can possibly be.

What about all the baggage that goes with the magic that's ascribed to you guys?
That's a symbiotic situation. That magic only happens when I'm onstage performing, and it only happens between me—or us—and the audience. They can't ascribe that magic to any individual, because when he's not performing, it's not there.

What people in many instances fail to recognize is that they are every bit as much a part of that magic as we are. It doesn't exist in a vacuum— it's magic that transpires between us and our audience. They're as much part of it as we are. That sounds like a huge platitude, but it's very real.

An awful lot of people out there—to whom going to see the Dead is the highlight of a year—they assume that you have to live a life of constant magic.
That'd get a bit rich after a while. Too much of a good thing. Everybody assumes that all celebrities are magical all the time, and it's just not true in my experience. Otis Redding, for instance, was an amazing guy, and when I met him he was a regular guy. Jimi Hendrix, the same thing. If they weren't one hundred percent magic all the time, then I don't think anybody is.

What I do take very seriously is the responsibility I hold to my audience to be as good as I can possibly be.

Is your attitude toward that at odds with your partners?

No. I don't think so. We may vary in our own interpretations of what excellence is—that's how everyone comes up with their individual styles, they have their own parameters.

It's been sixteen years now—
We've become more developed as individuals, and in some ways have become fairly apart. On a good night, that serves to expand the dynamics within which we work.

Whether you more or less like each other at various times, you all trust and respect each other—
Yeah. Whether or not we like a certain aspect of what another is doing. I'm going to go out with Bobby and the Midnites in January and I intend to have a whole lot of fun, and develop certain sides of my performance. When I come back and play with the Grateful Dead after that tour, I'm going to be a little different. There's no predicting how it's going to go over with the group.

I could hazard a guess that you're going to develop some more show-manlike attitudes—
I'm going to try to develop as much musically, if not more so. Basically, what I am is a musician. Showmanship I can kind of get into; it's kind of fun—to a point. But at the point at which it starts to detract from the music, it stops being fun for me. I'm not going to practice a bunch of moves or anything when I could be practicing scales. And I'm not going to come up with anything that limits my ability to play. But as far as showboating my licks is concerned, it makes it more fun for me. Like dancing.

That brings us back into the subject of maintaining two bands. What do you get from the one that you don't get from the other?
It's a different sort of thing. For instance, I like working with the Midnites, 'cause virtually everybody in the group sings. I can do big choral arrangements, and that's a lot of fun. The Grateful Dead is not as wide open on that level. The rhythm section in Bobby and the Midnites is a little less dodgy than the rhythm section in the Grateful Dead. The rhythm section in the Grateful Dead is unique, and can be a lot of fun, but I also like playing with the Midnites because it's real straightforward and solid; I can play a whole different sort of style with them.

Is Bobby and the Midnites commercial music?

I don't really even address myself to that consideration, ever.

You just said you want to make a whole bunch of money so you can beef up your studio!

Yeah, but I haven't the foggiest idea what "commercial" is. I know what I like; I know what seems appropriate in a given instance—or don't know what's appropriate and have to sort of guess—but as far as commercial is concerned, I'm just going for fun. I figure if it's fun for me, there's at least a chance it's going to be fun for someone else. Rewarding in one way or another. Generally with music, I go for fun. Obviously it's not always fun that you're singing about. Sometimes the feeling that you're looking for is not fun at all. I'm just going for the music.

What about Gary [Lyons]? It seems to me that a guy who's in the business of producing records is under some kind of compulsion to produce hit records.

Yeah. But he works with me not because I'm a giant seller—he has bands like the Outlaws, Foreigner, groups like that—he's got any number of offers to do some real major acts. But he's made about all the money he can deal with. As far as he's concerned, making money isn't his primary concern. He really enjoys what he's doing, and he has a knack for it. And people tend to like his production. He can take a band and make it more palatable, at least on record.

I believe in working with a producer, personally, because...I spend, I guess, ten months a year onstage or on tour or working on it, coming up with material and performing it. A producer is a guy who spends the bulk of his time in the studio. Whereas I've developed a whole lot of technique for my onstage presentation, he's developed a whole lot of technique for working in the studio. He eats, sleeps, and breathes studio, whereas I.eat, sleep, and breathe onstage. So he's going to necessarily be a little bit more in touch with what a studio is all about. It's an immensely complex instrument, and he plays that instrument. The stage is also a fairly complex instrument, and I play the stage.

Do you have any advice for young musicians who want to follow in your footsteps?

I guess that best advice that I could possibly give is to make sure you enjoy what you're doing. Make sure you're entirely engrossed in it and you enjoy it. Whatever you're doing—playing guitar, writing, performing, or recording—if you're not enjoying it, you're headed up a blind alley, I think. I kind of believe in fun. Music isn't about fun and nothing else for me, but still it should be fun. Otherwise, it's going to get old, and it'll sound like it.

Knowing what you know today, would you do anything differently?

Probably practice more; probably figure out some sort of regimen that included more practicing way early in life.

More discipline?

Yeah, a little bit, but not a whole lot more. The more disciplined I get, the more introspective I get stylistically. That's cool to a certain point, as far as I'm concerned, but if you get too introspective, you get insular; you're not really reaching anybody by reaching inside. That doesn't sit so well with me.

Whose recognition do you want? Whose approval do you seek?

Mine. And then, secondarily, my cohorts'. And then, thirdly, the audience's.

Doesn't Clive [Davis] matter at all?

Clive falls somewhere in between. He's not in the band. He's interesting to bounce off of for me, because he really is another country heard from...Without variety, you can't have no horse race. I do like to have opinions, and bounce stuff off of different people and different kinds of people.

Do you tend to do what [Clive Davis] wants in terms of making a record happen?

[*Emphatically*] No. If I made a record that I thoroughly hate—I'm in the business to make the kind of music that I like. It's no use banging my head against a wall doing something that I'm not going to be pleased with. That's going to shorten my career, because I'm going to end up hating it. Regardless of whether anybody else likes it, there's only so long you can go on doing something you hate.

But is it frustrating to you at all that the Grateful Dead don't sell more records than they do?

It's frustrating to me that we don't make better records than we do.

Why doesn't it happen? The material has always been good. The songs are the strongest thing—it's just that the performances in the studio are lacking, and the production values vary wildly.

One of the reasons we don't make good records, generally, is because we don't know the material when we're doing it. We don't know the material until years later. We should make a blanket policy of not recording anything that we haven't played onstage.

That's the opposite of the industry standard. The Doobies and the Eagles spend their lives in the studio writing the songs as they go.

But we're not that kind of band. The Grateful Dead differ from other bands—even Bobby and the Midnites, it's the same thing: I wish we could have had a lot of the material onstage before we'd taken it into the studio. There's a fair difference in the rendition—I think there's one song, "Book of Rules," that we'd actually played.

On your first solo album, Ace, *you used all the Grateful Dead.*

Yeah. That was a Grateful Dead record, as far as I'm concerned. And I don't do that material with my side groups.

Why was that put out as a Bob Weir album instead of a Grateful Dead album?

It was all me singing, all my songwriting. I started by using a couple of different musicians, and it just settled in to being a Grateful Dead record right quick.

It seems that you didn't really spring out and start carrying a fair share of the glory and the work until Pigpen stopped working. Is that a fair assumption?

I guess so. Pigpen was our showman. When he started to slide, I sort of naturally stepped into it. It's something I don't mind doing—in fact, I rather enjoy showboating and all that kind of stuff. [*Laughs*] Somebody had to do it. Garcia's been on a long, slow taper as far as his showmanship is concerned—he's become less and less showy. Way back when, he was a lot more showy—he used to move onstage almost all the time.

Your songwriting seemed pretty understated in the early days, too. That raft of material that came along on Ace...from that point on, it was Jerry-Bobby, Jerry-Bobby. Were you writing all that time?

No. Along about late 1970, 1971, I sort of got into gear finally. The time was right, I guess.

In the early days, there was what one writer described as a "long, lazy dialogue" between Garcia and Phil. TC was sort of in and out, and you were sort of in and out. I always liked what you did under those "Dark Stars," but it was so far back—

Yeah. I didn't have all that great a vocabulary as a guitarist at that point. And my role, then as ever, was a fairly difficult one. Being in between the lead and the bass and intuiting where the hell they're going to go and being there. It took a while to work up a touch for that. I'd get hot and find myself moving pretty fluently in that role, then I'd lose my momentum and fall out of it. It's a real difficult position to stay on top of.

So much about you seems contradictory to what people expect of the Grateful Dead: running, healthy, Lacoste shirts...

...We're a whole lot more amorphous than people are generally capable of viewing us, individually and collectively. Even if we were like somebody thinks we are, we're not that way anymore—no matter what it was. By the time anybody decided what we're like, we were different. That's always been the case, at least with this band. I think that's pretty much the case with life: people try to ascribe properties to somebody or a group, and by the time they ascribe those properties to a given entity, that entity has changed.

So many different musics are at work in the band. That makes it what it is, and it's also what makes it hard for people who are more superficially oriented to get a handle on it. You can't say, "What kind of music is the Grateful Dead?" Is it country-rock, folk-rock, jazz-rock, acid rock—

The Grateful Dead is a band that pretty much defies categorization. Interaction's what makes it happen. Everybody in the Grateful Dead has a fairly individual style. Nobody sounds like anybody else in the group, or anybody else. I don't play guitar like anybody I know; Garcia doesn't play the guitar like anybody I know; Phil doesn't play bass like a bass; the drummers are quirky, and Brent's fairly unique as well—getting more bent as the days go by, it's true. Given any conversation that goes on in that band, there's always going to be another country heard from. Any conversation is going to turn a corner. It's completely unpredictable.

How outside was it when Phil and TC were in there with their avant-garde influences? It must have been hard to muscle all those styles together into one thing.

It got cumbersome from time to time. When TC was playing with us was an era when the music was its most cumbersome. It was hard to turn the corner, because it was a little too outside. For me, nowhere could I find a handle on the drift when it started to get spacey, well enough to intuit where it was going. It was accidental music, but a little *too* accidental. Sort of like the difference between driving a car in a drift and driving a car completely sideways. If you're completely sideways, chances are you're going to run off the road.

Did they know where they were going?

No, oftentimes. When we were experimenting with accidental music, it was a little bit too far in that direction. There's a big difference between a happy accident and a real, genuine musical revelation—which do come to us with a fair degree of frequency, even these days. Happy accidents are wonderful stuff—you could almost live on a steady diet of that, but you need a little bit of control to get a genuine revelation. And at the same time, you have to get uninvolved egowise. It's sort of a tightrope you're walking: on the one hand, you're trying to forget yourself, and at the same time you're trying to maintain control and be assertive. About what, you only have a sort of an inkling—you have your intuition to go by, and that's it. Music for us happens best when we rely on our intuitions more and our egos less.

Bob Weir

November 14, 1981
San Rafael, California

Second of two for Music Exchange. *Two days later, at the Front Street studio.*

[re dyslexia]…it takes a humongous amount of concentration for me to read anything of any length. It's textbook dyslexia. Reading music is out of the question. I can count, and tell you what inversions I'm playing, you know.

Did "Born Cross-eyed" have anything to do with being dyslexic?
No. I was also born cross-eyed, and to this day I'm still slightly cross-eyed. That may account for some of the dyslexia—I'm not sure.

Let's go through Bobby and the Midnites title by title.
"Haze"…started out with a certain riff that I was playing to myself, and I decided it'd be OK if I could put a somewhat angular scale over the top of it.
As I was playing with that, I got the news that a friend of mine had died. The song, as it turned out, was more or less a eulogy for that friend, a guy named Bruce Baxter. He died of a multitude of excesses, but he got a

129

whole lot more living done in his forty years than any half-dozen normal people do all combined in their lifetimes. His liver finally gave out at the age of forty.

The next one is "Too Many Losers," which was originally called "Fuckin' With Fire." Clive [Davis] sat me down and said, "Listen: this one has a chance to make it as a single, and I'd sure hate to lose the Midwest and the South behind one line. Can't you come up with another line that kind of says the same thing?" So I came up with "Stokin' the fire." [*Laughs*] It wasn't just Clive, it was Clive and my esteemed producer, Mr. Gary Lyons—who, despite his lack of temperance in some situations, saw some merit in Clive's pleas. Between Clive and Gary, they managed to supply enough leverage to get me to change the line to "Stokin' the fire." That one I wrote for a couple of friends of mine. It pretty much says what it has to say.

It has a nice antidrug line, too, suitable for Top 40. Help live down the Grateful Dead jinx...

You can't sing about it, though, if you haven't been there. You don't know about it if you haven't been there. Maybe I can shed some light on it—but anyway...

Are you confessing?

Well...

The next track is "Far Away." Matthew [Kelly] came up with a riff for that song, and over the top of that a line came to me out of the blue: "Far away, far, far away." It took me a week or two to sort of flesh out the rest of the song, come up with a story line, which I did. That one was easy to write. [Guitarist Bobby] Cochran and I played around with the chords. That one happened real quick.

The next song is "Book of Rules." That has been one of my favorite reggae cuts for the last few years. It was a sort of a hit in England. I finally found the record and copped the tune, and recorded it, and then a few weeks ago—after the record had been pressed up and everything was happening—a friend of Barlow's found a compilation of verse, a collection of poems from the turn of the century to about 1930. There was in it a poem called "A Bag of Tools" by R. L. Sharp. The words to that went, "Isn't it strange how princesses and kings / And clowns that caper in sawdust rings / And common people like you and me / Will be builders for eternity / Each is given a bag of tools / A shapeless mass and a book of rules." The second verse is: "Each must make, ere life has flown / A stumbling block or a stepping stone..." So I'm going to sing it like that from now on. That's an example of what happens when you send a lyric through the Caribbean and back: you get some transfiguration, shall we say. It came back this way a little different. I had no idea that there was that original poem. I knew there was something that I liked about that song beyond the lyrics that were there, though the lyrics that I got off the record were kinda neat in their own right. But someone was singing a song, and these guys heard it and got the lyrics as best they could, and then I got the lyrics as best I could off their record. They wrote a third verse, that one about "Look where the rain is falling from the sky."

So you got yours from the Heptones?

Yeah. I don't know where they got their version of it, but I'm sure they probably wrote the music as well.

"Me Without You" was a song that Alphonso [Johnson, the Midnites' bassist] wrote. I couldn't understand the lyrics that he had, couldn't figure out what he was getting at, so with his permission I undertook to rewrite them. I didn't get too far, and then Barlow did a rewrite that I kind of liked, and so I used those. That one's sort of self-explanatory, as well.

"Josephine" came to me one day after I'd been up for a long time, a couple of days in a row. I was sitting at my dining-room table, staring blankly off into space, and "Josephine" sort of appeared to me. I guess most of the first verse just came to me in a flash. The melody—all of it at the same time. I didn't have a guitar in my hands or nothing at the time. I was just sitting there and it sort of popped into my head. That one couldn't have been easier to write, really. It came to me pretty complete. I wrote— god, I don't know how many verses to that one. We could do that one all night, pretty much. [*Laughs*] I've got 'em all written down. There are some good ones—I might upon occasion throw in some different verses to that song when we take it on the road, 'cause some of the other verses hang together, too. I can make that song say just about anything [*laughs*]—it depends on the night. I've got way too many verses for it.

I read that you wrote "[I Want to] Fly Away" for Bob Marley.

Yeah. It's another eulogy, a little statement on Prometheanism. It would be hard for me to elaborate further, beyond what I said in that song. There was that underlying current in Marley's work where "everything's gonna be all right." He wasn't lacking for a sense of adventure. It's sort of a belief, a faith that everything's gonna work out somehow.

Do you share that faith?
Pretty much, yeah. I consider myself fairly adventurous as well— musically...I'm not afraid to take a chance, onstage or offstage...Current situations don't bother me that greatly as long as I feel that I'm leaning into the wind, that I feel I'm committed to furthering the progress of the human race, or whatever it is I'm dealing with at the time—if it's just music, or whatever. I think that he [Marley] pretty much had that view of things as far as what I can catch from his lyrics and his performances and stuff like that.

He was very religious in a way that I don't feel that you are...
No. At least not in any classical sense, though I do spend a lot of time in philosophical contemplation of one aspect of life or another.

He was one of those guys who seemed not to fear death—that that was the reward, and not something to be avoided.
Surely.

Once again, the Grateful Dead is the closest thing to a religion that I've got—and a most forgiving one at that.
[*Laughing*] As soon as we incorporate, I get to be in charge of making the mitres and stuff like that. We'll get some great hats.

If the first Christians' rituals became the stylized things they are now, two thousand years hence, imagine what the little cults and cells will pass on— what the Grateful Dead eucharist will be—
It'll be interesting to see, for instance, when the Grateful Dead True Religion...As Christianity split up and headed to Greece and also down to Ethiopia, there were not altogether subtle permutations of the religion that ended up in those places. It'll be most interesting to see if the Grateful Dead True Religion undergoes such transmutations over the period of time, if it sticks around.

Of course, god knows I can't take it seriously enough to expect it to stick around that long. But we'll see.

I don't know how it will outlive you mortal beings, but somehow it will.
   Pop up two hundred years hence.

[Whispering urgently] Ze tapes. Vee haff to haff ze tapes or ve can't do the service! It functions that way for a lot of people—
   The tapes exist as icons. Perhaps we'll get revisitations…maybe the band'll get together every three hundred years and reincarnate or make a reappearance. We'll work something out—you'll be among the first to know.

Put me on your mailing list, Bishop Weir.
   [*Laughs*] You can refer to me as "Your Holiness" from now on.

I already have a spiritual adviser, I'm sorry. You'll have to line up.
Two more songs: "Carry Me" is the ballad—
   That's a love letter, simply.

And "Festival." What's the inspiration of that?
   I don't know—that one came to me in the middle of the night. Actually, the chords came to me right here—I picked up my guitar and played them one time through and put it down on tape, and just didn't think anything more about it. There was sort of a melody in the back of my head, then the words came to me about six months later. The chords came to me while we were doing Grateful Dead *Go to Heaven*, and I was all set up to record, so I put 'em down—I was the only one in the studio, everybody was cleaning up, I was playing with my guitar. You know how that sort of thing happens. About a year later, I guess, the words came to me—in the middle of the night, as they usually do; most of the words that I wrote on the record came to me in the middle of the night—

Just wake up, roll over, and write 'em down?
   Or spit 'em into a little Dictaphone, begrudgingly at best, because I really like to sleep. The muse comes and taps you on the shoulder and says, "Not now—you've got bigger fish to fry!"
   …it's not like you can always get back to sleep, because just about the time you get back to sleep, the next verse comes.

The price of being creative—
   The tortured soul of an artist. I'm catchin' up on my sleep now.

Just because there's an "Uncle John's Band" feel to the acoustic guitar line, it represents to me a lot of what's nice about going to a Grateful Dead concert, the festival—

It's sort of a celebration, a festival of life, etc., with the implication that it's happenin' everywhere, every day—all you've got to do is see things that way.

Like everything else about the Grateful Dead, there are loud arguments about the work you do outside the Grateful Dead. Many of those "purists" find it offensive—

Yeah, they think it's too pop.

Pop, and sexist—

They don't have to buy it.

How do you feel about dividing the audience?

I don't take it that seriously. They're taking me more seriously than I take myself, and [*laughs*] they're fighting an uphill battle there.

I'm not really going to sweat it much. Some people like it better, too. Some people consider this record, and Bobby and the Midnites, punchier than the Grateful Dead, and figure that if the Grateful Dead got a little punchier again, they'd benefit by it. I don't take that seriously, either.

Whatever medium I'm working in, I try to stick to that, and not worry a whole bunch about what people are going to say or think. The only given is that it's going to change. This is nothing like *Heaven Help the Fool*, and my next record—even if it's with Bobby and the Midnites, which I rather expect it will be—will probably be not altogether reminiscent of this one, because we're going to grow up a whole bunch if we do a tour—grow a face and it'll probably be a whole lot more clearly defined what the group sounds like.

One of the reasons this one sounds "pop" is because of the production. I'll probably approach it the same way next time, productionwise, because I really like working with Gary. The only way that this record could have happened was if it could happen fast. In this particular case, I had to write simpler tunes than I'm used to writing, though my more complicated tunes fall under the same criticism as my simpler tunes—they're still too pop for some people. If they want not altogether transparent, not altogether superficial lyrics, they can listen to "Fly Away." I did pretty much my best to make a completely philosophical, artistic statement there with absolutely no regard for commerciality whatsoever.

The other songs on the record..."Josephine," there's absolutely no regard for commerciality on that one, either, and very little on any of the rest of them. They were simple, by and large, so that we could learn them and perform them with a fair degree of authority. The players on the record all played quite aptly. I don't think I'm to be faulted for the lack of mistakes, the lack of out-of-tuneness.

Is that how you characterize Grateful Dead recordings?

There was a period when our trademark was more or less sloppy recording in general. The Grateful Dead is not as sloppy as it has been in the past, but if they want sloppy, they've got all the live tapes that they can choke down.

When we make a record, what we're trying to do is get an idealized version of the material.

I think the mistake a lot of people make is expecting anything to approach the energy they get at a Grateful Dead gig.

That's a big mystery to me. Bobby and the Midnites has a lot of energy—

More than the last couple of Grateful Dead albums—

I think the technique of trying to get everything done as fast as possible—because I had to, I had very little time—resulted in more energy and enthusiasm on the tape, because we didn't have a lot of time to nitpick or go over and over things or write complicated things. Not that I view complication as anything bad, because I have occasion to write a complicated piece of music every now and then...

Again, people make a mistake in expecting you to toe the legendary mark instead of exploring...

Without variety, you can't have no horse race. It seems obvious to me that if they want the Grateful Dead, they should go and buy the Grateful Dead, tickets and records. I'm not going to put together a band that sounds like the Grateful Dead—there would be absolutely no point in it.

You've already got a Grateful Dead—

Ask the man who owns one! [*Laughs*]

It wouldn't be a vacation. If it doesn't sound enough like the Grateful Dead, I'm sorry. It's not going to.

Jesus, there are people out there who go there just to watch you—I guess you know that—and they'll buy the record just 'cause your picture's on it. They're not all dogmatic Deadheads—"let's go into the flux"—

I would say by and large our crowd is a lot looser than that one dogmatic segment that has to have things a certain way. They're going to resist the changes the Grateful Dead go through, no matter what they are, more than anybody else, because those are the people who don't want it to change. It's going to have to change, for us! They don't have to live with it day in and day out, year in and year out, and we do. We would go stark raving bonkers!

Well, why do you keep playing the same old songs all the time!?!?!

There are new ones coming out. The reason we keep playing the same old songs is because we haven't had time to write. Now I have time to write, and I'm doing it.

One more Grateful Dead question: Songs are getting placed—a certain song only appears at the beginning of the second set, and so forth. There used to be a lot more latitude in how things would go. I noticed it opening up a tad bit again...at the Greek...usually we don't get that many trips into the void in one night. But there's an awful lot of that thing: you only hear "U.S. Blues" as an encore, and not an entirely welcome one at that, and "Sugar Magnolia" is always the set-closer—things are very well programmed. "Estimated Prophet" goes into "Eyes of the World"—

I put "Sugar Magnolia" at the end of the set because I'm going to blow my voice on that one. It's written in a certain register, and I've learned through the empirical process that if I'm going to sing that one, I'd better sing it at the end of the evening.

Except on New Year's Eve.

Well, I don't sing the end part. The end part is where my voice takes a dive.

You do seem to torture the high end of your range a lot.

You bet. I've been thinking that myself of late. If I intend to...I'm starting to think about taking my range into consideration when I start to write a song, or taking some vocal lessons and extending my range to meet the requirements of the songs I write—one of the two. I actually have taken some vocal lessons, and I have extended my range a bit.

What do you think of Jerry's characterization of a lot of your songs as being "strong on changes and weak on melody"; or that the changes come first?

I don't do it that way so much anymore. I caught myself doing that, and he pointed that out two or three years ago. I remember him pointing that out to me, and I've thought that over. It's been my observation in the past that if I get locked into any one particular way of songwriting—writing the changes first or writing the melody first...Typically for me it's writing the changes first and then supplying the melody and the words pretty much at the same time...then I come up with a melody that fits it....I endeavored particularly on the *Bobby and the Midnites* album to really mix it up. Ever since he pointed that out to me, I've been trying to mix up my approach. I guess starting with *Go to Heaven*, I started trying to mix up my approach to the chord changes and the texture changes and all that kind of stuff.

One thing that you're going to get if you have a given method of songwriting is that the songs are going to tend to sound the same. I guess if you've got a real successful formula for it, it works out nicely for you. But really, I would like more variation in the way the songs come out. One way I've found of getting more variation is mixing up my approach to writing.

Ever sit down without an instrument at all and look for melodies to sing?

Like I say, "Josephine" came to me almost entirely before I picked up the guitar. I had almost an entire verse before I picked up the guitar and started chasing it around.

"Greatest Story Ever Told" always struck me as being a great piece of rhythm guitar.

That one started out with a rhythm guitar lick. It actually started out with a pump that Mickey had—he recorded the pump and told me to write a song [*laughs*]. I ran the pump tape and built a chord structure around it. Mickey suggested that I pattern the song after "Froggy Went

A-Courtin' and He Did Ride." So I sort of patterned the melody after that. Was it Mickey who suggested it, or Hunter, or me? I forget. Hunter responded: "Froggy went a-courtin' and he did ride." Well, "Moses come ridin' up on a quasar" was about as close as Hunter could get.

Which came first, "quasar" or "guitar"?
   "On a guitar," I guess.

How did it get changed to "quasar"?
   Because I liked "quasar" better. In fact, I think I supplied that word...."Black-Throated Wind" I wrote all at the same time. It was a process—it took me a while. I was snowed in in this little cabin in Wyoming with Barlow, a guitar and his typewriter, and a bottle of whiskey—

The catalyst—
   The catalyst, a bottle of Wild Turkey 101. We just sort of pounded away at it. That one's a fairly strange song—I intend to redo the lyrics on it, and it may resurface.

Are you going to change them completely, or just fix them up here and there?
   Fix them up, I guess. I tried running it by [in its original version] one time and still couldn't get with the lyrics as they were, and so I've got to sort of concentrate on that one and get a good new set of lyrics.

How do the lyrics of your newer songs map into your personal life?
   Some of them do and some of them are just completely extraneous vignettes. If I write a love song, for instance, or what amounts to a love letter, then obviously that maps into my personal life as such.

I'm thinking on a more grand level. The image people might gather, alligator shirts notwithstanding, of the Grateful Dead guitarist doesn't jibe very well with the guy who sang "Shade of Gray" and "Heaven Help the Fool." I'm not asking this completely from my own standpoint, because I think I understand it somewhat. But there's more of a "Union Street kind of guy" singing on your solo stuff.
   I guess. Left to my own devices, I sort of revert to my own personality...the "lonesome preppy a long way from home," essentially.

Also who I'm hanging out with at the time... For what it's worth, I don't spend a whole lot of time on Union Street. In fact, I don't partake of nightlife at all. I have a very, very limited social life. Realistically, very, very little of it has that flavor to it, and oftentimes when it has that flavor to it, I'm not altogether singing the praises of that particular flavor of life.

Some of the stuff—"Haze" and "Too Many Losers" in particular—are sexually very hot lyrics. That's one thing about the Grateful Dead: there's almost no hot sex.

I'm basically a fully heterosexual, red-blooded American boy and have certain instincts that I wouldn't deny.

So why don't they show up more in the Grateful Dead?

They do, as far as I can see. "I Need a Miracle," though a little tongue-in-cheek, was still all that kind of stuff. All that stuff is tongue-in-cheek. Like I say, I don't take it all real seriously. If there are sexual overtones— it's just something to sing about. Hopefully, I can make it fun. Those are the songs I try to have fun with, essentially. If I'm trying to say something ponderous or make a pronouncement, it generally comes out more like "Fly Away," or sometimes it comes out like "Josephine." "Josephine" is a pronouncement of sorts, but I really couldn't get at it beyond what's actually said there. I was just trying to capture an esthetic, and I got about as close to it as I'm going to be able to do, because it takes the words and the music in that particular song.

That "Union Street" persona that a lot of people find offensive—they'd probably be pleased to know that I don't take it all that seriously. And they'd probably be pleased to know that if they looked a little deeper they'd find that there's a fair bit of tongue-in-cheek involved in all of it.

But those Grateful Dead theologians—

Fuck 'em if they can't take a joke. [*Laughs*] I've basically been trying to avoid saying that for a long time, but like I say, it's not there to be taken seriously.

It's amazing to me how accepting they are of some things, of the self-sabotaging nature of everything about the Grateful Dead... everything takes forever to happen, and they accept that, and yet they get so mortified when you write about temporal and exciting and physical things. Again, we're talking about a small minority—

And I really do try to balance it out with a fair amount of fairly contemplative stuff. For what it's worth, "Haze" came out sounding like a party song, but to me there's a fair bit more depth to it than that. The guy didn't take himself altogether that seriously. He had a way of coming up with some amazing profundity from time to time as well. It was hard for me to get that in there, but I gave it my best. What sounds like good-time rockin' party lyrics is actually a eulogy in that particular case.

I wonder if that's evident, though, to anybody but the one who knows— who's been told that.
I don't know. It takes the words and the music, and there's a juxtaposition there: it goes from a sort of party groove into a more formal harmonic progression at one point in the bridge—

That Beatle-ish part?
Yeah. At that point, a more formal statement is made, too, then it goes back into the other thing. I think the song stands on its own. If everything else on the record were like that, I would find it noxious as well. But I've tried to present as broad a spectrum of subject matter as is possible on a record.

Do you think about the whole record, then?
Yeah.

It doesn't seem anywhere near as calculated as some—
As I'm writing, you know—"We've got enough party songs, we need a ballad here...I've got this one that I'm working on..." I think about tempos, keeping it consistent.
The whole record is a work, and keeping it sounding like one work...I like to make it all in the same studio, or at least do all the basics in one studio and all the overdubs in one studio and all the mixing at one sitting, keep it happening like that. I like to take into consideration what kind of songs I have on the record and how they'll lead into each other and balance each other out, and the contour of the whole thing—where it leads to—and the lyrical content and where that leads to. More than anything, I take into consideration the musical textures—the tempos, the keys, the rhythms, the melodies, and where they lead to. There's a fair bit of thematic consistency throughout this record, as well.

It's sonically very consistent.
Yeah.

But so was Heaven Help the Fool, *and so was* Ace.
All done in the same sitting, all done in a short period of time…The records themselves sound quite different from each other…I'll be damned if I'm going to do the same record again. But when I'm making a record, I don't just concentrate on the songs—I concentrate on the entire record.

All these things you've listed about making a record—they're all things that you've either opted out of with the Grateful Dead, or you're aced out of…
Yeah. Well, they wouldn't be quite right for the Grateful Dead. I wouldn't try to do "Far Away" with the Grateful Dead, for instance.

I wasn't even thinking of material. The consciousness of a record—Grateful Dead records have a very disjointed quality to them—
You've got a number of different writers, and a number of different producers. It's gonna be real difficult under those circumstances…if we're working with a producer, everybody is at very least coproducing his own tunes. You don't stand much chance of getting real consistency under those circumstances, so you don't even shoot for it. With the Grateful Dead, the recording process is completely different. That's why I like doing this: I can make records the way I want to, or one way that I want to.

If you guys can be so wonderful together—if that committee can function so beautifully on a stage—then why the fuck can't it happen here [in the studio]?
We're kicking that one around. We don't know.

Phil said, "If I never have to set foot in a studio again I'll be a happy man."
That's one reason why we don't get great records—he hates it in the studio. He likes playing live—[laughs] very simple.

Why does that necessarily mean that going into a studio is a drag?
Ask him. I can have more fun in the studio, and I guess put out records that sound like they're more fun. I had a great deal more fun making this record than I generally have making Grateful Dead records.

Are Grateful Dead sessions fun?

They can be, but they go on and on and on. Grateful Dead records take way too long to record, in my estimation. What momentum you have that makes it fun at first starts to wane towards the third month.

Have you guys ever thought of going somewhere, getting away from all the people that are always here—

We're married to this studio.

Couldn't you all go off to George Martin's studio in Montserrat and record there for two months, the way some of those other big names do it?

Sure—I'd give anything a try at this point with the Grateful Dead. I think Grateful Dead records, we've got to do something different. There are some ideas forthcoming right now...less overdubbing and all that stuff. I think the Grateful Dead would benefit a great deal...a great deal more of it live. That would come as a consequence to structuring things so that they can happen quickly, easily, and naturally in the studio—and also as a result of taking the material and performing it in total as it should be and knowing exactly how we're going to go to it in the studio. That seems like a simple procedure, but we've never done it like that.

Was the Warfield stuff [the 1980 concerts that yielded the acoustic Reckoning *and the electric* Dead Set*] done with you guys conscious of trying to play a tad bit cleaner, with a little restraint?*

Yeah, I'm afraid so. What we got were some nearly letter-perfect performances that were a little lacking in the old punch department. But the old punch doesn't come across on tape and records. When you really lean into a chord and play it real hard, for instance, it might go a little sharp. Nobody's going to begrudge you that live, but on a record you're not caught up in that spirit and enthusiasm, and what it sounds like is out of tune. I think everybody had in the back of their mind the fact that the tape was rolling and that we were going for a record, and concentrated on a little neater rendition of a given tune rather than a more impassioned performance.

It wasn't wholly unsatisfying, was it?

No. We got to a pretty good balance at one point. Unfortunately, a number of the songs that we got that were really wonderful performances were also songs that had been out on so many records that we couldn't do it again. It would have been nice to put "The Other One" on, for instance—we had some just spine-chilling adventures there.

...*"Scarlet Begonias"*...
I thought that was going to be on there.

What was the first guitar you ever had?
The first was a seventeen-dollar Japanese guitar that I got a long time ago. It was acoustic—my first electric guitar was a Gretsch Country Gentleman.

How old were you when you got those two?
I got my first guitar when I was fourteen, I guess. It was unplayable. I didn't know that at the time, and went ahead and learned to play it anyway—not particularly well, though, because there was just nothing you could do on that guitar. Then I got a classical guitar and started playing folk stuff. That lasted for about a year, and then I got a steel-strung—I was about fifteen, got a Harmony Sovereign—and started playing a little bit of bluegrass, a little bit of country-blues, and sort of dove into the jug-band era of my life at that point.

What was your inspiration to get your first guitar?
I wanted to play and I wanted to sing, and it was portable. All of that made it impossibly seductive. You could accompany yourself with an instrument and do a fairly credible job of it without having to cart a piano around with you.

Who were your first heroes?
I liked the Everly Brothers, Chuck Berry a lot, the Kingston Trio, Joan Baez. I quickly tired of the Kingston Trio, but first when I heard them, here were three guys who could make a lot of music all by themselves. That seemed like great fun. I quickly dumped them as heroes as soon as I heard Joan Baez all by herself playing a guitar and doing real well. From there I started finding out about others, like Reverend Gary Davis and people like that. I also fell into the jug band, and through hanging out with Garcia and that crowd, learned a lot about the range of what was available in American folk music. I got fairly grounded in that by the time I got into rock 'n' roll, so my roots are pretty much still all there—American folk music.

How long had you been playing when you started playing with the guys you're still playing with?

Aah, three years, I guess. I couldn't really play the guitar much at all when I started playing with them. I could play barre chords and that kind of stuff, and I immediately came up with a whole lot. I had to invent stuff to do, because at that time, rhythm guitar was completely undefined. Rock 'n' roll rhythm guitar went no further than playing a bunch of barre chords, and I could already do that. From the start, since I started playing with the Grateful Dead, I've had to sort of invent stuff to do as a second guitarist—

Why did they have you? What were you good for?

I could play the guitar. I could play rhythm guitar about as well as anybody around, and I could sing and all that stuff, and we'd been playing together for a while and having a lot of fun. It seemed like the thing to do to become a rock 'n' roll band.

Was getting a guitar pretty much the end of your scholastic career?

Oh, you bet. I spent my last year in school learning to play the guitar. Didn't attend a single class. I was going to a real loose, progressive school at the time, and they figured, "Well, if that's what he's looking for in education, that's what he gets." By god, I got it, and I'm relatively happy that I did. I could probably speak French a lot better than I do if I'd taken another year of it. I was doing pretty well with all that kind of stuff. I went to a number of prep schools—

Is it true you kept getting thrown out of them?

Yeah.

And throwing yourself off the roofs of them?

Yeah.

What was your problem?

[*Shrugs*] Fun, fun, fun. I didn't get in fights or anything like that—I was just a disciplinary problem, I guess what they refer to as a yahoo.

Just 'cuz?

[*Laughs*] Yeah. I got decent grades. I couldn't read, so I learned how to listen fast and how to bullshit even faster.

They didn't do anything about your problem?
They didn't know.

Nobody ever discovered it? Didn't your family help you with it?
Everybody just figured I was lazy. I didn't tell anybody that I couldn't read. [*Laughs*]

Do you do much reading now?
I'm working at it. For what it's worth, I have ways of getting information: I talk to a lot of people about a lot of stuff.

You don't seem unworldly or uninformed—you may not be able to quote Rimbaud—
Right. But I *can* read poetry. Anything that has a real "roll" to it—the better the writer, the better I can read it, because if you can sort of intuit what he's saying as he's saying it, you can get into the roll of what a writer's doing, particularly in poetry or good prose...I can read that—not amazingly speedily, but if I can get into the sound of it, get it rolling through my head, then I can actually read it. But as for reading texts and stuff like that, it's really, really difficult, because letters turn around and stuff like that. It's classic dyslexia—reading sheet music is out of the question.
It hasn't hung me up that much.

Getting back to musical development: in pretty short order, you went from playing by yourself to playing in the band. What kind of songs did the jug band do?
Country-blues. We did some Jesse Fuller tunes—"Beat It On Down the Line" is a Jesse Fuller tune. "The Monkey and the Engineer," another Jesse Fuller tune. We did "Stealin'"—you know, a lot of jug-band tunes. "New Minglewood Blues," in the original form that we did it in the jug band, was a jug-band song.

How close was it to the version on the first Grateful Dead album?
Not that close. Actually, the one that we do now is closer to the original form. I attempted to get it as close to the feeling of the original version as I could. The guitar figure that I'm playing, for instance...
The words are undergoing a constant—it's the old folk process rearing its motley head again. The words'll just keep changing.

It's an interesting technique you use on that—fretting and using the slide.
   And also hammering on the slide. [*Laughs*]

You're pretty brave about that.
   [*Laughs*]

There have been times, I'll admit, when I've been a little embarrassed at your slide playing.
   Sooner or later, I've managed to get it down. It just takes a long time. And working on the slide is my hobby. It's not easy to play slide in standard tuning to begin with—you can't just hit any old note and expect it to be the right one like in open tunings. I'm still working on the tone that I get.

Again, back there in '78…there was stuff like "Stagger Lee" where it would go on and on and on…There were times when the Grateful Dead punished us some for showing up.
   [*Laughs*] I discovered about this time last year that the whole trick to slide playing is tone.

Too much high end, it gets brutal.
   If it's too thin…you've got to have a lot of sustain: either use a compressor or a lot of distortion—or a little of both—whatever. You've got to have a lot of sustain—that note's got to be real fat, especially in a loud band like the Grateful Dead, or you're going to lose where it is—you can't even hear the note if it's too thin.

Dan Healy

May 22, 1982
Greek Theatre, Berkeley

This interview appeared in Recording Engineer/Producer *June 1983, titled "The Grateful Dead—a Continual Development of Concert Sound System Design for Twenty Years." The conversation took place in Healy's dressing room at the Greek Theatre after a Dead concert. We were joined for a while by Owsley Stanley (a.k.a. Bear), who was the Dead's first sound man. The conversation does stray into heavily technical realms at times, but there's plenty of general-interest material as well.*

Healy The first PA I did was two [Altec] 604s off a seventy-watt amp that had a two-mic-input mixer. And that was far out compared to what was there the weekend before [at the Fillmore Auditorium].

So we started putting equipment together. What was available was Altec voice of the Theater stuff, crap like that. The first thing we did was go get tons of it, only to find that that was a stopgap measure. By no means was that what we were looking for. Where that equipment ended, so did the literature and research. All the questions we had, nobody had any answers for. So we set out to find the answers ourselves.

That's when we ran into [Ron] Wickersham, [John] Curl, and [John] Meyer. Those guys were real long in the design-and-prototype area, and we were long in the criteria. Basically, we were the guinea pigs. They were the guys who performed the magic.

We built a system and scrapped it, built another one and scrapped it. We never had a finished system, because by the time it was near completion it was obsolete in our minds and we'd already have a new one on the drawing boards.

How'd you get through a show?
Healy It was tough. It was tough.
Bear We found out you couldn't get there that way. The technology wasn't developed enough. [McCune Sound] hired John Meyer; he started to design stuff that Dan couldn't blow up.
Healy 1974 was the conclusion of our mainline involvement in the R&D part—the "Wall of Sound" system. That was never finished, but that was the most complete prototype that we'd gotten to. By '74, the gas crisis scene happened and the economy got weird, and it became impossible to continue R&D on that kind of level. We were designing it, building it, operating it, moving it—all that stuff—and it began to eat us up after a while. Actually, we were damn lucky; we got a tremendous amount of knowledge out of it before it became such a burden that it started to distract from the music.

By '74, we had realized what we needed, and how to get there. But it was huge and very inefficient, so it became a matter of taking one more step.

At that point we dumped it all in Meyer's lap and said, "go," because he was right along with us through the design and construction of it.

We had to pull back and regroup. We were involved in the movie and making records and stuff, so it became a matter of specialists. We had gotten to "This is what it's supposed to be. Now we've got to make it one-fourth the size and four times as efficient." The specialists had to cultivate it and develop it, which Meyer had done. This is already the fourth or fifth generation of this idea. He started with the JM-3s and JM-10s [speaker systems designed for McCune Sound], then he did the System 80 thing, then he did the monitors—which we call ooh-pahs (UPAs)—and then came to the MSL-3s. That's five generations of the new concept.

The first thing he did was hop up a 604. Then he hopped up some Altec shit; then he bottomed out on that and came out with the JM-3s and JM-10s. Then he went to Switzerland and came back with the System 80 stuff. This around '72, and we were ready to get back at it.

We got together with [Bill] Graham and wanted to do a system. One thing led to another and we ended up not doing it, but the idea didn't die.

Another year later, Graham put up some money through Santana, and they got Meyer to do the System 80. It resembled the center cluster of the [1974] Grateful Dead system.

Eventually there weren't enough trucks to haul enough speakers, and enough room at the gigs to put up enough of them, to get the right sound without blowing it up. It was a better-mousetrap thing through the JM-3 and JM-10 stuff. At that point he scrapped that whole shot and went into designing his own speakers.

Bear [Meyer] got a grant and went to Switzerland for a year, to this million-dollar laboratory, and he totally redesigned the interior workings of loudspeakers. He came back in the late seventies. I read an article about him in a trade magazine, called him up. At that point I was working for the Starship, in 1979. He was building loudspeaker systems for movies, trying to get subwoofers together for *Apocalypse Now.* I needed a monitor that [starship vocalist] Mickey Thomas could handle.

I went to him and said, "I'm working for this band, and the only monitors I can use are the SM-3s"—which he had designed—"and they're not powerful enough." I had heard his ACD monitors. I said, "Can you put this into a dense, small package with a very controlled sixty-degree pattern—where the horn and speaker have the same pattern, that is very coherent like that?"

He said, "I'm trying to sell speakers to the movies."

I said, "How much money do you need?" [*Laughs*]

Healy We had to take him off that project, because more important shit was going on. We needed his ass.

Bear The *Apocalypse* people never did wind up buying his stuff....

Healy Right. He was wasting his time anyway.

Bear Once he built that, then a little modification of that gave the UPA...then he decided he could go back into acoustics. Once he got started, his inertia carried him on.

Healy It's getting to where there's some significant efficiency going on. You don't have to carry truckload after truckload of equipment around.

When you guys played the Orpheum in '76, there was a huge speaker box in the orchestra pit.

Healy That was an early, early version of a subwoofer. It never really worked. The idea worked, but we were dealing with an efficiency problem in the cabinetry and the way the cabinets were loaded. The understanding, and all the research that had been done in speaker cabinets to that point...even though it all bore out mathematically, it actually became obsolete and had to be scrapped. We wound up with these huge boxes; we dumped lots of power into them and they'd flap and flap and flap. We had the right idea, but it needed some refining, to say the least.

First, you have to build a good, accurate speaker with good materials and accurate tolerances. You do it consistently enough that you can put two in a cabinet and they'll sound pretty much the same. Believe it or not, you can go buy ten JBL or Electro-Voice or any standard industrial sound-equipment manufacturer's stuff, and the variation will blow your mind. You have to have a certain amount of conformity; otherwise, when you go to try and treat a problem, each [speaker] will be so vastly different that the problem wouldn't even be the same. You have to start somewhere, so it became—for good or bad—making them as uniform as possible, and then advancing that as much as possible.

We went to JBL at one time and their attitude was "We're selling speakers faster than we can make them," and didn't give a fuck what we wanted. Conceptually, American speaker manufacturers are more into amplitude accuracy. One of our greatest realizations was when we said, "scrap that and go for linearity." As soon as we flashed on that and got to where we thought it might be possible to attain, we no longer had anything to talk about with Altec and JBL and Electro-Voice. To this day, they're in that space—although they're starting to try and catch up.

[Meyer] had to get down to the paper used, the glue—they very essential elements of it—and start from the ground up. And he's still going through changes. Every now and then he'll find a new kind of paper or say, "I found that this glue swelled up at a certain temperature," or something. Every day there's a new rap about all that stuff.

How long does the system stay in any one particular configuration? Does it change from gig to gig?
Healy On some levels yes, and on some levels no. It's becoming obvious what the direction is, and now the only difference is in implementing it with things like better materials....We haven't completed the research on this concept, although the idea is there and understood. Every day there are same things—new this, new that. We found a different connector, cable...

Remember that we're trying to take this across the country and interface with halls: set up the equipment, play a show for twenty thousand people, tear it down, show up the next morning in another city, and do it again—for three weeks in a row, or a month or six months. So a lot of the energy has had to go into making it efficient on those terms, too.

There was a time when we could go into the hall three days ahead of time and spend three days standing back going. "Well, what do you think? Let's try this." Now, man, you've got to hit and run. Nowadays it means a hundred thousand dollars to go into a hall for three days and fuck around with your sound system.

Bear Ideally, you ought to be able to go in, and, in about forty-five minutes to an hour, be ready to have a show.

Healy We've got that part of it together—it's easy to bring it in and set it up now. Now we're going through other, subtle changes.

How much do you learn from the SPL [sound pressure level] meter and the real-time analyzer?

Healy After enough years of doing this, you can pretty much just listen and know what's happening.

Bear It's boiled down to the ear.

Healy You have a speedometer in your car, but you don't have to use it, or even necessarily have it. You don't even necessarily need it to know how fast you're going, but it's there for reference. I use the SPL meter and the real-time analyzer on that level. I leave my filter set flat and when the show starts I dial it in [during] the first couple of songs, because of enough years of watching it and correlating it—I now know from what I hear what frequencies, how much, and what to do with it.

Bear And ideally you'll be close enough to the speakers...The tendency is to get further away from it, and it's hard to tell. You have to listen to it for a while. You put an instrument in the back of the hall, it hears the hall and doesn't hear the system. You can't adjust for that, because your ears will filter out the hall.

Healy It takes years to learn to have your ears not take care of it for you. You can trip right out...it took me a long time to say, "But wait a minute. This isn't right."

Eighty-five feet is my [optimal] distance from the stage, at least in the hockey-hall-type spaces. In an outdoor gig, the variables all change. In my opinion—and my opinion only, for that matter—the ideal combination of near-field and far-field is eighty-five feet.

Bear I want to be all near-field. Forty feet.

Healy I like to be able to perceive the far field. I don't like to be enough into it to where it's a distraction, but for me it's important what the audience hears.

Bear I've found that I can control the system better if I don't hear the hall, because I've found that if the system's right then no matter how far away you go, the sound is correct. If I get in the back, I start tuning the system to the hall, and invariably at the very back it doesn't sound as good. My experience has been to try and stay close.

It sounds better close up now, too…
Healy It sounds better everywhere.
Bear It's a very articulate system. The transient response is incredible.
Healy Transients of 136, 140 decibels are not at all fatiguing to listen to.

One of my philosophies is that I strive to have it be moving but not be fatiguing. I could take half this much equipment and make it shriek, make you jump right under your chair, but I don't go for that. From the start to the end of the show is a continuous progression of how to spend the watts of audio power that you have in such a way that it's pleasant and human.

Doesn't the band's level gradually come up during the set?
Healy Sometimes. Sometimes it starts heavy and goes down. You have to react to it—it's all part of the day-to-day gigs. Some nights it starts screaming loud and gets softer, and some nights it starts in one place and stays there. There isn't really any good or bad in it—it's just a different night in a different way. There are so many things involved in what causes it to be a certain way that—at that point you'd do better to spend your time worrying about more tangible things. You can say, "This is life," put in that bag: "Today's another day." It's kind of a waste of time to try and worry, because there's nothing you can do about it except live with it.

I'd like to hear about some of the experiments that failed.
Healy Every one of us has had many ideas—"This is it!"—and you spend a lot of time and energy and it goes *pffft*. There's dozens of them.

I remember one time, we were playing at Stanford,[1] debuting the first version of the '74 system. We got all these Electro-Voice tweeters and rebuilt them, got it all happening. We pink-noised the room from the booth to be exactly flat. It may have been from around a hundred feet. If you flatten a system from there, it'll sound like a buzz saw, and it did.

We spent maybe twenty thousand dollars on amps, crossovers, and stuff, started the show, and in the first two seconds of the song wiped out every brand-new tweeter. Smoked every single one. "Oh, okay, we learned

---

[1]February 9, 1973, Roscoe Maples Pavilion, Stanford University's basketball arena.

about that!" We went through all these changes to put these protection devices, and they never fuckin' worked—they blow long after the speaker's gone.

How did you get through the night? As I recall, it was a pretty good show.
Healy We probably opened up the tops of the crossovers from the 5s, equalized a little bit, and faked it.

No replacements.
Healy Shit, not on that magnitude! Hell, we blew eighty or a hundred of them. Maybe we had a dozen replacement diaphragms.

That kind of shit happens a lot; recovery is another thing that you learn after enough years of that kind of shit. Recovery is your backup buddy. A lot of nights some major thing will run amok, and nobody even perceives it because of various ways of recovering.

Also, by now we've had enough experience at it that it's easier to estimate what's going to work and what's not, so it's easier to avoid catastrophe.
Bear We have more reliable equipment, too.

How long have you had that [Jim Gamble] mixing board?
Healy This is maybe the tenth time I've ever used it. I've used hundreds and hundreds of boards—variations of people's ideas, rental boards....This is one of the nicer PA mixing consoles.

There are two PA mixers that I think are really cool, and the rest of them are mediocre for the most part. I like the Clair Brothers console, and I like these Gamble boards. Jim Gamble's concept is the hybrid race-car kind of version. It's real fast and real slick; it's not as comfortable as the car with the big cushiony seats...the way the gain stages are staggered from the front end through the combine buses and EQ [equalization] and output stages, the headroom window is narrow. You can't get up a mix and then turn your submasters down halfway, because you'll clip your combine without getting enough signal out of it.

What I do in this board is put all the faders—including the masters and submasters—wide open, and establish my mix from the preamp gain pot. This board works the best when it's wide open all the way from the beginning out the end. There are reasons why that's an advantage: it's easier to make a faster board, and a lower-noise board, that way. But there are disadvantages, like you can't turn down your submasters. If I want to turn down the drum submaster, I've only got about a 6-db window before it starts clipping the inner stages. That's a disadvantage, but on other levels it's enough of an advantage.

The Clair console has that sort of infinite-headroom capability. You have like 40-dB variation in any stage before you get any clipping or serious signal-to-noise problems. You don't have to continuously monitor it. But the disadvantages are, it's a little slower-sounding. It doesn't handle the transients as well. It's lower-noise than the Gamble.

The Gamble comes in twenty-four and forty-channel models; we've got a forty.[2] I have a little Biamp board on the side to take care of my overflow, but the overflow usually winds up being parts of the Rhythm Devils—little sound-effects mikes and things like that.

We cut the Beast[3] down in an attempt to pull it together physically on the stage so we could perceive each other's dynamics better. We've sort of thinned down our setup. We got rid of a lot of stuff and channeled it in closer so we could all hear each other better.

Was there a specific reason for Jerry and Phil switching places?

It was a matter of distribution of sound—who hears who, and what advantages and disadvantages the monitors have. It's a step in the direction of further refining how we're hearing what we're doing.

What was gained when Weir moved his speakers up in front of the drum riser?

He did that to narrow the line.

Objectively, if everyone was standing in a little clump like this...from a musician's point of view, blend and balance, it's better to be close to each other. The more spread-out it is, the more difficult it is to hear each other's music, and consequently the harder it is to get down to finer levels of playing together.

I would have thought that it'd be relatively easy to get monitor mixes to suit each guy.

[2] By 1991 there were fifty-six inputs. And they *still* needed more!

[3] The Beast is the percussion array at the rear of the drum riser, where huge drums hang from a metal frame and many electronic and acoustic percussion instruments are laid out for Mickey Hart's and Bill Kreutzmann's "Rhythm Devils" improvisations. The Beast was an outgrowth of the duo's work on the sound track of Francis Ford Coppola's film *Apocalypse Now.*

You reach a point of diminishing returns with monitors. We've taken it to that place. You can have your monitor scene so well set up, so efficient, that you can isolate yourself from everybody. But then look what you've done.

What was wanted was less monitors and more hearing. If you're standing onstage playing through your amp and speakers and everybody else is far enough away from you and have their own volume control, a duplicate set of speakers where they can hear you, then everyone can dial in their own mix—but then they lose track of the finer points of what they're trying to play.

You end up playing to the mix instead of the other guys, right?

Right. If you multiply that enough, you can get everybody into their own world, and no one's together anymore.

The other side of that is less monitors; hear each other from the same source that they're hearing from. It's best to hear Jerry from Jerry's speakers, etc.

When we began to reduce it down it became a matter of... Having Weir at the side of the drum riser widened the setup that much more, so we put him in the middle and we were able to move another three feet closer together. Then, when we did that, it turned out that it worked better for Phil to move to the other end.

Wasn't one of the principles of [the '74 system] that the individuals could control their sound in the whole thing?

That was the philosophy of no monitors. It was the ultimate derivation of IM [intermodulation] cleanliness: no two things went through any one speaker, so the intermodulation distortion was staggeringly clean—cleaner than anything today. The stuff we're doing today works infinitely better, but it's also true that we're putting multiple things into it. You have to live with that—but it's not a problem. That system still holds the record for harmonic—and most especially—intermodulation distortion.

Our IM isn't that significant now, for that matter. That '74 system was going crazy towards zero IM. There were fifty-five six-hundred-watt amplifiers. There was a separate system for the vocals, a separate system for the drums, separate systems for the guitars and piano. A complete sound system for everything there. You could get it amazingly loud, and it was amazingly clean.

There wasn't a board in the house. Weir's speakers went all the way to the ceiling, and his volume control governed all those speakers. When he turned up, it was the PA. Jerry controlled his volume onstage and in the house, because it was one speaker stack. I think those guys each had forty twelve-inch speakers in vertical columns. Phil had a quad system.

It took them a while to balance to themselves, didn't it?
It was the "as above, so below" theory: the way line arrays tend to work is, if you stack a bunch of speakers vertically and go up close to one speaker, you hear the volume of that one; if you move a little bit away you hear two, move some more you hear three, and if you have a bunch of them stacked up high you can move quite a ways away and the volume stays the same....What you heard onstage was what you got in the house. It was reasonably successful. The largest problem was blend. That's that super-clean thing, where zero distortion takes you. You can get to the point of too much space.

I recognize, and fully employ in my mixing, the concept of a certain amount of distortion—but not the really obvious kind. There's distortion that I know occurs, even though you couldn't measure it coming out of the system. I play "ear distortion," rather than equipment distortion. The equipment is really clean, but I know what constitutes various kinds of distortion within your hearing. By employing that, you can color and fill in spaces. It's like relief work in a drawing. Instead of fuzzing out your equipment, it's advanced to the point where the equipment remains clean but you can play on actual ear distortion.

If you play a high guitar note and a low bass note at the same time, clean enough and with enough amplitude, your own ear will create intermodulation distortion. The distortion used to be in the equipment, and now it's in the air.

So how many amps and watts do you have now?
Lemme think...there's probably about fifteen to twenty thousand watts here. It's at least twice as efficient as the '74 system, and it's heading towards being even more efficient, and that's really significant. Efficiency comes down to the number of boxes that you have to carry around, and it becomes a matter of weight in a semitruck going down the highway—and that's an important consideration in this day and age. It's no longer possible to have three or four semis, two stages, etc. And it doesn't really serve any purpose. The sound system we have now is better than the '74 wall of sound.

[A crew member comes into the room and speaks to Healy about a problem with the tapers. This was two years before the tapers were "authorized" with their own section in each arena. This practice is unique to the Grateful Dead, as far as I know.]

The word is out, everybody's really cool with their equipment.

The only thing that bums me out is when I see them shoving someone out of their seats. I was a junior tape jock at one time, and I have a reasonable amount of sympathy. But after a while it got to be, "Hey, man, we're here for the tapers," and pretty soon the kid that stood in line in the snow for ten hours to get his ticket comes in with tears in his eyes: "Me and my girlfriend just got thrown out of our seats by tapers." At that point, it was "What are we doing here?"

If never another inch of tape got pulled on any of our shows, it'd be okay with me. For me, it's for the audience: I don't do it for the tape machines. I fail to perceive the importance and gravity placed on pulling tape on every show. Whatever happened to the one that got away?

This rap can go around and around until doomsday. I'm not into stopping them, but I'm not into feeling that that's the ultimate responsibility of the art lovers, or whatever.

I became sympathetic with the tapesters from when I was that person. This was before rock 'n' roll. I started in this scene at nightclubs and jazz. I remember buying my first stereo tape machine and my first two condenser microphones and making payments, sweating to get my payments together. Eighty dollars a month or something…[at] the time it was big bucks. I remember going around to clubs and recording, so I have sympathy in that respect. I've sided with them, helped them and given them advice and turned them on to equipment. It only became a problem when the concertgoer began being fucked over. At that point it became, "Wait a minute, you guys. It's cool to tape, but it's not fair to throw somebody out of a seat when they went through heavy changes to get it."

Do you ever listen back to the tapes?

Of course! I learned probably everything I know from them. Microphones don't lie. If you put up a microphone in the audience and pull a tape, if it doesn't sound good you can't say, "It was the microphone," or "It was the audience." You've got to accept the fact that it was probably because it sounded like that. When you stick up a mike in the audience and it sounds cool, it's probably because the sound was cool. So it's significant to pay attention to that kind of shit. I've learned a lot from those tapes.

The digital tapes are okay, a digital version of the same music....Once it's digitized, you can do anything with it. The idea of digital recording is that it takes the heat off the medium.

I've discovered over the years that two things are true. One is that what you like is what you like, and two, it isn't necessarily the medium that you use—it's what you do with it. Some of the best tapes I've got were recorded on some of the funkiest machines. Conversely, I've gone through the most extreme changes to get super tapes and had 'em not be that groovy.

Yes, clearly and definitely we're moving towards digital tape recording. It will, without a doubt, eventually come to that point. But you may not suspect the reasons why. It won't necessarily be because they sound better; it might be because it's easier to store, convey, edit. When you talk about "is digital recording better?" do you mean "is it neater when you hook up a computer to it that you can edit tapes?"—there's a whole lot of things. It's too general....

I'm not adamant about any opinions about any equipment, because if experience has taught me anything, it's that there's a lot of ways to make things work. There isn't necessarily any one way.

Does Brent's automatic microphone switch work now?

Yeah, it works like a champ. We got the microprocessor program debugged. It's a solid piece of gear. It went belly-up a couple of times—there's always a certain amount of burn-in time—but now it's settled in. That's definitely a significant improvement.

The people who use these ideas are those who recognize the importance of not having a vocal mike on when there's no singing going on. That severely impairs the mix, because it washes out the blend. You have to know that the vocal mike is the loudest microphone in the mix; if it's just open on the stage, it's picking up sound twelve to fifteen feet away from the drums, for instance, or from the amp line. It's adding it in fifteen milliseconds later, which is that many degrees of phase cancellation. The net result is a washing-out of the mix.

On a rock 'n' roll stage you can't use audio amplitude to gate, because frequently the guitars are louder at the microphone than the voice standing right in front of it. I got tired of switching off the mikes when people weren't singing. A certain amount of me always had to be on guard for when a vocal was going to happen, so I wasn't free to listen on a more general level. That was annoying to me.

We were playing at the Paramount Theater in Portland, Oregon [October 1–2, 1977], which has a balcony that...you look down between your knees to see the stage. Up until then, I had manually switched off the mikes, just like anyone else—anyone who cared, anyway. I was never able to free myself from [riding the switches] to be able to, for example, concentrate on listening to just the drum mix. I needed to be freed from that level of mechanization so I could concentrate on a more broad level.

I was looking down, and—being a musician myself, as well—it all connected. Among some of the subtleties that you learn when you're becoming a performer is, when you're playing rock 'n' roll, bouncing around onstage, one of the first embarrassing things that happens to you is running into the mike and banging yourself on the lip—or you're a mile away from it. The first thing you learn is not to hit people with the peghead of your guitar, and the next thing you learn is how to run to your microphone without knocking it over or missing it completely—which is easier to do than you might think.

Your foot placement becomes important. There's a home-base place where you put your foot in relation to the mike stand. You know that if you place your foot there, you'll be right at the mike. So there's an imaginary mark there.

That night I was looking down at that and I realized that—there's a home base for your foot. Then I flashed...I had already tried using amplitude gating, and any other kind of gating that anybody had come up with. I used the same kind of mats that they use to open doors, taped down on the stage. Every time they intend to sing they put their foot in the same place, so it was duck soup: I taped the mats in the right place, then designed and built the electronics that gated the VCAs [voltage-control amplifiers], interfaced it all, and lo and behold it worked.

With a guy who sits down, that idea wouldn't work, so what could we do? That's when John Cutler cribbed the sonar trip off the Polaroid camera. The Polaroid people have a team that goes around talking to electronics people, trying to expand the use of that concept. They sent us a prototype in a box, and it worked. Cutler breadboarded it, spent eons writing the program, and it's a very sophisticated device that works like simple.

Has anyone picked up on it?
The Starship bought one from us. We used to just build one, but now we get like twenty extra circuit cards made. Now if somebody like the

Starship comes by and wants to try it, we give them the cards and a parts list.

Do you ever get burned out on Grateful Dead music?
Yeah, lots of times. Do you?

Lots of times. What happens when it gets stale for you?
The level that it gets stale for me on isn't from a continuum point of view. I react more to "tonight was a good night" or "tonight wasn't so good." It's also totally subjective to my own self. I don't ever burn out on a long-term basis. I can have a bad night and go home kickin' the dog, discouraged, grumble-grumble, but I'm always ready to start again tomorrow.

There's nothing for me to get discouraged with. It's part of my own self. You don't judge yourself on that level. You have good days and bad days, but that's about it. There's never any sort of conclusion—it is what it is.

For me it's a vehicle that enables an aggregate of people to experiment with musical and technical ideas; it's a workshop and a breadboard as well as a dream and a treat. There's no place in the world I've ever heard of or could conceive of that would deliver the amount of space that this delivers to me to be able to experiment and try new things. And also hear and appreciate good music and stuff.

I've been doing it so long, I don't even look at it [as a job]. I also recognize the fact...I don't hassle destiny—there's some reason why I'm here. I spent years worrying about what it was, and I don't care what it is anymore. I came here this morning with ideas from yesterday, and I couldn't wait to get up this morning and get here. That's what it meant to me. I was real pleased with what I heard today. I was glad, once again, that I had a situation where I could feel good about getting up, coming over here, and trying it again another day with a new idea. That's what it means to me.

My reward is when I look around the audience and see everybody having a good time. That's plenty reward.

Phil Lesh

June 30, 1982
San Rafael, California

Follow-up to the July 1981 interview. Musician *asked for technical information about Phil's equipment (all of which is obsolete now); I wanted to pursue the discussion of what it's like to play music in the Grateful Dead.*

Being the bass player, it's a little difficult to communicate the ideas that would cause the music to go in any particular direction, because in the Grateful Dead there's a lot of *playing ahead:* the drummers get locked into a rhythm; Jerry or Bob (less so Bob, I think, than Jerry) will get locked into a mode—a scale—and he'll play on this scale until you don't think there's anything else can be done with it. Sometimes he manages to go farther with the same scale, but frequently it starts piling up and becomes static. That's the point where if I was playing any other instrument—like keyboards or guitar, I guess not drums—

To throw some kind of bolt into it—
　　Yeah. Either that or just turn it a bit.

You can't do that?

I find it really difficult. Not so much because I can't think of what to play—there's so much going on...when I say that everyone is playing ahead, I mean that they're not listening.

Sonically, you can't wedge yourself in?
No, it's psychically, psychoacoustically. If you're playing along, all of a sudden you find yourself thinking about what you're doing, thinking the notes as you...play them. In my experience, when I do that, it means I'm not listening.

The thing to do is to get on the beam and "let the music play the band."
Yeah, and let the notes sort of come out.

It shouldn't be work.
No, and that's the kind of attitude that works best for the Grateful Dead, in my opinion. It works best for me when the Grateful Dead is happening. In fact, when everybody in the band is happening, that's how it is—there's no time to think about what's going on, no time to be thinking the notes that you're playing.

That second night at the Warfield [February 17, 1982] was one of those, wasn't it?...There were visible signs of ecstasy....
Yeah, man, it was good. Normally it's easy enough to just walk off the stage and be done with the gig...when those things happen, boy...And when they do happen I like to make it a point to eyeball everybody and [*gives thumbs-up*].

Are there ever times when you just come off of it high like that and somebody else comes off kickin' stuff?
Yeah.

It's not always mutual.
It's not always mutual.
It's possible for you to have that happen to you all by yourself, and come off feeling real good, and you still know...all you know is that you played well. You can even notice other people not playing as well, but it doesn't bring you down as much as it would if you weren't playing well.

When "it" plays—

When "it" plays instead of me—as Karl Wallenda said, "The wire is life; all the rest is just waiting around." I said that to my old lady once and she about cut my head off. [*Laughs*] You mean I'm just 'waiting around'?" [*Laughs*]

"I'm married to these guys, honey." Anyway, it's that kind of thing. It's really hard when the band is just playin' ahead, all ahead full...it's like a supertanker, kinda hard to steer.

Sometimes I think your rhythm section is...collapsing under the weight of its own gears. Bobby says, "But in a way it turns corners quicker than other rhythm sections."

Well, in a way it does, but only if everybody wants to do it....I've arrived at this attitude which I've just described to you over a period of years where I would systematically try out everything I could think of, literally everything I could think of—and that's plenty—to make a specific change at given points in a tune or a jam or something like that. And it took me a long time to realize that people just won't listen.

...I don't feel like I've slacked off trying to make "it" happen to the best of my personal ability....Let me put it this way: There are ways to make it easier for "it" to happen—things like playing dynamically, like listening to each other play. Sometimes we don't do that. For instance, sometimes we can come out on the stage and from the first note—[*mimes a rocket*]—it's like straight out from there. No problems—away we go! That's rare, more rare these days, but it still can happen. And there's the more common experience where we have to start from just about nowhere, and sometimes by the end of the first set or the middle of the second set we can get it up to a place where something can happen. Or there's the one where nothing you can do makes any difference. I don't even know whether the other guys in the band are trying as many different kinds of tricks as I am. I'll try to play more. I'll try to play less, I'll try to spread out my registers, I'll try playing one note—

Your commitment is to working at it—

Yeah! What else is there to do? You're on the stage—you've got to do something. We've got to play the show. If my outward demeanor...what I'm really doing when I don't seem to be enjoying myself is, I'm concentrating so hard on trying to make it happen that it's not working. You can concentrate too hard. I should know better, because when it does happen, it's always...spontaneous, in a sense.

• • •

I've always felt, from the very beginning—even before the Acid Tests—that we could do something that was, not necessarily extramusical, but something where music would be only the first step. Something maybe even close to religion—not in the sense that "the Beatles are more popular than Jesus," but in the sense of the actual communing. We used to say that every place we play is church. Now it's not quite as all-encompassing—it's not quite so automatic...the core of followers is not the reason it feels like church; it's that other thing, "it."

There are two sides of it, for me. There's the communion level, the strict psychic level, and then there's the "medium is the message" level. I snapped on this watching another band, I think it was Quicksilver. I said, "Wow! That's it!" The medium is the message, in the sense that people out here in the audience watching these guys perform together can, if they're so inclined, realize that that's all they have to do: work together with some other people, and it'll get better for them. It'll be like music.

It is true. It would be much more widely implemented were society more receptive to such things.
At the same time, it's what society needs more than anything. That's one of the reasons we're all committed to it—or I am, for sure....

The way we approach music is a different road than almost anybody else, that improvisational attitude. It's the one thing that we all agreed on at the beginning—subconsciously, because we didn't really talk about it until much later. Once we had the experience that we could do it, then we started trying to rationalize formal connections so we could extend even further. That's where it's sort of fallen down.

You mean as soon as you started really trying to quantify it, it slipped from your grasp—
Essentially.
Sometimes the tapes tell a different story; sometimes it'll feel really good and the tapes won't sound so good. Usually that's a function of the mix, I've found—on a statistical level. More likely, I'll think it's bad and it'll turn out to be amazing.

Is that because you're such a harsh critic of yourself and the band?
Myself, mostly—that's a key point I'd like to make.

You don't venture to criticize the other guys so much?

Not so much—not out loud, heh-heh. But I reserve my greatest criticism for myself. I'm always kickin' myself 'cause I can't make it happen. That's the dichotomy of the whole thing that I'm dealing with.

It's always going to be there.

Yeah, of course. I'm totally at ease with that.

You told me last year, "If it narrowed down in any one guy's direction, it would cease to be what it is."

With the Grateful Dead, there's more possible than you could ever dream of—even I could ever dream of. That's what's frustrating.

But it's only possible to the collective.

Mm-hmm.

As we said earlier, you either surrender and give yourself over to it—which you have to do to make it work—or you stand back from it, hold yourself aloof from it, and therefore interfere with the function of the entire thing.

That's right. And that's the big mistake that I make most of the time. I try everything, and that draws me further away from it, because I'm consciously trying.

Where the real thing to do is tune out and wait for "it" to find you—

Let it go. There's a really fine line about that, because you have to keep it going somehow, because you're still on the stage performing. Although I do, I've always done this—and it gets people really crazy—I will stop playing when I don't have anything to say or I know that what I do is not going to matter.

I've seen you do that. There was a time when Jerry started "Wharf Rat"— it might have been that Davis show [March 14, 1982]—you stood there with such a stricken look on your face—

I remember that. I couldn't believe what the fuck he was doing. I even yelled at him: "What the fuck are you doing?" He should have waited a little longer....This is my opinion speaking, but I know a lot about that shit; I've studied it all my life.

Everything has gotten so structured.... I loved those three-set nights back in '73 and '74 when things would get weird in the first set, weirder in the second set, and weird six times in the third set.

Yeah. That's the kind of shit that I love, too. I think every song we play, everything we do should be able to open up at any moment.... I'd just as soon just get outside! That's what we're all about! The rigidity of the set and the show that we do is a direct outgrowth of the decision to do the *Workingman's Dead–American Beauty*–style material, so that goes back a long way. In fact, this particular show that we're doing now, in 1982, has been ossifying since 1970.

● ● ●

All I know is that I want it to be different for me, so I'll do everything I can to make it different for me, or better for me, within the limits of what I've got to work with. And really what I've got to work with is me and my equipment; it's pretty difficult to deal with the other guys—"Hey, could you tune the bass drum a little different?"

It astounds me again how it can be so good and so lame at the same time.

That's a pretty good way to put it. At exactly the same time. You have to keep believing there's a payoff somewhere. If it's not happening right now, there's always the future. But the little details tend to frustrate you, on a day-to-day basis. They pile up; it starts to grind you down.

I've characterized the Grateful Dead as "America's longest-running musical argument"—

The very definition of musical argument is something that keeps going, and you uncover new details and new combinations. A musical argument is not the same as a verbal argument. A verbal argument implies that there's two sides; a musical argument makes the two sides one thing, like counterpoint. A fugue is like that; a double fugue, at least, takes two different ideas and shows you how they relate, and it shows you how they're the same thing. That's really a good description, in sort of an abstract verbal sense.

John Barlow

November 25, 1982
Montego Bay, Jamaica

In 1982 I was senior editor (West Coast) for Record *magazine, a Rolling Stone publication. After bugging the editors of* Rolling Stone *for several months, I was given an assignment to do a story on the Grateful Dead. Relations between GD and RS were none too cordial, I gathered, and the assignment had been somewhere near the back burner for several years. A number of different writers had been assigned but no story had ever materialized. Ben Grevatt, the Dead's East Coast publicist at the time, arranged for me to join a press junket to the Jamaica World Music Festival, where the Grateful Dead and Bobby and the Midnites were scheduled to appear on an impressive international bill.*

John Barlow, songwriting partner of Bob Weir (and later Brent Mydland) was in Jamaica with the Dead entourage. I introduced myself to him and he agreed to an interview, which took place in the patio bar of the Intercontinental Hotel at Rose Hall.

You didn't just pop up out of nowhere for Bobby's first solo album. You prepped with him—is that how the legend goes?

Well, I wouldn't put it that way.

You got kicked out of schools with him?

167

Well, that almost became the case. We both went to a prep school when we were about fourteen which specialized in fairly bright but temperamental types—basically a lot of intelligent miscreants. He'd been kicked out of a couple of schools already, and I'd just managed to make such trouble in Wyoming as a fourteen-year-old that my father, who was a politician, was told that if he didn't want to get shitcanned in the next election he was going to have to get me out of sight. So we went down to this school in Colorado.

What was he?
He was a state senator.

And you were just raising a little hell...?
Raising a lot of hell...mostly just petty vandalism. Bunch of young kids...

And that's where you met Bobby?
Yeah. He was weird and I was weird, I mean even for that place. So we got sort of thrown in together, and we've been real close friends ever since.

Then he got kicked out of that one, too. I didn't get kicked out, but I didn't want to go back very bad. I almost went to the next school that he went to, which was a real interesting place called Pacific High School in Palo Alto, where the students would do projects like build a submarine in a pond. But I decided at the last minute not to, and then we didn't see each other for a while.

But along about the time things started to really cook, '66 and '67, we started spending time together again.

Where were you?
I was in college at that point. Wesleyan, in Connecticut. Small liberal arts college.

Had you guys done anything creative together before that? Or were you just destructive?
No, not even very destructive. We were just real close friends. And I spent a lot of time in San Francisco in those days—took time away from college and spent the summer there twice.

Did you know he was in this psychedelic rock band?

Oh, yeah. I'd been out at Millbrook taking acid with [Timothy] Leary and those people, so I was aware of what all that meant. It was just that [the Pranksters and the Grateful Dead] had an entirely different spiritual overlay on what they were doing, if they had any spiritual overlay at all. It was in the form of circus rather than Eastern mystic rites, which was the way in which we were conducting it. I finally decided that I preferred the combination better, and started going back and forth with it.

And then there was a period where I didn't see too much of him again. I got sort of serious about college for a while.

What did you study?

What it amounted to was theology, as much as anything else. I mean, I got a degree in comparative literature, but it was basically a theology degree. It was just an independent study program where you could put together pretty much any mishmash you wanted to and come up with some kind of dilettante's degree.

One of those kinds of schools.

Oh, I was serious about it. It wasn't Goddard by any means, it was a serious university, but they were going through a period in the late sixties like every place else where they were being forced by their students to be very experimental about things.

Anyway, then I became a poet of sorts. I was writing a lot of poetry, mostly because I knew that if I were invited to a New England girls' college to read it my romantic opportunities were greatly enhanced.

Were you published and all that stuff?

Yeah. I look back on that poetry and it's kind of amazing to me that I was, because it was pretty adolescent stuff, but you know poetry magazines—there are a lot of them and they'll publish damn near anything.

And then I wrote a novel and got an advance from Farrar, Straus and Giroux to finish it. It needed many more coats of wax—in fact it needed a second half, and I took the money from that and went to India instead.

What year was that?

Sixty-nine, something like that.

I went to India, and just got completely scorched by that experience, and came back and struggled through the second half of it, and handed it all in to Farrar, Straus. They spent about a year trying to figure out whether or not there was any way to put it into enough order to print it, and they finally decided that there wasn't.

Were you furious?

No, I wasn't, particularly. I think they were right.

During that time I was just on hold, I wasn't really doing anything. I wasn't in college any more, I was just waiting to find out whether or not they were going to publish my novel. Writing a few articles here and there, you know, but I wasn't being very serious about it.

And at that point Bobby had just started writing songs, really, and he and Hunter had worked together on a few of them, but very few. Their relationship as coconspirators was a bit flawed; but they didn't quite have the same rapport. So Bobby said, "Well, you write poetry. You might try your hand at writing some lyrics." I wasn't doing anything else, so I did try my hand at it. I sort of made up some things that sounded like song lyrics.

The first one was "Mexicali Blues," and I was just *stricken* when I heard what kind of a setting he'd chosen for it. It was a whole different thing from what I had in mind. But it turned out to be okay after I got over it.

You didn't expect a brassy polka. More of a desperado feeling?

Yeah, that was what I had in mind. I thought, "This is gonna be swell."

And since then he and I have been working on things more or less continuously, sometimes over the phone, sometimes at the ranch, sometimes in California. Sometimes hardly at all.

It is not easy trying to write with somebody. But those things have a certain advantage, in spite of the amount of turmoil that goes on. It's a lot like being married, actually. Sometimes we just can't stand each other, over what are fundamentally aesthetic differences. But fortunately, as with being married, we've been good friends for so long that we've got a fallback position if things get too scary.

And you know that eventually it'll work out.

Right. But there's something that two people can often do that one person can't, which is to provide a kind of synergy in the sense of two entirely different points of view coming together in a way that may not be all that pleasing to either one of them, but it works in a way that their own vision all by itself might not.

Any comment on Hunter's observation that Weir "uses a lyricist like a whore"?

Well, let me put it this way: I have referred to myself over the years as the Grateful Dead's word nigger.

He's actually only that way when he's feeling a bit uptight and overworked. Then he gets very headstrong about certain creative decisions, and I'm not in a position to gainsay him because he's got to get out in front of a whole bunch of people and sing that stuff. And if he doesn't want to sing it, I'm damn sure not going to try to make him.

That's the bottom line. The guy whose mouth it comes out of...

Yeah. So I grit my teeth and watch a lot of good lines go down the tube, or what I think are good lines.

The difference between writing lyrics and writing music is that you are dealing in concepts as opposed to sounds.

When you're trying to make a song work—I mean, I know that Bobby in particular deals very much in the textures of the words that he sings. Syllables have to sing well.

Oh, very much. Well, sometimes I think that he would be better served by my syllables for pure purposes of phrasing. But he also has his own particular style of phrasing things, which I've always thought sounded a bit like the way in which a man would walk if he had two knees. But it seems to work. [*Laughter*]

It's always interesting to watch his songs develop.

And that's been a great problem, because both of us are procrastinators for one reason or another. I'm a procrastinator largely because I've got this entire other life that I live that is very consuming, and it's difficult to come in after a ten-hour day, whether it's driving a tractor or feeding bales or riding horseback and pushing cattle and that kind of thing, and want to sit down and work on a song. There's not a song in my heart at the end of some of those days. And he procrastinates because he's got to get up onstage about 180 nights a year. So as a consequence we end up writing the songs right before they hit wax. And those are never the songs as they are two years later. I wish to god we could change that.

We're making some positive strides in that direction. We've got a song now that they've been playing a couple of months that they aren't going to be recording for a couple more....

"Throwing Stones"?
Yeah.

"Lost Sailor" and "Saint of Circumstance" worked that way too. That one got toured a lot before the album.
Well, yeah, but that was written with the idea that the album was going to happen right away.

Oh. So you got a reprieve on that one.
No, I didn't really get much of a reprieve. Because actually the [basic tracks] on those two songs were done probably six or eight months before the thing was finally mastered. We were stuck with the basics at that point.

So within the gross musical structures, you and he had a chance to play with the lyrics a bit.
Yeah, a little. It now, to me, sounds exactly like what I had in mind. But when it came out on the record it certainly didn't. I think he would probably tell you much the same thing.

There aren't that many changes in the words....
No, changes in the way in which they're delivered, actually. The words aren't messed with, usually, in any case, except additions and subtractions of a minor sort. But it's just a matter of getting the delivery down so.that the words are set in the way that they're intended to be set.

He has to grow into a song.

A lot of his songs start out, it seems, as chord changes, and they're sort of, as Jerry observed, melody-weak at times....
Yeah, and that's correct. He's a rhythm guitar player. It makes my job a great deal harder, because often the first thing that I hear in a song is the rhythm part.

Doesn't he give you a melodic idea sometimes?

No, he says he'll work it out, usually. And, you know, there've been occasions where I've had the opportunity as a result of that to make some contributions to the melodic idea. But it is a little more demanding that way.

And the other way in which it's happened on occasion is where I gave him the set of lyrics and he took 'em someplace. It wasn't always someplace I wanted to see 'em go. But they went there anyway.

And then there've been a number of really serendipitous cases where I gave him a set of lyrics just knowing that I was going to see my baby slaughtered and impaled before it was all over with, and it came out sounding just right. So I don't know.

There was one called "Money, Money" that I had the notion of as being some kind of a Mose Allisony kind of jive blues thing. It sounded like Mose Allison done by the Grand Funk Railroad by the time it was done. I was really upset by that and refused to write any lyrics for him for quite a while. I mean, I went on writing his lyrics, it was just that I had to hear the music first. I got stubborn and decided that my judgment regarding what music meant was better than his judgment regarding what words meant. And that was kind of a silly attitude. The way it works best, I think, is when both of us are trying to develop something together and have the opportunity to spend some time together and get it done that way.

The other thing is that sometimes things work out okay as far as other people are concerned and didn't work out so well as far as I was concerned.

There's a fundamental problem in creating art. A, the only person that you have to please ultimately is yourself. And B, you really don't have the right to criticize anybody else's opinion of what you've just done. That's their song then. You can't take that away from them.

Joe Jackson said, "What am I supposed to do, go around and interview everybody and ask what they think of it? Or tell 'em what they're thinking wrong?"

Right. No, it took me a long time before I got to the point where somebody could say, "Hey, I really like such-and-so a song"—which I felt had come out poorly—and not sort of say, "Well, I thought it was a piece of shit." What I say now is, "Well, thank you. I appreciate that. What do you suppose it means?"

And the interesting thing is that usually what they come up with is something entirely different from what I had in mind, but it sounds, in some cases, even better than what I had in mind, so I tell them, "Yeah, that's what it means." But what they've essentially done is to write their own song. I just provided them with the raw working materials.

I think that line of thought is central to the way in which this organization tries to do things, which is in a participatory fashion.... You're producing the raw material for somebody out there in the audience to become his own form of creative listener. Involving him in the creative process in some way.

At least Hunter has the wonderful opportunity to go out and play his songs himself if he doesn't think the Grateful Dead do them right. [*Laughs*] Which I'm afraid is not afforded me.

Do you play music at all?

I don't play. I never have. Music is really one of the first loves of my life, it's just that I, for some weird reason—at this point I think it was practically a cosmic denial—I never learned how to play an instrument. Unless you count the clarinet in the high school band.

Actually, what it comes down to is that at the time one would start taking piano lessons and should, I was living in a pretty raw town where the kids were tough on each other. We were all cowboy kids and cowboys don't take no piano lessons. So I got tired of fighting it and decided that I wasn't going to, either. [*Laughs*] Biggest mistake I ever made.

But that doesn't necessarily deny a person the ability to understand how music works, and I studied fundamentals of music theory and I can follow a score if I'm at an opera, for example.

I'm sure you know that a lot of the Grateful Dead purists, or those whose involvement in the cosmology of it goes back to the beginning, sort of had a hard time with the original Weir-Barlow compositions. There are some who still don't deal with it.

Well, except for the fact that I go back to the beginning, and I think they're being doctrinaire, as adherents of a religion are inclined to be.

But I'd have to admit that most of my favorite Grateful Dead songs are Hunter-Garcia songs. I mean, those guys sound like the Grateful Dead, what the hell? And an enormous amount of this is about the inner workings of Garcia's mind, unfortunately. I think it's unfortunate for him, to the greatest extent.

The responsibility of that?

Yeah. It's not easy to have people going around thinking you're God.

How much do you suppose he had to do with promoting that concept?

Oh, never any. *Never any*—except for the fact of reverse promotion turning into promotion, you know, in the Howard Hughes sort of way that it does. The more elusive and unavailable you become, the more people are going to get nuts over who you are. But he became more elusive and unavailable, I think, *because* people were getting nuts over who he was. You know, it's like that Bob Dylan song ["Idiot Wind," from *Blood on the Tracks*]—"People see me all the time and they just can't remember how to act." Happens to him practically everybody he meets, and a person gets tired of that.

Anyway, to a very small degree, people will periodically hit me with the same thing. The Deadheads are an especially devout bunch and they all have their icons within the general pantheon of things. So I get maybe four or five Deadheads a year showing up at the ranch—

What do they say to you when they show up?

Well, usually they seem to find it hard to say anything, because they've got this real strange concept. And I actually welcome these opportunities, even if I'm fairly busy, to spend an hour with them and give them a real good view of the fact that I'm just another guy running cattle in Wyoming. I'm chairman of the Republican central committee of Sublette County, Wyoming—

Well, that must throw 'em for a loop Republican.

Yeah. Well, see, all the jagged edges start to enter into this serene, smooth picture that they have of how it is, and they're forced to—most of these people are really pretty intelligent, and they realize that you can't get too carried away about being devotional to something that is this complex.

Who perpetuates it? How does the myth stay so strong?

Well, I sure don't think any of us do.

…They do work awful hard, and they've been living a life that is, to me, impossible to live. I road-managed them on their fifteenth anniversary tour, and every time I see the life on the road I'm stunned that any of them are alive. I couldn't survive that life. A person gets tired.

They're used to that.

Well, I don't know. It takes its toll. There is such a thing as the human organism. Which is not to say that they've gotten old and tired, it's just that there are a lot of times when they are tired. But I still think that on a good night they're the greatest rock 'n' roll band on the planet.

A lot of what that seems to have to do with, and this is strictly my own opinion, is the same kind of creative synergy that I was talking about when two people get together, that I was talking about when listeners participate in the creative process. The audience and the band create something that is really unusual and unique. Nobody else does that, and I hesitate to call it mass hysteria, but there've been plenty of times when I went to a Grateful Dead concert where I thought it was just the best goddamned thing I had ever heard in my whole life, and I was happier than a pig in shit to be there—and I listened to the tapes afterwards, and I kept thinking, "Wait a second. Christ. Phil's off-key. And what are all these notes where Weir's supposed to be there—was the amplifier down? I didn't hear the vocals get so out of sync at this point." What I'm saying is that there's something transcendent about the experience itself that probably causes people to get into a spiritual kind of relationship to it that they wouldn't with a lot of other very fine bands.

I sat with Bobby after a particularly weak Midnites show at the Keystone Berkeley a couple of weeks ago...on the heels of a bunch of good gigs. We had dinner in this fancy restaurant and everybody had had a little too much wine, and the food was rich and a little too close to showtime, and everybody was a little too enthusiastic and overextended themselves.

After the show we're sitting in the dressing room and all these [fans] are coming in going, "It was awesome, Bobby.... It was just..." And we had just gotten through talking about what a bum show it was.

I wonder how they deal with the uncritical thing.

I don't think the artist has the right to deny anybody else their opinion of his work. And the corollary of that is that you don't have to listen to it, and you shouldn't.

So he just politely endures them saying, "You're magnificent," and he knows it was shit, so—

Well, as I say, I quit worrying about people telling me that lyrics that I didn't think were so hot were great, because if it did something for them that was fine by me. I continue to have my own opinion of that work, and don't intend to do the same thing twice, but if they like it, then I'm glad they do. I mean, genuinely glad they do. I don't begrudge them their liking it. *De gustibus non est disputandum,* right?

One of the things I have to tackle here is the Grateful Dead as an institution and what it all means seventeen years down the line.
Well, it means that for one thing we are a community ourselves. Which I think is damned important. I mean, we are a *community*. We're not a commune, and we're not brothers—we're a community like a small town in Iowa, where everybody farms right outside of town.

Even though you're so far away you're part of that?
Sure. And what's more to the point is that one of the ways in which I find myself undisturbed by the intense devotion of the Deadheads is the fact that very few people in this country come from a community in the first place. They come from a suburban area where you live in your house and the next guy lives in his. That's being lost hand over fist as America becomes more suburban and less country-oriented, which is the natural environment of community. And these kids feel something lacking in their lives, which is that kind of relationship with other people where you don't have to ask somebody hardly, if you need help you get it. And when they need help they get it. Because that's how it works. It's a wonderful thing to see down here, the extent to which that happens.

They wouldn't have a community on the basis of where they came from, but they have a community now, in themselves, in the floating community of Deadheads. You go to a Dead concert and you see Deadheads that you've seen before. Lots and lots and lots of them. There are people who go on the road with the Grateful Dead.

There was one great scene there in New York a few years back when they were playing Radio City. Weir and Garcia were on "Good Morning America." And they were both dingier than pet coons, and they had some real scrofulous Deadhead down in front of Radio City, and they did a live take down there to show them how they were waiting in line for the tickets at seven o'clock in the morning, and there's this guy that looks like he's maybe taken a little too much of something for too long, although he's only about twenty, and they said, "Well, what do you do for a living?" And the guy just says, "Oh, whatever I can do to get by. I spend all my money going to Grateful Dead concerts."

So quick they go back to the studio and the straight lady asks Garcia, "What do you think about somebody who spends all his money going to Grateful Dead concerts?"

And Garcia says, "What the hell do you think we do?" Which as far as I was concerned was as clear a description of how it was with the Grateful Dead and how it was with the Deadheads and how it was with each other as I've ever heard.

Bob Weir

January 4, 1983
Mill Valley, California

Another interview for the Rolling Stone *article that never happened. We started at Weir's house, went out for dinner, then came back and talked for several hours—including taking turns hanging from the ceiling in gravity boots.*

Weir: We may not be the most professional outfit on the face of the planet, but as has been dutifully noted in the past, once things get rolling there is something that happens. I'm a man of fairly discerning taste myself; if I didn't like it, I wouldn't be around.

We even seem to get back the fans who'd completely written us off as has-beens. From time to time they come drifting back, hit a good evening, and they're reborn.

If we go on the pat hand—what we know we can do—it gets stale real quick and we can't do it anymore. That should be plentifully obvious.

So the band not only encourages change, it thrives on it.

Yeah....We're always going to play real loose; we're always going to play kind of open, and we're going to try to create an opportunity for something new to happen every night. We do that, even when we get

179

trapped in a situation where we have absolutely no material and not a whole lot of new ideas—which happens from time to time; bound to happen with any group. It's part of the ebb and flow of any group.

But there's always the possibility that something new can occur. We're going to go for it every night. . . .

One of the reasons a lot of people can't latch on to the Grateful Dead is that the downbeat is taken for granted. . . .

So we're a cultured taste. . . .

Everybody does something a little more sophisticated, which can be read as "less accessible."

That's a fact. That may be a basic fact. I've never heard it quite so succinctly stated. . . .

Musically, that's something I can appreciate. But I sense that a lot of [the audience] aren't really even listening that closely for musically specific stuff—but there's a vibe, an emotional tone, that you don't get anywhere else. That's what they hear.

We have our own esoteric approach to music that's been cultured over the years we've been playing. It seems to me obvious that under those circumstances, we're going to come up with some fairly quirky modes of presentation. But even so, whatever it takes to get us off—as long as it actually does get us off, summons whatever spirit it is that we're called upon to summon—as long as we can supply that, I think our listeners will be pleased.

Even among musicians, we're a cultured taste. Even if you can perform the kind of music that we perform, it's questionable as to whether you would want to. We're just those kind of people.

We leave things awfully loose. A lot of people just naturally don't like things that loose—in life, in art, in music. God knows, they're certainly entitled to their tastes, as we're entitled to ours. So we play it loose.

Has there even been any conscious effort to steer it?

The approach? No, because none of us really understands the approach. The approach is only established in action, by all of us at the same time. It seems ridiculously hypothesized, but it's true. On a good night it's fairly evident; on a bad night, it's fairly evident that we failed. The hell with it.

There are those little niceties, like organizing the endings of tunes.... There are nights when everybody intuits it, and it's beautiful; there are nights when everything works perfectly except how to get out of there. And there are nights when everybody, with the finest intentions, ends up half a beat or a beat apart....

There are nights when we're playing "Estimated Prophet," or any other tune that's in an odd time signature, where we get off the *one* [downbeat] and we just can't find the *one* to save our souls. And there are nights when we'll play those same tunes, and absolutely no one will ever play the *one* because everybody always knows where it is. I guess maybe one or two percent of the audience know that the tune's even in an odd time signature. But that's for musicians to understand and appreciate.

Whether or not the tune works is another story. Sometimes the *one* has been lost and is given up for dead, and everybody's playing their own seven/four and waiting to hear someone resoundingly establish the *one*— but still playing within their own framework—there are nights when that makes what I guess they call accidental music, or found art, or whatever. But it works. There are surprises to be had on bad nights, by that example. Sometimes a complete disaster will amount to something, a genuine phoenix out of the ashes of what was supposed to have been a song. We'll go back and listen to the tape, and by god, there's the basis of another song there. That does happen.

...Part of maturing as a musician is learning to listen as well as to state your own case.... I figure my good nights are when I can listen better than I might normally....

It can be argued that that level of showmanship you've been embracing lately is not essential to the Grateful Dead experience.

I agree. I think I probably look out of place bounding around on stage, but for what it's worth, the more I move the less I get stuck anywhere— musically as well. So I think I actually play better when I move more. I'm not doing that just to elicit crowd reaction. I'm actually doing that because I feel like it. I enjoy it, and the more I enjoy the music, the more I feel like playing it.

...On the other hand, you have a guy like Phil, who already had—way back when—a really good notion of what the music could amount to. He's been waiting for, for instance, my musicianship to reach his ideals of what the music could amount to—and he probably still is, and he probably has a long wait in front of him.

When it's happening, it happens! There's something that happens in the Grateful Dead at its own pace that just transcends any other rock show....

We have something more than...We just went four nights without repeating ourselves, except for the new tunes....I guess we have about twelve hours' worth of material at this point....We're not going to be able to get a real pat show down.

Let's fact it: we're a jazz band. I won't say we're nothing but a jazz band, because our basic premise is rock 'n' roll. We just approach it from a jazz point of view.

Jazz syntax with a rock lexicon...

Something like that...The Grateful Dead is a process....The only question is, How strong are we going to pursue this, and in what manner?

What makes you so proud that you'd stand on top of the roof and holler about it?

A good night. A good night makes it all worth it. I've said that a million times....

● ● ●

If the Grateful Dead continues just the way we have for the rest of our lives—assuming that we all live for a while—we're guaranteed a living. Beyond that, what more do you want?

I like to play with side groups. I learn a lot, and I'm not going to stop—not soon. At the same time, to throw away approaching twenty years of practice at making one instrument out of several—that's stupid. Just on an individual basis, that would explain some of my commitment. Beyond that, the guys in the group are the closest thing to brothers I've ever had. I enjoy their company. We have good times together, offstage as well as onstage....

We never know if [something] worked until it's over. That's a given. I can be flipping out onstage about how good or bad it is, and walk backstage and get the exact opposite from a fellow band member, and then the varying opinions will start to filter in from the observers. So we can't even know after the fact without some study.

The tapes always lie....They tell me what I expected to know in advance when I listened to the tapes: how well the notes were turned, how in tune it was, how in time it was—

All the empirical stuff.

Well, feeling is empirical, too, but they don't report that at all. On a really good night, oftentimes—this is not just myself; I've seen this true in many cases—on a really good night a singer or guitar player might get enthused and go sharp—a lot. And the people who are listening don't mind at all, don't even hear it, because all they hear is the enthusiasm...That's the difference between the real-time experience and the relived experience that you get on the tape....

The saving grace of our live records is that they have sort of halfway conveyed some of the enthusiasm of our live recordings....

• • •

[Reading from my notes] *"Bob at times seems compelled to create a demonstrably unique structure with his music." A lot of your stuff is intellectually really satisfying. Your sequence of seven-beat rock tunes...a danceable seven-beat thing is pretty neat...But a lot of your songs are highly evolved, and could be characterized as forced—*

—and constrained, right.

Intellectually satisfying, but not necessarily as viscerally satisfying. Not as immediate.

I once observed that Jerry's stuff is more immediately accessible, but some of it got pale in a hurry, and your stuff takes a little longer to appreciate but holds up better. I guess the tough question about this is, Where did that intellectual drive come from?

A lot of it came from Phil. For instance, back when we were the Warlocks he turned me on to Coltrane and a bunch of classical music that had completely escaped me. That expanded my conception of what music could entail—popular music, or whatever. I just couldn't see where the bounds of popular music should be so constricting as to deny the possibility of, for instance, odd time signatures or harmonic modes. Though I've never formally studied music, it doesn't take a lot to adopt and appreciate those areas of music....

"It's a sin to bore your bandmates" [a note I wrote at a concert]. You just wouldn't bother bringing in an unsophisticated tune.

I wouldn't dare do that with this band. We'd butcher it. If I brought in a tune that fell completely flat in everybody's tastes...I can't imagine what would happen to it.

How do you know [with a song]?
 One way is, you wait until an idea occurs to you that you know is going
to hold universal appeal to the rest of the guys. You wait until the goody
arrives. That's why it takes us so long to write material for this band....

How do they let you know?
 I hate to wax metaphysical on you, but I think they let me know in my
dreams, before I even start to write. I don't put pen to paper but what I'm
sure that what I'm doing is right to bring to the band.

Have there been any spectacular failures of judgment in that regard?
 Yeah.
 That tune "France," for instance [on *Shakedown Street,* never performed live]. I didn't actually write that one—it just sort of happened. But
it sure as hell didn't happen right...It just wasn't satisfying.

*Your [songs] are less traceable to any one particular style....You don't
write anything that seems like a real country tune these days, and you
don't use particularly jazzy harmonic structures either, although the
complexity of some of your stuff suggests jazz. It's unique.*
 Actually, we write simpler stuff now than we did a few years ago. I think
that's probably good, but it's not a goal....
 We go through those phases, where we'll borrow substantially from a
given idiom and come up with our own translations of it. Then we'll get
real inventive and come up with stuff that sounds reminiscent of almost
nothing. Then we'll go through another phase where the stuff is
reminiscent again of given idioms....We don't so much grow as molt
through eclecticism.

• • •

We were born outside of any current vogues...

That would seem both a curse and a blessing.
 Yeah.
 We're not a real temporal band. We haven't come and gone like
numerous other bands before us. On the other hand, we haven't made the
dent that numerous other bands have made.

I really think in the final analysis Grateful Dead music is a significant accomplishment in the history of Western music: a genuine synthesis of musics.

It has yet to be seen, in my estimation.

By whom?

By us, for instance.

We espouse the American musical tradition. Actually, we espouse American traditional music—foremost, as I can see. And we'll borrow from other idioms, but pretty much…I think we've built our own little aesthetic around American traditional music, or our own generalized ideal thereof. And I don't see a whole lot of that being done these days.

If we become so unhip and out of vogue that everything we hold dear also falls into that fate, then we will have failed. We could as easily serve to bury that aesthetic as to rejuvenate or revitalize it.

I would propose that it's an amalgam, a synthesis of an impressive variety of stuff, that transcends matters of style.… Rather than speaking in Muddy Waters' voice for one tune, you acknowledge having heard Muddy Waters and taken him to heart; you use the timbre of his voice while using, say, the vocabulary of John Cage. The idea of it being an extremely open-minded experiment is defensible by virtue of how long it's been around.…

Each sequence of tunes [in a Grateful Dead show]…touches a different ground and conveys a different progression of emotional tones. There's something that goes on in this conversation, this complex feeling that's put across with the music, that is very much a function of the characters of the musicians involved. That thing has evolved with your technique—and Phil's, and to a lesser extent Garcia's.… You created that voice together and have worked on it together.…

We have learned to appreciate and intuit each other's version of that elemental color that a given song is supposed to evoke.…

We have fairly similar attitudes about what music is supposed to evoke, but at the same time, fortunately, we have fairly divergent views of what music is supposed to evoke, too. We have a lot to learn from each other. I guess we're all gifted with fairly prehensile intellects, at least as regards our musical endeavors.…

I'm not surprised when somebody comes up with some completely off-the-wall lick that just makes sense.

[Hanging from the ceiling in gravity boots—Bob first]

Do you have any sense of being privileged to have grown up in the times you did and been involved in this unique thing, and not had to work for a living?

You bet. To the point where it, for better or for worse, sort of stokes my sense of purpose....

What you have in the Grateful Dead is a bunch of guys who would probably amount to neighborhood heroes but for the fact that they've fallen in with each other. Their innate understanding of each other and their concerted sense of quest coaxes out of them what on a good night I would equate with genius. And that's hard to find. Nonetheless, I've seen what pretty much satisfies my criteria for genius displayed by the various members of the group, almost always in response to a stimulus offered by someone else in the group.

Was it evident from the beginning that something special could happen?

Yeah.

...Our first responsibility is to amuse ourselves. If we can't do that, then we can't entertain anyone. It's a sham. Also, it's a given that we're going to have to go through some stuff that ain't so much fun, such as bad nights, in order to learn how to be more flexible—so that in the end, when we evolve into angels, we can make anything fun. We can make fun out of hell.

[Down comes Bob, up goes David]

The most I've ever amounted to is through concerted effort with other people. The better I can do for them, the better they'll do for me, in general and in specific....That's been a pretty consistent lesson life's been hammering me with....

If what I'm doing doesn't relate to what everybody else in the band is doing, no matter how good I'm doing it it's not making magic with the rest of the band. And making magic with the rest of the band is, number one, how I've always made my living, and number two, how I've always received my greatest gratification.

If I practice a given solo over and over again until I can play it really dazzlingly, if it doesn't relate with what the rest of the band is playing—directly, every moment—then it doesn't sound as good as if I'd practiced playing with the band over and over in that same context and learned to intuit and play with what the rest of the guys are playing—and maybe render something a bit less technically dazzling but more cogent in the framework of the music that's going on.

We practice a lot…onstage, in front of people. We practice chasing that elusive goody. It's drama.…I still do to some degree, but I used to always watch what my fingers were doing. At this point, I really have to watch the faces of the rest of the band to read better what they're up to. I can hear what they're doing, but I need to look at their faces to see if they're happy about it, or if they're really intent about it.

[Both parties on the floor now]

The record that made the most difference for us in our recording career was *Workingman's Dead*. That was recorded and mixed in nine days.

The first one was recorded and mixed in, I think, five days. And not bad. *Workingman's* was actually something of an achievement.

How did the process of making Grateful Dead albums become such a drawn-out, tooth-pulling affair?

Because we had the finances and perhaps misplaced knowledge to…spend maybe a little too much time getting basics too close, and all that kind of stuff—to go for a conventional kind of product, which means real tight basics and spare but aptly rendered and perfectly placed overdubs. And that's not what we're really well versed at. The more we belabor our songs, the limper they come out sounding.

…It's a viable direction, as far as I'm concerned, to come up with a whole bunch more material, go in, and just jam like we do onstage and put out records like jazz people do—and not expect to sell very many of them, but in the end come up with a pretty fair catalog.

If we're going to do stuff that's more complicated, that's more extended in one regard or another, then I think we should either save it for live records or at least have it onstage for a good long time before we try to record it. I would cite as an example the songs on *Ace* that we still do. They're much stronger now, and they were much stronger a year after they were recorded.…

I've learned a lot about "Throwing Stones" in the dozen or so times we've performed it. I know the band knows a lot more about the song than it would have otherwise.…You can't do that in the studio. You can only do that in front of a live audience. I think we should play everything live before we record it....

We played at the Melkweg in Amsterdam [October 15–16, 1981], on borrowed and rented equipment. Did "Lovelight" for the first time in a long time, and "Gloria." Everybody got real loose. It was too hot for words. We didn't last very long, but I think everybody had fun just being in a different environment. I like what happens when this band gets force-fed different circumstances. I may be atypical in that regard, but that's my preference.

We played reasonably well in the Melkweg, given that I was playing a borrowed Japanese imitation of a Telecaster through, I think, a Twin Reverb. I think I got lucky and scored a Twin Reverb. Both drummers played on borrowed drum kits, and Brent played, I think, a borrowed, real funky Fender Rhodes. Couldn't get a B-3 to save our souls. Garcia played a borrowed guitar and borrowed amplifier. Phil might have had his bass; he might have been playing entirely through borrowed equipment, too.

And for what it's worth, the Us Festival [San Bernardino, California, September 5, 1982]...Given that they put us on at nine o'clock in the morning...We'd never experienced that kind of thing. It was as foreign as going to Egypt to us, to get up at nine in the morning and go play—much less to a crowd that wasn't a hundred percent Deadheads. Hell, it put us into emergency mode—"Holy shit, here are all these strange faces, and this is a weird time to be playing"—the only way to deal with it was for us to lean into it. And we did, and I thought we did real well. There were a lot of breakdowns in the first part of the show, but toward the end, I thought that—at least for my taste—we kind of pulled it together. We were all busy waking up, our equipment was busy waking up, the crew was busy waking up—and the crowd was busy waking up. By the time everybody was awake, I don't think anybody can fully remember· the equipment breakdowns and the breaks we had to take to rectify all that stuff. By the time we got rolling, we just kept rolling until they were about to break out the hooks and drag us off. We were having fun, in the most absurd—at least by our standards—circumstances.

I had a great time playing in Egypt [September 1978]. There were a lot of Deadheads that followed us over there—several hundred—but the audience was about five thousand each night, and the great majority of them had never heard rock 'n' roll before. It seemed to me that they caught on pretty quick. Part of rock 'n' roll is derived from African traditional music, which is some fairly elemental stuff. Those folks are at least in part African. The Nubians that opened up the show for us played Bo Diddley rhythms, and that was Nubian folk music. They didn't do it with guitars, they did it with tars and a lot of hand-clapping and foot-stomping and singing. But it was the same kind of rhythmic motion and drive that rock 'n' roll has…

• • •

It's that impish facet of the human spirit, that no matter how good you've got it you think it should be better—not just for you, but for everybody. It's the same thing that drove a bunch of relatively well-off suburban kids from California to band together and make music that was in some way expressive of a fairly critical view of the social structure that spawned them. Not because they were starving, but simply because they felt that it could be better. They had a vision.

And if art can serve to further civilization, then it's performing its ultimate goal, in my estimation.

It doesn't necessarily have to transmit a political message of any immediate, specific nature—

Hell, no. If it just makes people happy. If you get off listening to revolutionary songs, then that's wonderful. If it makes you go out and bomb an embassy and kill innocent people, then that's not good. But I don't think rock 'n' roll has ever really done that. If it makes you get up in the morning and feel that maybe you can punch it out with life, and the social order and the situation you've been force-fed up until that morning, then that's wonderful.

For those that are drawn into whatever it is that we do, through whatever avenues or for whatever reasons, we can and do supply a little genuine joy. I speak for myself as well as for people who I've met who have told me this, and from what I've been able to discern. I don't know if that's a complete reason for being, either for me personally or for the band, but it's a good holding pattern…until we figure out if there's something more to go for.

What about being the spiritual home to so many Deadheads?

I don't understand that very well. We aren't accomplished masters at any sort of spiritual realm, and for people to ascribe to us those qualities...either they're seeing something in us that I have yet to see, or maybe my standards are impossibly high—but I don't think so.

I know the guys in the band pretty well, I think. By and large they are some philosophically adept individuals. But I wouldn't go so far as to call any of them spiritual masters.

But the Grateful Dead, and what happens when the Grateful Dead play music, certainly meets several of the definitions of what a church is, or a spiritual gathering place. Maybe it's not something that you've fostered consciously or that the band embraces, but there it is.

And some people even go to the show for those reasons...Our bad nights are their bad nights, and our good nights are their good nights.

Or maybe every night they're in the presence of that thing is enough...

These guys are like brothers to me. They're my oldest friends, and I know them for their best qualities and their worst faults. God, they're humans, and for people to hold allegiance to a bunch of guys that I know be eminently human seems strange to me. I've said this before, and the more I say it the more it seems to happen, so I'm beginning to accept my role as perhaps a misbegotten demigod and accept the responsibility of doing the best I can to live visibly within the bounds of a reasonable, acceptable cosmology.

It seems silly that I should have to worry about anything beyond doing the best I can musically and perhaps poetically, but I guess these days no matter what you do or what you intend to profess—art or whatever business it is—if you become relatively successful at it, you become something of a celebrity and then more than simply what you do, who it is you are, and what you amount to well beyond the bounds of your realm of expertise comes into critical view. You become a celebrity....Being the focus of what amounts to a quasi-religious cult is just weird! I don't really change what I do that much....

...for us, regardless of how well we play our individual instruments, at this point what we amount to is how well we play to and with each other. If we keep playing and touring the way we are, it'll get better and better.

Any idea what you might be doing if this hadn't happened?

Nah. I never wanted to do anything but what I'm doing. I used to fantasize about being a cowboy, and one of the guys that made the music I heard on the radio—though I had no idea of what that was all about. I just liked the whole idea of it.

Tried being a cowboy. That was most like work. At the tender age of fifteen I ran away from home, got a job on a ranch. . . . Being a cowboy was most like work, especially since the new kid in the outfit gets all the shit gigs like shoveling stalls.

How ambitious was everybody [in the band] at the beginning? Or was it just something to do?

Nah. None of us ever figured at that point that we were going to make a life's work of it. Garcia was a banjo teacher, and he had gigs on the side. He was a professional musician. Phil worked for the post office, and at the same time he went to school and studied with Luciano Berio and various notables in the classical world. Pigpen and I swept up in the music shop, and I was lucky enough to get a job teaching beginning and intermediate students on the guitar, and beginning banjo. I was actually pretty good at it. I was good at working with kids.

Billy [Kreutzmann] was working in various bands, as was everybody. I think he was working at a wig shop, or something like that, whatever genuine paying gig he could get. He was married at the time I met him.

Pigpen would work at the music store because he could hang out with musicians, but basically he didn't want to work any more than he absolutely had to. But playing was different—that wasn't like working, for Pig.

We fell together, New Year's Eve of 1964, I believe. A friend of mine, Rick McCauley, and I were wandering the back streets of Palo Alto. We were way too young to get into any of the hot clubs. We'd worked it out so we could get into this one folk club, but there was nothing happening that night—or at least not yet.

So we were walking the back streets of Palo Alto, just talking things over and walking around. We walked by the back of this music store that we used to frequent, Dana Morgan Music, and we heard banjo music coming from within. That seemed strange to us, because it was New Year's Eve, so we knocked on the door.

It was Garcia. We recognized him from the numerous bands that he was in at the time (I didn't personally know him at the time). He was the local hot banjo player. He was in there playing banjo, waiting for his students to show up. Of course, it was New Year's Eve and absolutely none of them were coming. He was absolutely unmindful of the fact that it was New Year's Eve, so we acquainted him with that information....

We started talking, and Garcia had been playing for a few hours as far as I could tell, and he was hot to play with somebody. We talked him into...He had the key to the front of the shop and we knew it, so we talked him into breaking into the front of the shop and we grabbed a couple of the guitars—the ones we'd always wanted to play. He had a good time playing and singing and kicking stuff around all night, and by the end of the evening—I don't know what time it was—we decided we had enough second-rate talent there to throw together a jug band.

We called a rehearsal for a few days from then. I knew a guy or two, Garcia knew several guys, and we sorted it out when we got there.

A few of us sort of struck a chord together. And I mean I really couldn't play at all, but they figured if anybody's got to start from scratch it probably ought to be me.

The next day I got a washtub and a broom handle and a piece of string, and a bunch of different kinds of jugs, and showed at the next rehearsal. God knows how, but on the spot I figured out how to play them all. I could make notes happen with a washtub bass; I'm actually pretty good at it. Jug, too. We listened to a bunch of old jug band records that various guys had rounded up, and then we started working on the songs. We actually became a fairly good jug band.

People dropped out as the rehearsal schedule got a bit more rigorous. Then we became really popular around the mid-Peninsula area. Had work just about every weekend. We'd rehearse either in Garcia's garage or in the music store.

At one point Garcia left on a tour of the South, more or less to study bluegrass music. By that time I'd advanced on guitar to the point where he decided that I could probably take his beginning and intermediate students. So I started working at the music store.

All the time that we were first getting started, we were real happy playing jug band music, and we were getting real good at it. But we got to be real tight, and then started wondering what we were going to do. People started quitting the band, to go away to school or this or that. In the fall, we didn't know what we were going to do.

About that time the Beatles started to become popular. For what it's worth, Garcia had all along been playing in rock 'n' roll bands—pretty much to bolster his income. He was playing guitar or bass, whatever was required of him.

We started kicking around this idea of maybe firing up the old guitars and at least maybe playing some blues, Chicago-style or Jimmy Read style or whatever. We got Pigpen involved, and finally through the shop we got Billy involved. The son of the owner of the shop wanted to be the bass player, and suddenly we had a band—especially since the son of the owner of the shop could supply the instruments.

Along about New Year's Eve of the next year, we had gone from being a jug band to a rock 'n' roll band. Called ourselves the Warlocks. We played for about six months that way, and then the son of the owner of the store couldn't make our rehearsal schedule, not to mention our gig schedule, and had to drop out. I think Garcia knew Phil—I don't know where from—so we invited him to sit in with us. By this time Garcia and I were both working in another music store anyway, part-time. We had large clienteles.

We sort of hustled together. . . . We already had a following at that point, so we just sort of added Phil and we were a working band. Then we got a gig in a bar that lasted for two months, working from eight till two every night—seven till two, maybe.

Did that get you started making stuff up as you went along?
You bet. . . .

Phil Lesh

February 5, 1983
San Rafael, California

Another interview for the Rolling Stone *piece. Dennis McNally, the publicist and official biographer of the Grateful Dead, had mentioned the influence of the science fiction book* More than Human, *an interesting tale of a group-mind entity—homo gestalt—that may have had some role in helping the Grateful Dead understand what was happening to them.*

There's an interdisciplinary experiment going on here, on more than musical levels.

Oh, yeah. It's sort of like the music is the message, but the messengers are the music....

I want to talk about the Grateful Dead as a significant little corner of human history...a cultural phenomenon...in a way that doesn't seem completely hysterical.

It's a paradigm of something, a model of *Homo gestalt.* I love it. That's probably not all it is.

[More than Human][1]...*accounts for the other human synergies....Dan Healy looks down from the steep balcony at the Portland Paramount and*

---

[1]*More than Human,* by Theodore Sturgeon. Ballantine, 1981.

194

realizes that singers always plant their feet in the same place relative to the mike every time they sing so they don't bash their teeth in, and thinks, "If I put a treadle right there I could gate the mike automatically." It was an inspiration that led to something totally utilitarian, totally unsung, and totally wonderful.

So it accounts for the music, it accounts for that attitude, plus the fact that nobody supervises anybody as near as I can tell.

This whole thing, really, is a lifestyle.

It's a lifestyle and a life work. I've come to really accept that; it was a joke at first. The joke was we were going to stick 'em with the shit and split, but it got too serious right away. This was '65.

You weren't planning to do it for long?
I said, "I don't want to be doing this when I'm thirty."

Was that because you were a beat kind of guy and didn't think anything was worth doing for very long?
I didn't at first realize it could be art.

When did you decide it could be art?
Oh, about two weeks after we got into it.

Once you figured out it was art, when did it become a karass from which you could not escape?
Immediately. Well, no. After the Muir Beach Acid Test [December 18, 1965], say. Somewhere in there.

Was it "forever" in the sense of "we've got forever because that might just be tomorrow," or was it "forever" in the sense that "we can invest the rest of our lives in this and do something"—
Well, at least as many years as it takes. The flash I got was "We're on to something here, and it's worth pursuing as far as it takes us." And so far it's taken us plenty far. A long way.

The case to be made is that it's a life's work to be proud of for what it represents as the process if not the product, because there may not be any presentable product along the way but the experiment itself is a worthy thing.

Okay, but it's not over yet. It's the kind of thing you can only see as a whole, especially if you're part of the process. When and if it's all over—

I'm thinking of starting [Playing in the Band] with this quote: "There is only one success: to be able to spend your life in your own way." That seemed like a suitable keynote, in a way.

The deal is, "This is what it is. We're not sure how it happened, but it did because it was possible in those days for people to get together and declare themselves to be something. It wasn't possible for long, and this lucky little circle of people declared it, staked it out, and fucking well stuck with it—"

Yeah. In a sense, though, we didn't declare it. It declared us.

At one point, personally I knew—and I assume everybody else did. I couldn't walk away from this. It was too good, too interesting. Not interesting in the sense that you say about a new play or paperback novel. I mean really *interesting*—and fraught with meaning, dare I say, of greater breadth and scope and significance than I had ever imagined, even in other forms of music.

Did [More Than Human] have anything to do with believing it was possible?

Yes and no. It might have helped me with the conceptual basis, but at the same time [the reality] was so immediate and experiential that it was not to be denied.

Acid helped, also.

Is this the only acidhead organization that has thrived this way?

I have no idea. I have no idea. I don't really feel like the Lone Ranger, personally. In my organization it's impossible to feel alone, unless you have an unpopular viewpoint, temporarily.

Yeah, but you belong.

Very much so, yes. We all do. We belong to each other.

When I make my assessments and analyses of the Grateful Dead, they always seem kind of derogatory in a way. There is a very ungainly kind of homeliness to the Grateful Dead society. Mickey talked about how it's easy to see why people wouldn't like the Grateful Dead, and the Grateful Dead really doesn't care whether you like it or not.

It doesn't even care whether *we* like it or not.

• • •

[*More than Human*] is a book of subversive literature. You can tell from the style of the writing.... This book would be redundant if it were written now, because it wouldn't have any originality to the ideas.

To you.
You mean there's somebody out there in America who's never heard of LSD and what it does?

There are millions of people in America who have no idea that LSD has anything but the most horrifying effects.
Yes, unfortunately.

You saw through it into a whole 'nother realm of possibilities, as a great tool. You were looking for tools.
Yeah—and what a great tool to have handed to you!

There was such a short period of time in which—
—that was possible. That's right. Just about two years—

And that door slammed shut right after you guys jumped through.
That analogy works [when] talking about the music business, too. The Grateful Dead could never have been signed [to a record contract] except in that year when everything in San Francisco was hot. They had no idea what they were getting into, and you guys didn't, either.
[*Laughs*] We had a better idea than they did.

Had they known what characters, what ambitious souls—
They found out. And the whole San Francisco thing, right after that happened it just....We were too proud of the scene.
Did you ever flash that if you hadn't turned so many people on to pot the prices would be lower [*Laughs*]? It was kind of like that.

I have a friend who said, "I don't want the Dead being more popular—it's hard enough getting tickets now."

[*Laughs*] That's about right. I don't think we'd want to be more popular. The only thing that would help would be the money.

I guess it would diminish further the intimacy of it.
It's bad enough now. We can still manage to play in smaller places....

Listen, when it's happening between the six of you, it doesn't matter how big the place. There are so many people I know who don't even know when the music's good. They're there for something else entirely.
A party.

It's more than a party.
Well, soulful party. No, that's too shallow.

It's much too shallow. It is the spiritual core—
Usually what's happening out there is a large version of what's going on onstage....

People go there for something even other than a ritual thing. There is the ritual aspect, and some are just there for that, the dressing up—
The time-warp aspect.

Yeah. And some are there to party. Like Bobby says, in these small towns it's "What rock 'n' roll band is coming through?" It's Foreigner one week and Grateful Dead the next....And there are some who ride the music— much more forgiving people. There are fortunate times when I can stop listening critically and be one of those and enjoy.
It represents a spiritual center for a lot of people. Dick Latvala—a truly committed, idealistic, thoroughgoing, positive Deadhead if ever there was one—talks about the responsibility of being a Deadhead, turning as many people on. It's not work.
No, and it's not like being in a fan club.

There are those adherents who live for the Grateful Dead at great distances from its true heat. That speaks loudly of its power.
Like the line from that "Free Man" poem: "A low-voltage sun." Ever seen that? It's from St. Valentine's Day 1968, from one of the *Anthem of the Sun* sessions. This guy, during the Haight era, there were a lot of people who changed their name to Freeman—Free Man. Even women.

[*He leaves the room and returns with a poem.*]

Tonight we danced to the Grateful Dead
In a ballroom hung with gold
And while we hung our acid heads
They made their dream unfold
They began in red and black ribbons
    of silk shantung
Sequined with gold and pearls
Bold as antique heroes
Humble as hometown boys
They led us down a flaming trail
Of flowers and creepers and low-voltage suns
Half-hidden [in?] messianic volcanoes
Did you see God? the people all around were asking.
Did you slip through the fire without getting burned?
Til one cool head, turning out his inner eye, said,
I made the trip
God's not dead
He's a beautiful joke.

I fell in love with this when I saw it. I thought, "What a great version of
that experience."

• • •

*From time to time I'm sorry I came and learned how the Wizard of Oz
really works.... I've gone past being embarrassed about having seen that it
is a machine, not a miracle. Now I can see the miraculous nature of the
machine itself.*
    It's pretty fuckin' amazing. It's amazing that it turned over once, really.

*There are so many people that I know in the mainstream of the music
business and of Bay Area society.... So many people who've crossed paths
with the Grateful Dead and say nice things about them as people....Although the industry as a whole takes the Grateful Dead as a
whole as a ludicrous example of ill-conceived music, or whatever.*
    *Brent says that when he was in [Silver] a few years ago, the manager
used to say, "You guys can practice all day or you can be like the Grateful
Dead!"*
    [*Laughs*] Which means, "Practice practice practice, and make every-
thing just the same, and make sure that you never take any chances."

Hey, the Grateful Dead used to practice all day, for years and years and years. Used to play *every* day. The whole band. I guess it was about 1970 that it stopped being every day, and that was just because of logistics. Most of the time when we weren't practicing we were recording or playing gigs.

• • •

There are obvious technical things that happen.... I know it happens to you guys because it happens to me. Sometimes we'll play really satisfactorily, and be really high all the way through it, and at the end of the song I'll realize that I didn't play what I usually play, but I never didn't know what I was going to play.
That's a good feeling.

It doesn't always happen in a jam. In a song, I'll fill in the verses in totally unusual and satisfactory ways, and play a solo unlike any I'd played before. We all have our terrain we're exploring.... You'll basically worry that same section of—
Yeah, at least until you get it right to your satisfaction. When you've explored that part to your satisfaction, you can go to your next step.

But isn't it also true that sometimes you play something, a real phenomenal thing, and not ever be able to play it again?
[*Nodding*] That used to bug me.

Not to be able to recall that—
Not so much not to be able to recall it, just not to be able to put it out again...It's not always what you're playing that makes it—it's what everybody else is playing, too. The holes are just in the right places, or whatever.

Was there a time when "it" remembered things that the various of you couldn't?
Yes, but... You don't ever repeat the exact musical details, but you go to the same place. And it's a recognizable place: "This is the highest we've been on this song, and now we're back here again." You recognize that you're there again in the context of that particular piece of material.
For instance, we'll play "Sugaree," and one night I'll be playing rhythm. The next night I'll be playing melody and counterpoint throughout the *entire* song—sometimes slow, sometimes fast, sometimes loud, sometimes

quiet—and I wouldn't even want to try to be able to do that exact thing again. But I know that when it's right, I'll be able to do something very similar, and something will have that effect or a more profound effect on the music.

You'll have the right emotional tone, anyway.
Not so much emotional as textural…The details don't really count on that level.

How arguable is it that the Grateful Dead was more or less an antisocial bunch of guys individually who found more comfort together—
Oh, sure. Misery loves company. [*Laughs*]

Were you all pretty alienated characters?
Let me think. I would say Pigpen, Jerry, and myself were more alienated than Bob and Billy [Kreutzmann, the drummer]. But Bob was on his way.
When I met Billy, he was just out of high school and already married with a child. He was under twenty-one at the time, because we had to get him a phony draft card.…It was a real draft-card—we just had phony information on it. Both he and Bob were underage at that point, and Billy was Captain Straight, because he had a job and a wife and a kid. But it didn't last very long.

In other words…It happened, and there you were.
Essentially, that's really it. I could never have preprogrammed that for my own life. It was an extraordinary set of circumstances. When I look back on it it's so amazing the way it all led for me to be able to do that, even.

Any idea what you'd be doing if you hadn't done this?
I don't know, man. I don't know. I probably would have left music forever. I already had.
If I had never taken this road, who knows what I'd be doing? It's so impossible to even consider it. I had quit my job at the post office. I was living off my old lady, taking acid. She had the job, and I was fuckin' around, man, having a wonderful time. [*Laughs*] Blowing my brains out.

It wasn't just…fun.

No. It turned out to be life. As soon as the first rehearsals started happening and I got over my nervousness over maybe not being able to play the bass with any degree of musicality—that got blown away in the first rehearsal.

When did you start realizing that there might be something of greater human significance available to the Grateful Dead?

Acid Tests. That's when it really hit me. I knew we could make music before that....Let's see, I went down there in June, and two weeks later we played a gig....I guess some time around when we had the [gig] six nights a week, five hours of forty-five minutes on and fifteen minutes off....It was great, boy. That's when I knew we could be a band. I thought of being a band in terms of being a jazz band like the Miles Davis Quintet. That was my idea of a band: even though personnel came and went, it was really a band. It wasn't just Miles' boys.

I'd be willing to bet that not all of your partners conceived of a band—

In that way? No, I'll bet not. Pigpen had a sense of it, because he got a lot of his shit from the Muddy Waters, blues-band stuff.

Where music was your life, not just your business or your trade?

Well, no, the conception of them being a band and the music they made. The lifestyle was such that Pigpen and Bob and Billy were all living separately, and Jerry had a house....We didn't live together until LA, and then we lived together for about a year, and then everybody split off again. It didn't really last that long.

The "family" thing came together after the music did. In the beginning, there was only the five guys—and a few fans, friends. It was the five guys, Billy's wife, Jerry's wife, my old lady—

When did it become clear? Was it ever a discussed and articulated thing?

I think it probably came across when we decided to change the name. That sort of meant we were getting serious, because we couldn't make a record if some other band had the same name as us.

I often wonder if I hallucinated that record, because I never saw it again. I was just thumbing through 45s, you know, in a record store—I don't even know where it was. Probably San Francisco.

I could have hallucinated it. I never saw the record again, never heard a word about the band called the Warlocks. Never, not a word.

I went back and told the boys that I'd seen a record with the name "The Warlocks" on it and if we were serious and wanted to make a record we ought to start thinking about changing our name.

"Grateful Dead" has so much meaning to it—
I'd never heard that phrase before, and when Jerry recited it to me— "Hey, man, how about 'The Grateful Dead'?"—it went [*makes a rapid ticking sound, like the tumblers of his mind going around*]...

It so long ago lost any kind of macabre overtones. We're so used to it that we don't even think of mortality, or of the gruesome meanings of it. It means something else: tie-dyed shirts, granny glasses and loud, loud music.
That, for sure, but it also means a whole segment of folklore—and a bunch of spurious, if I'm not mistaken, Egyptian trips. I've never seen any of those quotes in the Book of the Dead—they're all from hippies.

Childe was real, the guy who catalogued the ballads—
And this book by a guy named McNutt, called *The Grateful Dead*. It's a rundown of all these folk stories about the grateful dead. It's a two-hundred-page book. The stories come from all over the Continent and England.

So this is folklore about satisfied ghosts?
Well, ghosts that have a debt—of honor, usually...[For example], if a husband dies and leaves a debt of honor and the wife just goes on with her life and doesn't take care of business...It's essentially the spirit of the departed hanging about until the debt or point of honor is settled. Then they're the grateful dead; before that they're not...They're essentially ghost stories in the classic sense: the spirit of the departed appears to his friend or his wife or husband or mother.

What about as a rationale for hedonism? "We're already dead—let's party!"
Sure. Hey, what do you think the Acid Test was, partly? [*Laughs*] You're dead when you're born.

You could run an analysis of this business and drive an ordinary consultant berserk with the contradictions and waste in it. And yet...that's the thing: everybody works hard when they have to, and they have the leisure to work leisurely. It's a forgiving organization; it demands absurd things at certain times, and it gives you complete free rein the rest of the time. It may not bother you for weeks on end, but it'll call you at four in the morning to run naked through the snow to deliver something to someone.

[*Laughs*] That's happened.

And nobody seems unwilling to do what needs to be done.

Yeah, as long as it's clear that it needs to be done—and also that it's not just some jackoff.

There's a lot of that that goes on. And furthermore, there are people who in any other place but the Grateful Dead scene couldn't talk to each other. You look at the range of human types—intellects, characters—all the bikers, the hackers, the intellectuals...they all can hang together and find something to talk about.

It is a slice of life.

It's a microcosm.... But how did it happen? How does it transcend... You couldn't build it with girders—you had to just randomly toss rocks into that pile until it created that beautiful thing, whatever it is. It's accidental, like building the Golden Gate Bridge by randomly putting things together.

Yeah, five hundred monkeys with typewriters.

And you can't explain its continued momentum. Maybe you can.

I can't. It's a mystery to me. I think it's wonderful! I'm so glad that it's still going on, because I know I'm not finished with it yet. There's still plenty to be done with it. The great thing is that it has some kind of an audience.

More than audience, though.

Oh, yeah. Let's say that's the basic requirement. As long as we're going to be a musical organization, the only thing *that* really needs for its survival is an audience, right? But somehow it's become more than a musical unit. Like we were talking about earlier, when we were playing those five-set shows six nights a week, we knew it was a band that could be a good band—maybe even one of the best. But then the Acid Tests took it beyond that. That was like somebody says, "Okay, now we're going to go warp speed." Boom! Push the button and away we go.

Kesey used to call us the "faster-than-light drive." I always thought that was great.

How come nobody else ever played music like this, took this approach to it?

You got me.

You probably couldn't have gotten five more diverse musical types, musical traditions, personalities, and approaches together in some forced anarchy where nobody was allowed to be in charge. Maybe that's how it worked, because everybody got to shout as loud as they wanted—and you all, out of necessity, forged a language together.

The Acid Test was partly responsible for that, too, because whoever was in charge at the Acid Test was really in charge. But nine times out of ten if somebody tried to *take* charge, it would just dissolve in their hands.

You mean if somebody was commanding enough with their instrument—

Well, not even with their instrument. Neal Cassady would do it with his hammer, or just weaving around and staggering, looking weird. The Pranksters had their band; they didn't play what you could call music—but "music" is a pretty narrow frame of reference in a certain sense—but they sure played stuff. Did you ever hear that Sound City *Acid Test* record? It's Kesey and Babbs raving on, and Jerry and Pigpen—Pigpen, of all people—went in and played with those guys [in a studio] for two, three hours. I was so stoned; I was talking to Owsley. This was at Sound City in San Francisco, in '66.

Where were you and Owsley?

Out in the anteroom.

You missed the jam?

[*Laughs*] Yes. I was too interested in talking to Owsley. Jerry did the same thing at the Watts Acid Test. I was crazy, because I wanted to play real bad. I really felt like playing, and Jerry was at that place where "Wow, man, playing just isn't really important right now. I've got something on my mind." He was talking to George Walker—just rapping shit back and forth, about what it all meant, I guess. George Walker was one of the main Pranksters.

Anyway, at the Acid Tests the music... The only time our music has had a real sense of proportion in an event, you know. Even at the Trips Festival, we were playing a gig. At the Acid Tests, it was like, sometimes you just couldn't play. I mean the original Acid Tests up here; when we went down to LA, that was also gigs. All the ones up here, boy... Even the Fillmore, that was the last one... That was sort of a gig, too, but boy—that was really the Acid Test. That was the last time we all really got crazy together, because after that it was the Trips Festival, and that was a gig—a real gig, for money.

We all split up the proceeds from the Acid Tests—we charged entrance money—but normally it wasn't much more than getting gas and food for everybody. That was so great [*Laughs*]....

I guess that sort of attitude just sticks with you, because I know that if the Acid Tests had never happened we would have been just another band. I'm pretty sure of that.

But not everybody in this thing was there.

That's true, but at the same time, you can also say that without the Grateful Dead the Acid Tests wouldn't have happened, either. Not in the same way. Or that we would have gone ahead, and ended up with our own version of the Acid Test sooner or later. That's what we were all into.

The facts are that that's who was there. The people who were there—Kesey, Babbs, Cassady, Mountain Girl [a Merry Prankster who later married Jerry Garcia], everybody—those were the right people. And I guess that's the proof of the pudding.

And most of them are still around.

Yeah. They all know that this is some kind of nexus, I guess. The Acid Test itself, the Pranksters, it was a naturally dissipating kind of function. By its very nature, it's centrifugal—

Throwing things off?

Throwing people off, I guess, in a sense. People leave and go their own ways after something like that.

Why did this become more permanent?

Well, because we were a band. When the Acid Tests went their way, we still had a band to operate.

In other words, you had a commercial reason to exist.
Yes and no. I guess that could be right—

In terms of surviving in society, you had to have it. Kesey didn't have enough money from Cuckoo's Nest *to finance a perpetual party. Grateful Dead could generate enough income—*
Besides that, nobody in the Grateful Dead was interested in a perpetual party. We were all interested in being musicians—if not together, separately, although it never came to that.

So the ideal that was created came along with it.
Yeah...

And all the other bands just turned into bands.... This one turned into something else.
Yeah—a time capsule [*Laughs*]. Hey, nothing wrong with being a time capsule, depending on what time you're coming from.

But I'm all prepared to present this argument that there's nothing "sixties" about this band except a commitment to humanity. Everything else—if there ever is a band that plays a gig on a satellite it'll be the Grateful Dead, because by its very nature it's an experimental, forward-looking thing.
How can they accuse us of being old geezers when Bob Weir is doing what he does, Mickey's making three albums at once, you just came up with a bass that never existed before[2]—this is not a tired old thing.
It ain't trendy, that's all....
The chemistry in a good band—even Miles Davis's bands, or the Rolling Stones, any band that's either played together a long time or where the musicians are so great that despite being different they can play together and make great music. That's still just bands. This, apparently, has gone to some other level....
I can't see it from outside; I just know what it feels like.

---

[2]In 1982 Lesh commissioned a six-string bass with one string a fifth higher than the usual bass and one string a fifth lower. He has been refining and developing this instrument since the fall of 1982 in association with Geoff Could of Modulus Graphite Products, Inc., of San Francisco.

Jerry Garcia and Phil Lesh

February 24, 1983
San Rafael, California

*I always figured if I could get two of these guys together the result
would be considerably more than twice the fun, and Phil Lesh arranged
two sessions that proved me right. This session with Garcia and Lesh
took place at Lesh's house; it took a while to get the two men to stop
goofing on me and talk, but we did cover some interesting ground.*

Garcia: Because of the fact that it's ongoing and continually changing,
there's no way that any amount of telling of it is ever going to reveal it to
the point of demystifying it. It's much too complex!

Lesh: If we could explain it to ourselves, we would. But then, we'd
probably lose it.

Garcia: Yeah, right! It's always skittering out of our grasp.

You wouldn't want it any other way, would you?
Garcia: No! Fuck no! It wouldn't be interesting.

Lesh: This is the best.

The fact that it changes, the fact that it's a dynamic—
Garcia: And there's no place in the world where you'd find guys willing to play in this level. That's the thing about it, you know.

Lesh: Realizing your life isn't in your own hands anymore and not caring.

Garcia: We're having faith in it. We're saying, "Let's have faith in this form that has no form. Let's have faith in this structure that has no structure."

Lesh: It's your own subconscious. Sometimes you do things and you don't understand why you do them, and so do we.

It's okay to go on with no stated goal.
Garcia and Lesh: Yeah.

Lesh: Except to stay conscious.

Garcia: Yeah, except to keep it going. Wherever it goes.
    Most job descriptions are narrow, and what we're looking to do is expand, rather than narrow, you know what I mean? Rather than thinking of your job being this, it's open it out to this. Why do you only want to define yourself as a person who does only this, this, and this? You know what I mean? And why should your job be less than you are? If your contribution can be greater, then what we'll do is invent a reason for it to be greater. Dig?

Why does it work?
Garcia: It works because it can. I don't know why it works. I just know that it does. It works because we think it will, probably.

Maybe that's it. The collective will keeps it going.
Garcia: I think that's what all things like that are about. Faith healing, all that shit. Everything like that works because the people involved in it

believe that it will work. The belief system gives form, and the energy has some channel through which to work, and somehow it works. I don't know why or how or any of that stuff about it, but we know that it does work. It might work real fucked up, compared to some other ways, but I really don't think so. In a way, what we're trying to do might be the most efficient way to do things, considering the reality of the way some things really are.

Lesh: I certainly feel like that. Like, we have a paradigm here that could be really meaningful in the new age.

Garcia: That's right. In view of what's known about the nature of the universe, say...this is more of the successful way to go.

Lesh: There's less ego involved here, for one thing....

So the Grateful Dead doesn't correlate a job to human worth.
Garcia: No.

Lesh: And the way the Grateful Dead works is three-dimensional; every move has three dimensions to it.

It affects things on other planes.
Lesh: Yeah, and the interaction of the people in the Grateful Dead organization is more akin to the way a three-dimensional chess game works. In other words, a move at the office will resonate much faster in the Front Street studio than if it had to go all the way across the board to the "distribution of information manager."

Garcia: It's quantum stuff.

It's so dependent on the exact people involved.
Lesh: Even the people who are a little twisted and fucked up sometimes still function. It's hard to understand. And even though I've seen it going on, I hardly believe it myself. But yet it's still happening.

Garcia: It's because you have to be able to allow the entire range of human possibility. Here. Right here and now on this earth, in this life...

It's not often that things fall into a kind of focal plane where you can look at them and talk about them and say, "Hey, maybe it's this or that," you know what I mean? Sometimes that level of comprehension isn't around for years. And then every once in a while it drops in. It's like that moment of clarity, at which point we can look across things and say, "Look, here's where we are now and this is what we seem to be doing." And it seems possible to talk about it and describe it for that moment. And that moment will be as much as we can explain ourselves and that will have to hold everybody because we won't know any more about it than anyone else…until the next time it comes up. It's kind of like that. It's dynamic.

I have walked toward the center from the farthest edge….I've often felt like Toto the dog, pulling back the curtain and exposing the guy working the machine. I would have been much happier believing in the wizard. Knowing how it works can take the romance right out of the situation.
Garcia: I don't think so. How it works is the romance of it. That great Hypnocratic saying, "In the sea of Hypnocracy, the shore is just another wave." That was Saint Dilbert. Isn't that fabulous! That says it all right there, Jack. That's the whole treeth. The truth and the treeth.

The treeth?
Garcia: Yeah, there's the truth and the treeth. The treeth of the matter. That's the treeth of the matter.

There's another good reason to never write again.
Lesh: I promise to play only anti-notes from now on. I've reached the peak of my career and now I'm going to reverse it!

Garcia: Right! Inverse notes! I'm going to play everything I used to play, only starting in the other direction. Going back from now.

• • •

Garcia: It's truly been fantastic.

Lesh: Yeah, beyond our wildest dreams.

Garcia: Totally. Way beyond, way beyond.

You never had any expectations of this? You just fell into this?
Garcia: Yeah, hopes but never *this!* [*Laughter*] It doesn't let up, you know, it keeps going.
   We were lookin' for something else, in a way.

Lesh: We were old friends who happened to—

Garcia: We were looking for good times, really, but extra-special good times with a capital *GT*. Our kind of good times: good and weird.

How did the personal, collective quest turn into this incredible myth? That has grown independently of you guys, obviously.
Lesh: That's not our problem.

Garcia: We don't know, really.

When did it happen? How did it get transferred to the crowd?
Garcia: I don't know. It seems to me that as soon as we were playing at the Acid Tests, you'd look out there and you'd see that guy and he'd look up and go, "Yeah, I know what you guys are doing. I know what you guys are up to!" And you knew that they knew. It was one of those things. It was like one on one. Recognition, it was flashes of recognition. No telling what, really, but that thing that you recognize. And you recognize it because it's there. I could never say what it was.

Lesh: It's communal, in the sense that it exists—

Garcia: In that moment, when that guy look at you and goes "Yeah, I get it."

Lesh: You're both in the same place.

Garcia: That's right. You know, and he knows, and that's that moment.

Lesh: It's as close as you can come to being somebody else.

Garcia: That's deep, there. That is a moment of true knowing.

Lesh: What it is is suspicions confirmed. Yes, there is something like this between people. We've known it among ourselves, and now we know it can happen between us and total strangers.

Garcia: That's right.

Lesh: Mostly it's subconscious. We've trained ourselves in a certain way.

Garcia: That's right. We've had faith in that unspoken, unseen, unknowable in that frontal sense, you know? You've got to trust it just because of reportage. What so many people say about the Grateful Dead has that objective ring about it because they all report it. The reportage is consistent. You've got to say, "Hey man, it's like flying saucers. Are all these people lying?"

Lesh: Are they all deluded? Are they all drugged?

Garcia: They're all experiencing something.

Something more substantial than a leap of faith—
Lesh: No, it's a continual experience.

Garcia: Right. And it's something that's working on some level, and that's the thing that counts.

But I can report to you guys lots and lots of different people whose perceptions are so far from what I know to be true.
Garcia: It doesn't matter. Perceptions are always individuated. There's no contradiction in that.

I could bring people into this room and have them tell you what the Grateful Dead means to them and you'd be amazed.
Garcia: But they would be right.

Lesh: They would be right. We wouldn't necessarily be amazed.

Garcia: It might be one of those recognition things, where they would remind us of something…we already know about. There's nothing to say that we know the most about this that can be known—because we're it—

Lesh: We're just a piece of it, too.

Garcia: That's right…we're not *it*—

Lesh: No. *It* is informing all of us.

Garcia: That's exactly right. So our opinions are just that. They're our opinions, in our tradition.

Lesh: And our position.

Garcia: That's true. A unique experience. But everybody who experiences it, on whatever terms anyone experiences it, is right about it.

Lesh: It's like we're all orbiting around the sun. By the very nature of that situation, we each look at it in a different way.

Garcia: Right, and its warmth falls on all of us.

Lesh: Yes.

But it does function as a religion for a lot of people. It may not be a religion—
Lesh: Well, maybe we're talking about different things.

Garcia: That word *religion* has a whole lot of…negative to it.

It fulfills the societal role of religion to a lot of people.
Lesh: It used to. I don't believe that it fulfills that role anymore. There are other things, like games, like sports.

Deadheads belong to this to an exclusion. They are as devoted to this, and ascetic in pursuit of it—many of them—
Garcia: Well that's okay to me, too, because it's a religion to me, too, on a certain level.
    I don't like the word *religion*. It's a bad word. I'd like to not have that concept—

Well, let's assign a new word to it—
Garcia: No. I don't want to assign any word to it. Why limit it? I want it to surprise me, to continue to surprise me. I don't want to know anything about it.

Santa Barbara, California, June 4, 1978. Bob Weir (left), Jerry Garcia. (Photo by Bruce Polonsky)

Blair Jackson (left) and David Gans interviewing Jerry Garcia, June 11, 1981. (Photo by Dennis Callahan)

Jerry Garcia, June 11, 1981. (Photo by Dennis Callahan)

Bob Weir at Front Street, November 1981. (Photo by David Gans)

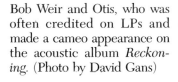

Bob Weir and Otis, who was often credited on LPs and made a cameo appearance on the acoustic album *Reckoning*. (Photo by David Gans)

San Francisco mayor Dianne Feinstein and Bob Weir at a press conference in the mayor's office to announce the Bay Area Music Awards, February 25, 1983. (Photo by David Gans)

Jerry Garcia, Irvine Meadows, California, March 27, 1983. (Photo by David Gans)

Working on Bobby and the Midnites' *Where the Beat Meets the Street*, Mill Valley, January 1984. Producer Jeff Baxter (left), Bob Weir, engineer Larold Rebhun. (Photo by David Gans)

Mickey Hart warms up at the Greek Theatre, Berkeley, California, July 1984. (Photo by David Gans)

Phil Lesh at the Greek Theatre, Berkeley, California, July, 1984. (Photo by David Gans)

Grateful Dead sound designer Dan Healy and the tapers, Berkeley Community Theatre, October 1984. (Photo by David Gans)

Phil Lesh taking calls from listeners on the Deadhead Hour. KFOG, San Francisco, August 25, 1986. (Photo by Mary Eisenhart)

Grateful Dead, 1987: Bob Weir, Jerry Garcia, Mickey Hart, Bill Kreutzmann, Phil Lesh, Brent Mydland. (Photo by Herb Greene)

Bob Weir, December 30, 1986.
(Photo by Glenn Mar)

Photo for *Jerry Garcia Acoustic and Electric* at the Lunt-Fontanne Theatre, New York, 1987. (Photo by Herb Greene)

Robert Hunter (right), David Gans. Black Oak Books, Berkeley, November 3, 1990. (Photo by Mary Eisenhart)

Grateful Dead, fall 1990. Phil Lesh, bass and vocals; Bill Kreutzmann, drums and percussion; Bob Weir, guitar and vocals; Mickey Hart, drums and percussion; Jerry Garcia, guitar and vocals; Vince Welnick, keyboards and vocals; Bruce Hornsby, keyboards and vocals. (Photo by Susana Millman)

I experiment with it as much as I can, with my little part of it. That's one of the reasons why I know that it isn't us. It's not something we're cookin' up—

Lesh: Who could have cooked up something like this: None of us, in our wildest dreams.

Garcia: Right, you can't manipulate or control it like you could something like a religion. It isn't something that I'm doing, and that's what makes it real special. It's not something I'm causing. We're not originating, we're not making it happen.

Lesh: It's got us, and it's so good. For us, myself, it's faith. I don't know about the Deadheads, but I'll tell you what it is for me. I have faith in this thing, whatever the fuck it is.

Garcia: Yeah, me, too. And it's taken a long time to get it…to get comfortable with it.

Does it wax and wane for you like it does for us?
Garcia: Yeah, because I'm a terrible skeptic. We all are. We've seen the elephant, we don't believe nothin'! We're the hardest to convince of all. If anybody is skeptical, it's us.

Lesh: I still believe in it. It still works. It's slow, it's anarchic, and sometimes it sputters and fuckin' won't start.

But when it pays off, it makes it worth all the dues.
Garcia: Yeah, it comes up triple bars, man. Pours out all the dollars, all the golden yummies.

Lesh: For a short time.

Garcia: For seconds on end!

• • •

Garcia: You'd be amazed at the mundane levels you never get above at the most highest concert, as far as consciousness goes. I mean there are times—

Lesh: "Oh, shit, my feet hurt!"

Garcia: Right! Or, "This string doesn't look right."

Lesh: That's where consciousness is a burden.

Garcia: That's the stuff! The ones I love are the ones where it's like, slippery. The best of everything is all around. I don't know how to explain it, but it's just, like, easy. It's just the coolest feeling in the world...the best, it's just so special.

Lesh: You can't put your fingers in the wrong place. It's impossible. I've tried. And you hear it back and it's still cool.

Garcia: That's all stuff that tells you about the objective nature of it, you know what I mean? How it's out there, it ain't in here. That's one of the reasons why you can trust it.

Lesh: It's finding out that something exists outside of you.

Garcia: That's the special, great special treat of life. Hooray!

Lesh: Hooray!

Steve Parish, Jerry Garcia, Phil Lesh, et al.

March 10, 1983
San Rafael, California

In any other band an interview with a "roadie" might be for the purpose of finding out what gauge of string the guitarist uses, the model numbers of the amplifiers, and some arcane lore about signal processing. In the Grateful Dead, members of the road crew—as well as the office staff— are virtually full partners in the operation. Ram Rod, who has been with the band the longest, is responsible for the drums and is also the president of the corporation. Bill "Kidd" Candelario handles the bass and keyboards and is also the head of Grateful Dead Merchandising. And Steve Parish, who takes care of the guitars, manages the Jerry Garcia Band.

Phil Lesh arranged this interview, which took place at his house. The transcript doesn't do justice to the hilarity and chaos of the occasion. At times there were two conversations going on at once, and various people

217

left the dining-room table for a while and then rejoined the discussion later. Parish is not what I would call approachable, and I was grateful to Phil for making the interview happen. I had long suspected that getting any two of these guys together would yield exponentially higher quality storytelling, and the Lesh-Garcia session a few weeks earlier had borne this out. But I also knew that a session like this had the potential to turn into a feeding frenzy or a torrent of unusable bullshit—so I was relieved and gratified when Parish turned out to be so warm and Phil and Jerry also rose to the occasion.

Jill Johnson, who appears late in the transcript, is now married to Phil Lesh and the mother of his two sons, Graham and Brian.

When did you join this thing?
Parish: I started hanging out heavy '69 to '70, end of '69. I started back East, working at this theater. I met the guys, and then I just moved out here. I'd been living out here in '68—

Lesh: This guy was such a natural—

Deadhead?
Parish: Yeah, believe it or not, I was a Deadhead.

Lesh: —just a good guy—

Parish: But I didn't know how much of [a Deadhead] I was, really, till I got—

Lesh: "Who's Jerry's new pal?"

Parish: Jerry sorta could see something in me, and he tried to help me. I had to pay my dues like we all do. I didn't know anything—you had to learn everything. I had some really good teachers, and that's the main thing.

Philosophy, electronics, drugs, what? All of the above?
Parish: You got it, man. I was just the raw material, somewhere in there.

Grateful Dead made you the man you are today?

Parish: Yeah, definitely. They take the raw material and mold it—

Lesh: You had something going for you—

Parish: Yeah, but I blossomed. I had to positively blossom—
But I'd like to talk about the crew, because that's an amazing thing. All of us have been working together for a very long time, and we've seen a lot of people come and go. There's an amazing bond that we have. We've been through so many different scenes in so many different places that we could never even tell people, that hold us together. That's something that you always know. . . . We never even understand how strong it is until it's called on, and then it's a really powerful force. All of us together create this one thing, and can do something together by doing our little parts of it. It touches you sometimes, when you think about it, even though it has its humdrum side. But it never gets a habit, see, because when you start getting [into] habit you always make mistakes—and you can't afford to do that. You fall into habits, and that's the worst thing that can happen to any of us. When we just start doing stuff because it's there, and we stop feeling what we're doing—it's really easy to do, because you start getting into a routine, and you want to do the same thing every day. The brain, when it gets into one little pattern, it stops branching out and seeing, and that's a bad thing to happen for some people. But it doesn't happen to us, because we don't let it. You've got to fight that—it's like a creeping fungus or something, falling into a habit. But a gig always is a gig, and anything can happen. That's the thing that's good about it.

Mickey said, "Ram Rod has to set my drums up exactly the same every time, because if a cymbal is half an inch too close I could break a finger. . . . That's a big responsibility. If he's going to go to all that trouble to do that job so well, I sort of owe it to him to play well."
Parish: Ram Rod is the guy that taught us all that dignity. He really did bring that into it. He just has a way. He's a really good teacher. He never withheld any information that he had, if he believed in somebody—and he did believe in me, I was lucky . . . he started teaching me stuff.
I worked for another band, Quicksilver, for a while. I remember one time when it was getting pretty strange. [Rex] Jackson took me down to LA when we were doing a show in El Monte, 1970-something. . . . I worked like half of 1970 for Quicksilver, because a job came up there. I was

hanging out in our scene here, but it was time to get something together. This job came up....

All my friends were on the Grateful Dead crew, and we were pretty close at that time. There was a tight scene; the two bands were both located in Marin, they shared a lot of history, and stuff like that. Anyway, I couldn't leave the Grateful Dead feeling behind for another band. Everybody understood it, and they helped me to get in and start working for it. It was just a clear choice. When things start happening, they start snowballing.

The first time I had to do all this equipment for Quicksilver, I really didn't know what I was doing. You can't fake it, because the amplifiers won't let you. Then I learned about amps firsthand; before that I was watching a lot. I started learning, and then I realized what the bottom line to it all was: electricity. [*Laughs*] You get a couple of good shocks, you really get a respect for it. You start learning what you're doing—you want to learn to preserve yourself and your friends. [*General laughter*]

It is really an adventurous job in a lot of ways, because when you drive somewhere in the middle of the night with all this band's equipment on your back...You saw it go...you set up for that show, with all those things that were happening, then it's all folded up in these boxes, put together just right in the truck....

It's that whole carnival, circus, "pack it up in the middle of the night and move" trip that's really an adventure—and an American trip all the way. But it's also universal...

Are we getting anywhere?

Yeah! I just wish the tape recorder was invisible.
Parish: It doesn't bother me at all. I'm just looking at it; I just like to watch the lights....

So what do you want to know about?

[Jerry Garcia arrives.]
Garcia: C'mon, Steve—what's it all about, man?

Parish: It started fifty-seven years ago when a lonely doctor in Germany invented cloning—

Lesh: And then Steve was born.

Parish: Back to dignity.

Garcia: Dignity above all things. Did you ever see *Singin' in the Rain?* It's got a great song at the beginning, a thing about dignity where Donald O'Connor and Gene Kelly are coming up to a premiere. Gene Kelly's all dressed in white, and he's saying, "Above all, dignity." Then it goes through this series of flashbacks of him and Donald O'Connor playing these sleazy sideshows and medicine shows, snake-oil things—where they learned their chops.

It's not like a typical employer-employee deal—
Parish: Not at all. You've got this common ground: the equipment. The equipment is our common ground, and we have this sort of responsibility to each other for it.

Garcia: We rely on it, and it relies on them.
   It's one of those things where you could split it all different ways. You could opt out in favor of one hundred percent total efficiency and have somebody that you didn't like doing it....A guy like Steve isn't totally efficient, but there's lots more levels to him than that. It's not just the fact that he lugs the equipment around and keeps it in good shape or any of that shit—'cause he doesn't. He fucks up all the time. [*Laughter*]

Parish: If people have faith in you long enough, eventually—if you're a decent person and if you're not a bad person—it kind of starts to sink through the ooze eventually. But we have a good teaching scene.

Garcia: You worked for us for a long time before you actually got into the technical odds and ends—

Parish: Yeah. I was doing a lot on just a physical level for a long time, and I didn't really take the initiative to learn what I could have.

Garcia: And you weren't called upon, really; it wasn't necessary.

Parish: And you could do a lot of things that were highly technical but not know what you were doing sometimes. You were just sort of going through the motions. And from doing that so much, but still trying to figure out what's happening—and having good teachers around, which we always did—that was the most amazing part...If you ever wanted to know anything, you could ask.

Garcia: [Dan] Healy is a fantastically good teacher. He's really good; he's the guy who taught everybody in the crew. He's got a good way of being able to talk about any number of technical things without losing you. He's really got a gift at it.

It's better to know; it doesn't do to have it be arcane. When Owsley was doing it it was esoteric, 'cause he was not so good of a teacher, in that way. He's another kind of teacher, really. Ram Rod will tell you that he learned a lot of stuff from Owsley, but it's one of those things where you learn stuff from Owsley sort of by osmosis, by hanging out with him or living with him, like Ram Rod did for a long time.

Parish: Ram Rod can explain to me things....He can tell me how to do something, but maybe he can't tell me why I'm doing it. I learned from him—he was a good teacher—but he taught...We were talking about that dignity thing, and he has that thing down. He really cares! If you treat all that stuff like part of us—and it is, really, it does talk to us—

Garcia: It makes its presence felt.

Parish: There's another thing about dignity on the road: When the show's over, that's pack-out, everybody leaves. And you've got to still take the stuff. That's when you've got to keep your dignity; that's one of the really amazing things—you've got to do that.

There's got to be something in it for you to put up with the long hours and the tedium. You don't even get to get up and play!
Parish: It's this adventurous thing that you can do, man, and—you couldn't actually put those people together any other way except the way they did.

Garcia: It fell together, really. It's one of those things.

Parish: People have come in and out of it, but the skeleton is still there, sort of. It's grown and changed a little, but—

Garcia: And they're on the line, really, when we play. They're up there sweating it out like we are, too.

Parish: Yeah. You have to pay attention a lot.

Garcia: 'Cause we go nuts when something goes wrong onstage. That's when those guys are really under the gun. Every one of us turns into a bug-eyed monster [*shouts wildly*] shrieking, and Steve'll be sweating and tearing things apart—

Parish: You'll be around, hanging out back there, and all of a sudden there's a noise that just rips through you. You can hear it, and you know what it is, instinctively, just from living with that stuff. We always do—we spend many, many hours with it, and we always did and always will. You can never do enough. Electricity is a strange thing.... It likes to mess with people.

Something strange will happen sometimes. It's just a magical touch, either one way or another. Things will come so close—they'll teeter, and then something'll happen. And you realize—only one or two people would know what happened, you know?

Garcia: And there's a perceptual, a credibility gap, too. You know something's wrong, but nobody will believe you. It's one of those things—

Parish: Yeah, that's right.

Garcia: It's something real subtle, and you know damn well there's something weird about your stuff, and you'll say, "Hey, man, there's"— and a lot of times it's so subtle that I can only tell it from touch or something. But he's learned to trust me—

Parish: Eventually it works itself out. It took a long time—

Garcia: He's running little tests on me [*Laughter*]. I loved it that time when you changed all my strings but one. He just wanted to see if I'd notice. [*Laughter*]

...Equipment stuff has a weird personality all its own, and sometimes it can be real ornery. I know that I've evolved all my shit based on the way it talks to me, how it behaves.

Parish: There's all these different levels of it, too. When you're driving the stuff at night, all the equipment's back there and it's talking to you in a different way than it talks to them when they're playing onstage. Then it's telling you, "Hey, man, come on! Take it easy—don't whip me around....Put me over here." It teaches you how to put it, over years—to learn what you can put what way, or it'll break and you won't have it when you need it at the show. You have to come to this place with it, and it tells you that, too. It's real strange, you know.

There's that time when it's onstage, and these guys are playing on it—and then there's this other time when we've got it. It's ours, and we've got to do a thing with it, and it talks to us. And you'd better listen when it talks—that's what I've learned. It takes a long time; you say, "That can't be"—you don't believe it, but then it happens....

Within the Grateful Dead, laws of common American business physics are suspended. There's this whole other thing that happens here, you know.
Parish: Maybe these guys would see somebody playing something somewhere, and then you say, "That guy's fucked—he ain't playing that right." I see a guy drunk doing equipment, and I think, "That ain't right." So you just learn what your own responsibilities are going to be, because you're in a world where everybody is trying to party—and trying to get you to party. You're trying to do something else sometimes and still party with them, and it gets to a place where you can get really out there. But you can't lose responsibility. That's the thing you've got to remember.

Garcia: It's not as though we're a business trying to be a loose business; what we really are is like artists trying to survive in that half-world of entertainment, which is much more conscious of its entertainment self than it is of its artist self.

Lesh: It's still the only place we could possibly survive.

Garcia: Right. It's the only niche there is—

Lesh: That twilight zone between art and reality...

Parish: Plus, the crew has a group therapy thing that we do. You get it right out. We spend that night [on the bus], and that always helps. Plus you'll be made fun of if you fuck up—

I noticed that—everybody busts everybody.
Parish: That keeps you going; that keeps you on your toes. Like, no one was waking us up on the crew—you had to learn to get up. Then you'd wake up on time, because you don't want to get left in Nebraska, man! [*Laughter*]

Garcia: The road thing is, some people can adapt to it and some can't. Some people really go to pieces on the road—

Parish: We've had some people we took out, and they only lasted like one trip—guys that worked on the PA or something, some great genius, and they just couldn't do it.
   They tried to replace me—[*he leans over and enunciates it again right into the microphone*] They tried to replace me [*laughter*]—and the guy got flaky, that's all. I didn't do anything to him.

Garcia: We had three normal idiots to replace Steve; no matter how we wired them together, they still didn't go off at the same time.

Parish: You can get on the carpet in this organization, too—don't think you can't. When everybody's mad at you at once all of a sudden, then you know you did something wrong.

Lesh: But it only lasts for a very short time—have you ever noticed that?

Parish: Yeah, the quality of our mercy.

Belonging to your job is kind of neat.... The social end and the business end are all tied up, so if you're ostracized in business you're ostracized in life as well, right? It's not like you can go home from your job and kick the dog, because the dog belongs to the Grateful Dead, too.
Parish: Also, everybody was always playing practical jokes on each other for the first about six years, constantly. If you ever let your guard down your foot would be on fire, or you got a real weird haircut—and a lot worse stuff that I can't talk about.
   There was a high level of spontaneous comedy that used to come down. It just pops up sometimes, and that keeps you going. If you can laugh at it, then at least you know you're OK. That really helps.

● ● ●

Garcia: I'll say to Steve, "Let's go over to Leo's [music store] and check out all the new shit," because I'll want to see if there's stuff that adds novelty to what I'm doing, things that I can do to my sound that are going to be useful in some way. Or I'll try new amplifiers...I'll just get on a kick, 'cause I'll be thinking that there's something I need to add to what I'm doing, just because I'm bored with where I'm at.

The band has a similar rise-and-fall thing that's different from the individual thing. The band's music has a certain periodicity to it, where it's fresh and novel and we're approaching it new again; then after a certain amount of playing it'll start to get a little stale. That's much shorter than what I go through individually.

I suspect that there are a lot of subtleties to it—
Garcia: There are a lot of subtleties.

There are long-throw cycles and short-throw cycles.
Garcia: Yes.

Parish: It takes a long time on some stuff. I can't believe some of the simple stuff that I should have been paying attention to that it took me a long time to realize....You take them for granted if they're right there in front of you, you know? You don't give them the attention that they need, and the stuff really likes attention.

Garcia: Like my effects rack.

Parish: Even the speakers, or the smallest cable; if you take it for granted—ever—it'll catch you. And that takes so many years—you wouldn't believe how subtle it is. My father dabbled in electronics and stuff like that, and I knew about it....You take things for real simple, and you don't realize how weak a lot of things are in this world. If you put them to a test, mechanically, a lot of things would break when you need them not to. You've got to learn to take care of things, and that's a responsibility that you couldn't learn any other way unless you cared about it.

Garcia: I try to make Steve's gig easier by coming up with a setup that's fairly straightforward and fairly direct so he hasn't got a whole bunch of extra wires and shit to fool around with. When something goes wrong onstage, you don't want to have to be going through every little thing— you only want to have a few things to deal with.

Parish: That's where that trust thing comes in, because when he tells me what he thinks it is, I have to zero in on that; otherwise, like he says, we'd have to follow a very myriad path—it would be a lot of things.

Garcia: I could be wrong about that, too, so I expect Steve's help; I expect him to be paying attention. He might notice that a speaker has frozen up before I do, or I'll know that something's wrong but I won't know what it is. I'll just complain in some vague way—sometimes that's all I do, say "something's wrong"—and he has to go at it from there.

Parish: Usually you can find it if you just sit there and think about it.

Garcia: It's on me to try to communicate more clearly to him what I think it is....But I feel that equipment wants to be as streamlined as possible, and as hard-wired as possible, so that there are few weak links in the system itself. That makes it easier on everybody's level.

Parish: Jerry's had a lot of patience. He could have said, "This guy doesn't know all the stuff I need him to know right now," but instead he looked at [me]—I think—in the larger sense and said, "This guy has enough heart and wants to stay and has passed so-and-so points, and maybe I can teach him." Because he's the one who really knows what he wants it to sound like. That's a very personal thing, a man and his equipment—for anybody, any musician. I learned that from playing an instrument in school: you and your instrument are tight—it's part of you. It's like a bike or a car, where you have to become a substructure of another structure other than yourself. Then you can only be as together as your guy is, and our guys are together. They know what they want, and it's so hard to express it—but through years and years of knowing what the person's up to, what can go wrong, what this thing sounds like...A lot of it is just hard knocks, and if you think someone can take it, well maybe you could teach him anything. You could take any person—

Garcia: You've got to have faith in the guy. If I didn't have a fundamental faith in Steve, he wouldn't be in the position that he's in of responsibility in relation to me and my stuff. It can drive me crazy, and it can also make me really happy. It's a place of real importance, but it's also important to me that the human level be cool, too. I would rather make allowances and work on the efficiency of my own stuff to make it so there isn't so much to go wrong, because it's important for me to have someone who's a cool person doing it. That counts. That's why I don't want a mindless automaton who's just a fuckin' technical expert—that's not what I want. I want somebody who's a real person. There's more to life—and there's more to rock 'n' roll, and there's more to our jobs—than just the level of our specific work. Sometimes he finds himself in the role of a security guy, or something. The way of life means that he has to wear more than one hat—and all of those things require somebody who has some sense of a higher vision. What we're going after here is like higher, really—there's more to it, and not everybody is capable of having that kind of vision, and rock 'n' roll doesn't encourage that, really. The whole roadie thing doesn't particularly encourage that. That's one of those things that's built into our scene because we want more to be there.

Parish: I've seen guys that had the same chances, and they couldn't respond to that. They either went too far into something, or they decided, "I've got to be somebody else in this scene," and tried to shift, and that didn't work for them. They couldn't really be happy with what they're doing. If you can be happy with what you're doing and realize that you're getting a chance to do it—if you don't respond to it, then you don't belong there, anyway.

Garcia: And then they've also got to be able to get off the road and come back here and duke it out with the rest of us, you know, in our ongoing—and the office scene, and the rest of it. The Grateful Dead is truly a twenty-four-hours-a-day thing. It doesn't ever stop, so there's got to be that level of participation, like it or not. Everybody adapts to it as individuals—no way you can take somebody and train them for it. It's formless, you know. It requires people who are sensitive, people who have a sense of humor, and who are a little bit out there—who embrace a little bit of misfit power.

Like Barlow says, it's a real community.
Parish: It is. And you know something? Our people are really honest—honest with each other. We might do whatever we have to get down the

road, but to each other there's a certain honesty. You can't lie. When we're together out there, it'd be useless if after all these years we lied to each other. If a guy asks you, "Hey, have you got so-and-so"—and he needs it to do his job—you give it to him. He might have something you need an hour later, or a day later. You might have a big fight with a guy, because you're living together and there are things that happen, but if something happens for the show then all of a sudden he'll be there, handing you a light or a tool or something.

Garcia: You do have to be honest with everybody.... That's why we can get through all that: there's something bigger at the end of the road, something that counts. It helps make it easy for you to be honest.

Parish: We have to cover each other—it's like an all-for-one, one-for-all thing. You can't deny it. And we've been out there long enough now to see cycles in the public that have shown us that we can't ever forget the old lessons that we've learned—because they'll come back again to haunt you if you forget being cool.

Garcia: If you don't pick up on them the first time you'll definitely have to pick up on them the second, or third, or fourth, or twenty-fifth time. They do keep popping up, recurring.

Parish: You've got to try and second-guess the worst things that can happen, so they don't. Like you get a flat tire or something, or there's a place with a lot of cops and they don't like rock bands in that town—you have to mind your p's and q's.

Garcia: There's certain human weirdness that falls in with it. There's what we call the "moth to the flame" syndrome. There are certain people who get fixated on the Grateful Dead, obsessed with it. You don't want to have those people locked up, or you don't want to have to beat them up and leave them in an alley somewhere. They definitely are going to get in your face—they could be weird, potentially, but it's one of those things that you have to handle as you go. You have to be able to roll with it, to some extent. You have to have a little bit of empathy for people, because the Grateful Dead can be very powerful and people can get sucked into it in a way that can be harmful to them. You like to be able to spare people—

Parish: You've got to like people to do it. But if you do it for all these years, gosh! there's so many nice people, there really are.

Garcia: Yeah, there are so many good people in that. That's one of the things that help give you the strength to keep on doing it—that plus the fact that occasionally it's beautiful and perfect. When it's happening...

Parish: And when things are going against you and you pull it together, then you feel really good—because you did something as a team, and you can't beat team spirit. It really is a good feeling.

Garcia: Yeah. The thing of getting off and just having your thing together is neat. The crew guys have lots of levels of that that it's hard to notice from the outside and hard to see except for when we're on the road and we've been on the road for a while. There's times when those guys are really clicking, and nobody gets a chance to see it, really. When they're at their virtuoso level, when they're warmed up—like when the band is warmed up, really cooking, from the first moment to the end it's happening. Nobody gets to see the crew at their peak, when they're having their magic times.

Parish: Usually at our shows, there'll be one person that'll come up and say, "Thanks," or something. Then you feel good.

• • •

Parish: If I could tell you all the funny little things that happened to bring me here—it's amazing. And I won't forget them, either, because they're part of why you're supposed to do what you do. If you remember how you got there and know where you're going—hope that you have a goal.

You mean cases where some third party—some totally unrelated thing—bent your course?
Parish: Completely!

Garcia: Just like all of us, really. Our lives were suddenly altered by random elements. That's what's fascinating: the synchronicity, how we all arrived by these weird, circuitous routes. None of us ever planned to get to this place.

Parish: The guys in the crew all come from different places. It's a strange thing in that way.

Garcia: And the crew really invented itself. There never was a time when any of us in the band hired Ram Rod, for example. Ram Rod was suddenly there working. I remember: "Who is that guy again? That guy with the blue eyes—an Oregon guy? He never says anything.... Ram Rod—oh, yeah, he's a good guy." I didn't know when exactly he attached himself to it.... Somebody else in the scene got him working because he was around and he was a good guy. He was part of Kesey's scene, so everybody trusted him. However he got in there, he got in there. Jackson, too—[1]

Parish: He just came...he was Ram Rod's old friend.

Garcia: And so all of a sudden here were these guys. It wasn't like we hired them. They invented themselves—kind of like the band, really. It's fascinating.

Parish: We went through a lot of strange stuff. We came so close.... People snaked in and out of it, but the skeleton is always there. It's amazing.

Another thing Barlow said was, "You're not going to find a weak mind in the bunch."
Parish: That's true, too. That's an amazing thing.

I haven't run into anybody that's boring.
Parish: We wouldn't stand for it. They couldn't make it through the grueling, rigorous initiation, man, which goes on for years. You have to prove yourself on so many levels.... Little games that we play, sort of like initiation rites, on the crew. You have to run a certain gamut, and I couldn't figure out why—

Garcia: You've got guys like Kidd [Candelario] nippin' at your heels day in and day out. [*Laughs*]

Parish: That was all part of it. When you're getting yelped at, you love to

[1]Rex Jackson, longtime crew member and eponym of the Dead's Rex Foundation, died in a car accident in 1976.

yelp at someone else. We used to have some fights—people would look at us and say, "They must hate each other," but we loved each other. If somebody else from outside messed with us, they were like opening up Pandora's box.

But also, you can't fake it. You can't pass those tests—
Garcia: You can't pretend to pass them.

Parish: There's no way you can bullshit and travel on the road.

Garcia: It's making itself up as it goes along; it's making up its requirements and its identity as it goes along. You've got to be light on your feet.

Parish: You've got to be able to take a hotfoot as a joke at five o'clock in the morning when you're trying to sleep sitting up in a seat and you're pissed off and your back hurts, maybe you're wounded....

Garcia: Or your heart's broken.

Parish: And then everybody's laughing at you, so maybe then you'll laugh. Or maybe something else. It's that old thing of travelin' on the road—baseball teams have it, circus people have it—it's what you keep going on.

Parish: It's esprit de corps. You're proud of yourselves, too.

You're real fortunate to have something so trying and rewarding to belong to.
Garcia: It's not a matter of fortune....It is fortune that we're successful at it—

Parish: You have to work for it.

As a life experience, I don't think anybody could choose—
Garcia: Sure you could.

Could you? A more interesting, more challenging—
Garcia: We did. You could choose something as interesting, as challenging, just by saying, "I am not going to go for any bullshit, and as long as

we've won this much territory let's go on and be as uncompromising as we've been so far." And if it ever lets us down, fuck it—we had a good ride, and it's back to the gas station. You must keep upping the ante— that's the only way you do it. You keep parlaying what you've got, because the whole thing is a dream when you come right down to it. The worst that happens is that you end up back where you were, and back where we were is something that we can all handle anyway. So since you're out there in a dreamland to begin with, the thing to do is to keep going for it.

I feel like it's a responsibility, for me, just because events in my life suggested to me that it was maybe going to be my responsibility to keep pushing it back. When I was in that accident, man, back in '60, it really changed a lot in my life—an automobile accident....A guy who was part of our social scene then, Paul Spiegel, who was a painter—and really the most talented person in our scene—got killed in this accident. For me it was crushing, but I had this feeling that my life had been spared to do something; I felt that I had to live somebody else's life for them—a little of that energy. But I felt that whatever, it's important to not take any bullshit, to either go whole hog or not go at all. So as soon as things started happening—as soon as the first lucky little thing started happening—I felt, "Man, we're duty-bound to push this as far as we can push it." If this situation says, "Be outrageous," be as outrageous as you can possibly be. Let's go for it, because what else do we have? We had nothing else, and we'd all paid some version of those kind of dues.

Parish: In a way, we're all misfits....

Garcia: Anybody who wants to can do it, you know. Who are we to have been able to do it? We're not somebody special—we're just regular people. If we can do it, any-fuckin'-body can do it, man, that's my feeling. If you go at it with people you genuinely get off on, people who you dig.

When I say "fortunate," I mean I'm delighted to be able to earn my living as a writer....If you don't enjoy what you do for a living, you're not living.
Garcia: Really, man. You've tried to convince people that's the case, haven't you? You've spoken to people who aren't doing what they'd like to do—

It makes me feel like I'm rubbing it in—
Garcia: That's right. I've spoken to a lot of people, and they say, "Gee, I'd sure like to be able to do something like that." And the only thing that's

keeping anybody from doing exactly that is the fact that they don't believe they can do it. It's frustrating, because you say, "Hey, man, it's the easiest thing in the world: all you have to do is just do what you want and don't do anything else."

Parish: One time this guy called Jerry and said, "I want to be on the crew—I think I'm right."

Jerry said, "Call Parish; he's in his room. He can probably give you an idea." I started trying to explain to the guy; I didn't just hang up on him or laugh it off. I said, "Man, it's a strange thing. I can't explain it to you. We were friends, and then these guys taught me something; it took years of just hanging out on one level...."

The guy started crying on the phone. He went, "Oh, no, c'mon, I've got to do this." It was the weirdest thing. I said, "Man, if there was a test, you just failed it." And I hung up on him.

Then about two years later, in London—it was the end of the show and the band had left. It was Wembley Pool. This guy comes bounding up the steps and says, "Parish, Parish, it's me! I'm the guy"—here's this happy idiot, telling me, "I'm the guy who called you. Remember, I cried on the phone and everything."

I said, "Great. Glad you're here, but get out of the way—we're busy." The guy had so little idea—he was standing there, and we were lifting stuff, packing it into cases, totally at the peak of our thing. It's like a guy walking out and talking to you while you're onstage or something.

This guy took it the whole route of being a complete idiot. He got in the way as bad as he could. I don't think we've ever seen him again.

Garcia: Certain people I'll refer to Parish. I got a wonderful call on the phone from somebody this last year when we were out, somebody who gave Parish a rave review. Steve had gotten up and talked to some people in the hospitality suite. He was almost in tears—but he was real beautiful, the way he talked about Steve. He said great things about him. It made me feel good, because I can do that. If somebody calls me up, and I know they're weird—and maybe they're even hurting, you know, looking for something; it's that moth-to-the-flame syndrome—if somebody's coming from that point of view of wanting to be on the crew or something like that, I know that I can honestly refer them to Steve and he won't shine them on if he's in the right space. But I know that Steve will be honest with them. If he ain't in the right space he'll just tell them to go fuck themselves, but I know he'll be honest. That's the key. If he isn't in the space to communicate with them, he'll communicate honestly, and he won't bullshit the guy.

Parish: We always have to have new blood boiling in.

Garcia: Yeah, you want to communicate to people that "Hey, there is a possibility to get into something that you'll love. If it's not this, it could be something else."

Jill Johnson: Remember in Jamaica, when we first got there after a long flight, a couple of little girls at the hotel...I know you must have been tired—

Garcia: I remember. I was tired.

Johnson: And you were really nice, talked to them and let them take pictures—

Garcia: Well, because I think they're real people. I remember how hard it was for me—in fact, it was so hard for me that I frequently didn't do it—to talk to the people who were my idols, or people whose music I liked. It was very hard for me when I was a fan. If I had gone up to somebody and they'd been mean to me, it would have crushed me.

Parish: We can't forget them, because they're everything—really. We wouldn't be anything—there would be no need for them to have a crew or a show or anything if it wasn't for those people.

Garcia: I care for them, you know, because they're letting us do this.

Parish: Yeah. I look out for them as much as I can. I really love them, because they're really good people.

Garcia: Yeah, and I'm only human. I have my short times.
  I try to be who I am and do what I do, you know what I mean, and...I try not to be an asshole. You do feel some self-consciousness on that level, but I also know that it's important for me to try to demystify that role and to be human with those people. So I allow a certain amount of it. I get

paranoid if I keep my door closed too long. People knock on my door and say, "Can we get your autograph," or talk to you, or turn you on, or something—if I don't let some of those people in and talk to them one-on-one, I feel like I'm losing contact. There's been times in my life when I burned myself out doing that, when I'd sit up all night five nights in a row raving with some hippies. I've burned myself out often enough to know that what people really want me to do is play well. And I know that if I approach them on that level and say, "Listen, it's important—I haven't had much rest, and I want to play well tonight," they'll usually give me a pass—even if they've waited for months to talk to me. If I'm polite to them, they're usually kind and polite to me. They're good people.

Sometimes they get a little excited, but if you remember what the whole thing is like, that's the key to it for me. I used to do that same stuff, like standing in line for hours for a ticket. I did all that shit—drive for hundreds and hundreds of miles to see someone. I've put in my dues on that level, and I know what it's like. All I have to do is project myself back to that and remember what it's like. That helps. And the other part is that I remember that those people are real people—they're not some kind of half-people. There's all kinds of temptations in rock 'n' roll to shine them on and bullshit them, turn into an asshole. But for me, it's important not to—and it's important to maintain some level of contact. It counts for me.

You never know who's going to bring you a message. That's another thing, on another level. On a more psychedelic level, I know that there are times—especially back when things were very psychedelic—sometimes a strange person in the crowd, a stranger would appear and say a sentence to me, and that sentence would say everything that I needed to hear at that moment. It was like God speaking to you, and if I hadn't been receptive enough to let that happen, or if I had shied away from it or locked my door, or done any of those things that I could have done, I would never have caught that stuff. I remember all those things—they all mean something to me, because they're lessons that I learned the hard way. I learned them by losing a lot on those things.

I've oscillated wildly. The Grateful Dead has been together for a long time; for a long time I was real skeptical about it, and I did what I could to fuck with it—because I distrusted it.

Parish: Everybody does that.

Garcia: You want it to be bigger than you—you want it to be more than you, and you don't want for you to count so much in it that you can upset it. That's the thing that I discovered, finally, by testing it. I wouldn't know unless I tested it that it is bigger than me, and it has more stability than I do and that I can't fuck with it personally, no matter what I do. That gives me a pass—it gives me more slack—because I know that it's not me.

But you still have your responsibility to it.
Garcia: That's right, and…my responsibility is almost neurotic. I can't overcome that, you know—it's just a part of me; it's part of who I am.

Parish: The other thing about the road: You let your guard down, it runs over you like a steamroller. Someone tells you a story and you get real sad for them and say, "I've got to help this guy." Then they fuck you over completely—lock, stock, and barrel—they charge breakfast to your room, they call the police on you—

Garcia: —there's a message in lipstick on your mirror—

Parish: So to strangers, you sort of put up this front until you get to know them.…Then you really hate them [*laughter*].

Garcia: Steve oscillates between being—

Parish: —the nicest guy in the world and the meanest guy in the world.

Garcia: The job requires it, in a way.

The duty cycle may be only fifty percent, but the impression is a hundred percent. People always see you as intimidating—
Garcia: Except for the smart ones; except for the cool ones—

Lesh: [*Laughs*] You know he's a real sweetheart.

Garcia: Yeah, or know that there's more to him…

Parish: There was meaner guys, man, than me.

Garcia: There've been meaner guys—Steve ain't that mean.

Parish: You get tested, though. People do some crazy stuff. He used to test me.…

Lesh: Now when Jerry breaks a string, he's lucky he doesn't get garroted by [Steve]—"How dare you break a string?"

Garcia: [*Laughs*] Right..."I don't want to have to ask that big guy for something....I'll just play without the string. God knows what he'll do, holy shit."

Lesh: "I'll whistle the top notes." [*Laughter*]

Parish: This promoter, Jim Koplik—he loves this story. He says, "That guy threw me off a fifteen-foot stage at Watkins Glen!" He kept telling me he was the promoter, and we didn't know him; nobody knew him, and he was bothering us. Me and [another crew member] just looked at each other and gave him the heave-ho. He landed in grass, you know....He loves it! That's how he introduces me to people.

Today this girl pulls up at Front Street in a BMW, and her speakers are blaring. Me and Billy [Grillo] were standing out there. I just smiled, and she hits the brakes, pulls in, and says, "Hey, man, what do I have to do to get a pass for the show at the Warfield?"

I said, "It's just not like that."

She says, "Come on, now. I know there's a price." People think there's some price. "What do I gotta do? Come on, what is it?" That never works. I've seen people bring all kinds of gifts, and they'll be the first people that you get rid of later, because they're just obnoxious and they can't ever change that.

Garcia: Just the vibe of who can be backstage or not—that's been going on all along, even since the very beginning. It's one of those things where you have to go on vibes more than anything else. These guys have to go through the changes, because it's real easy for somebody to come by and stumble over stuff, unplug half a dozen instruments.

Parish: You can't give them license up there.

Garcia: You have to be on guard about it, because there's always the thing of the poles—"Fuck it! Let everybody on stage," or "Keep everybody off stage—it doesn't matter who they are." It's the event nature of the thing—

Parish: [*Talking right into the microphone*] I can't go on with this any longer, man. This is all bullshit—these guys are holding us captive! Gans, you've got to do something, man! It's crazy—

Garcia: Help! We're captive in a print interview!

Parish: Pleeease, you've got to do something. Every time, we pay the bus driver to go where we tell him to, but he never listens to us—we try to leave....

Garcia: Waylon Jennings and his bus driver...the band had been playing poker with the bus driver for years, and losing steadily to him, until finally the whole band, Waylon and everybody, were into him for thousands and thousands of dollars. He ran the whole show. He was like the manager—he ran everything, he owned everything. They were fundamentally working for him. That's an example of how weird it can get. We found out about that when we played in Golden Gate Park with him [Kezar Stadium May 26, 1973]—it's funny as hell.

Parish: I must admit, we tried to do that with the Grateful Dead once, too—we started playing cards, but the only guy that would play with us was Kreutzmann, and he'd only break out five bucks. After he lost five dollars, he'd break everything in the room—and he cheated, too! So we couldn't get past that. [*Laughter*]

Garcia: The goal, as far as I'm concerned, is for it to be fun. I've opted for fun in this lifetime.

Parish: It can be fun, but it's never easy.

● ● ●

What is the Grateful Dead teaching the human race?
Garcia: How to fuck up.

Parish: Don't worry—by happy.[2]

Garcia: Don't worry—be happy! That's it! That's the best thing I've ever heard that anybody should ever hope to want to teach anybody else. That

---

[2]N.B. This phrase was associated with Meher Baba for many years before Bobby McFerrin made it into a hit record.

about fills the bill. Honestly—if there was something that you'd want to say to everybody that you'd want them to take seriously, that'd be about it.

Parish: There's a second clause to it: be responsible, with dignity.

Garcia: Oh, well, OK. Sure, whatever.

Parish: Because that's all we've got.

Garcia: But that just has to do with doing what you have to do to be happy. Do what you have to do to not worry. That supersedes all governments and everything—dignity and responsibility to people.

Lesh: Dignity with humor!

Garcia: Yeah! Dignity with humor—I'll buy that.

Parish: There you go! Yeah, yeah, yeah.

Garcia: I have never thought about whether there was something we were teaching everybody—or could, potentially. But maybe it's something like that.

There are object lessons to be found in this that other people could learn from.
Parish: There isn't one thing—it's so different all the time.

Garcia: There are so many. And lots of them are inconclusive.

Lesh: Why should we explain?

Garcia: And besides, why wouldn't each set create their own versions of the answer to that question?

Parish: Sometimes it's a different thing at different times.

Lesh: It's not supposed to be easy. It's not easy for us—we don't know—

Garcia: If we knew the answer to that question in some clear way, I'm sure…I would certainly try to lay it on you.

Parish: There is no answer.

Lesh: We agree that it'd be better for everybody to know what the answer is—then we could go faster—but of course, it's not like that.

Parish: And at the last meeting, we all voted that we didn't want you to know, man. [*Laughter*]

Garcia: The results aren't in—we're still looking. Hopefully, everybody else is looking, too, because we need all the help we can get.

What we have here is a knot of really bright, interesting people living a life that they're real satisfied with—right? This is like a little society—
Lesh: Wellll, yes and no.

Garcia: Yes and no. It could be better....I could see the whole thing in the sense of, "Well, if I work as hard as I can in my life, I may be able to end up building this thing that nobody can tear down after I'm dead," you know. And that may be the greatest function that it ever fulfills [*slight laugh*]—that it can't be torn down after I'm dead. [*Phil laughs.*] Or, I might be involved in this mysterious thing in which there is no individual me anymore, but there's this other thing that may be way more fun—and I no longer have the responsibility—

Lesh: As epitomized by Neal [Cassady]—

Garcia: Right...Neal was part of this whole idea, you know....

Parish: That's another weird thing. There's a spiritual side that's really weird about some dead people that we've all known, that have helped us.

Like whom?
Parish: Like some real close friends of mine that had died that I still feel help from. The whole Grateful Dead—on another level, the name refers to a whole thing on a spiritual level of being helped by departed souls of people that you once were friends with or helped. They look out for you, and if you tune into that—then I start taking it farther and farther. What if my grandmother, who is dead, is still there helping me in some way? If you tune in on that, then you get the help that you need on a cosmic level—plus you start getting turned on to it by things that happen to you that you can't explain in a concrete way.

Garcia: It might be a completely functioning, already existing reality which has always been energized by humans for this purpose—which is largely invisible, and largely magical or some such. It might have always been there, and people have always been activating—and still is, and that's what we're involved in: rediscovery of it.

As long as life goes on, as long as there's energy, this thing might always want to express itself—and need to. Part of what being human is is this thing that wants to express itself. It could be like that, because it feels that natural, certainly. It's not something freakish; it's not new in that sense— it's another kind of new. It's not that common, but it's not unusual, either. It's not unknown, either—that's the thing about it.

Parish: I can tell you so many stories about that....

Garcia: Its components didn't come out of a total vacuum. We'll hear ideas....

Lesh: It's us. It's just us.

Garcia: ...And this invisible component is tough to even speculate about, because it's invisible—[*laughs*] it's the unnameable.

Parish: One time I left a gig, and my truck was full. I was coming from Santa Cruz, and Buffalo Horse—this friend of ours who was the son of a very spiritual Indian leader—smoked[3] my stuff. I got in that habit...Mickey taught me that. He was down there, and he smoked my truck and all this other stuff. Anyway, I'm driving home, really haulin' ass on Highway 17, whippin' around those curves—I was speedin'. I go all the way home, and I get to Park Presidio; I stop at a light, and I started to go, and all of a sudden I can't turn. The wheel wouldn't turn.

I get out, and the tie rod...the metal had ripped off, and it was hanging by a thread the whole way. If it had gone on 17, there would have been no control of the truck. I definitely would have crashed and wrecked everything. But just when I came to a stop, it gave way—I could feel it. Now, you tell me: was it because I let him smoke my truck that day, or was it just one of those things?

---

[3] Also known as "smudging," a Native American purification ritual involving the burning of sage or other herbs.

Garcia: A high level of coincidence, synchronicity. There is definitely that—there's a certain amount of these extraordinary kind of symptoms that sometimes happen.

Parish: Road dreams, and stuff like that. Really strange.

Garcia: Yeah, weird coincidences that happen way too frequently for what would seem to be normal. There is a certain amount of that shit, yeah.

Parish: For any one of us, being involved in it was just a matter of being somewhere sometime, until we were almost pushed by some other hand.

Why did all the things happen for us in our lives that made it right for us to do this with each other? That's the other thing that we can't explain, because—we didn't all like each other at first, either. That's not something that's just taken for granted.

Lesh: But more of us have been together ten or more years—

Garcia: A long fuckin' time.

Parish: On a close level, through some deciding stuff. It worked, and we have that satisfaction.

Lesh: I thought you were an asshole when I first met you, man—

Parish: Right. Well, you always gave me a chance—you never slammed the door.

Lesh: I knew that you were OK, because of certain things....

Garcia: It takes a long time to get interested and to like people.

Parish: We were on the road for many years, but you always talked to me. And that time with the Quicksilver thing—I never told you this before, but...At the hotel, when Jackson took me down there...He knew the Quicksilver thing was getting really weird, and you were the one that told me: "Hey, look, it's a choice"—there was a chance of working with the PA, [Bob] Matthews might have given me a chance....You were in Jackson's room, and he was letting me hang out with him....We discussed it, and you said, "It's a choice of doing the good thing you want or working at this thing that you don't feel right about." And you told me, in a sense, to go for it. You were real encouraging.

And we've known each other for several years, but we didn't really get close until—even though we've been through a lot of life-or-death—

Lesh: The thing is that once you have tenure—

Parish: You can get to another level of understanding.

Lesh: Then it's automatic.
I had a lot of trouble with Kidd.

Parish: Everybody does.

Garcia: Yeah, he's a hard guy to get to know, tough guy to get to like.

Parish: But we know who he is, and we know what he's there for. He's real special to us. It's incredible.

Garcia: That's one of the things that makes it interesting—

Lesh: The most unlikely kinds of people.

Garcia: Yeah. You might not normally go through the trouble of getting to know somebody. There's a lot of people—just in the Grateful Dead, really—like Bill [Kreutzmann]. I don't think I would get to know him in a regular life, in a way, because he's a very different kind of person. It's been interesting getting to know him. He's always been very different. The whole thing has got a lot of dynamics to it on those levels.

Johnson: How did you happen to call Phil the first time?

Garcia: Me and Phil had bumped into each other for a long time before....He recorded the very first radio program I ever did, around 1960 or 1961. We were just in the same social world, really. We knew the same people. And I always knew that Phil had all kinds of amazing musical things—I knew certain stuff about him.

Lesh: We partied together.

Garcia: He was a friend—that's the reason I called Phil. I didn't call him as a stranger, or even some guy I knew that played.

Now Kreutzmann, see—I got hold of him because I knew he was just a player, not because he was a friend.

Johnson: Did you have some idea in your head when you started doing this?

Garcia: No, just that if I had a choice to do things with, I'd rather do things with friends—you know? [*Laughs*] 'Cause you want to turn your friends on—

Lesh: "Hey, man, why don't we do something together?" As opposed to going, "Hey, the union says you got a job here for thirty minutes."

Garcia: Right [*laughing*]. You don't do it that way. It's like a turn-on. We were all in the same world, in a way; the Grateful Dead just kind of grew out sideways, out of the side of this social scene. It was random—it could have been anything.

Lesh: It was random. Absurd! There's no reason it should exist at all.

Garcia: There's no logic to it at all. It's kind of the way things fell together one day [*laughs*], and it seemed okay.

Lesh: Jerry and Pigpen knew each other—

Garcia: Right, and I knew Weir, and Kreutzmann.... Bill was not a guy I knew socially. He was not a part of our scene, socially. Phil had been out of town for a while, off in Las Vegas, over in Berkeley. He always was a guy you ran into once in a while.... You'd juk it up for a week and then not see each other for six months, or something.

It was so obvious to me—"Right fuckin' on, Phil would love this." It just seemed like that kind of thing. And I knew he could do it—I didn't even think about that. I told you, man. I knew it all along.

Johnson: His mom is coming to the Greek Theater.... She's only been to see him once—

Garcia: I remember when she came one time—Walnut Creek. I remember that. My mom came to one show, even. That was incredible. She came when we played at the place out on Mission Street.

Lesh: We owed his mom for all our equipment....

Johnson: Where is your mom?

Garcia: She's gone. She's dead. She lived in San Francisco. She came when we played at the Rock Garden out on Mission Street, with Charles Lloyd, back in around [March] '67.

Johnson: How did she feel about it?

Garcia: She liked it. In a weird sort of way, she liked it. She asked me, "How do you get the guitar to sound like a horn like that?" My mother was a little on the far-out side.

Lesh: What a hip question!

Garcia: Yeah, my father was a musician.

Lesh: I would have shit if my mom had asked that.

Garcia: That was the first thing she asked me.

Parish: I always thought my parents really helped me. The things I learned from my father and mother helped me a lot for this life—more than they knew.

Garcia: I got a boot in the ass, actually, from my mother. My mom always encouraged me—she was into music....[My father played] clarinet, saxophone. Clarinet, I think, was his primary instrument.

Johnson: Was that his living?

Garcia: Yeah. He was an orchestra leader...big orchestras and stuff. He played all through the Depression, apparently. I remember seeing pictures—I wish my brother still had them—of my father's big bands and big orchestras. Some of them were really impressive, forty pieces and stuff, with a harpist and strings—amazing. He played at Treasure Island and stuff—there were all these things, but they all disappeared over the years. There's a few pictures of my father when he was young—he had small bands, like Dixieland, five-piece and four-piece. There's a few of those left, but I wish we had some of the old ones. They're cool, because the instruments were all so neat-looking.

● ● ●

Parish: I know guys that have been off the road with us for like ten years, and that's still the high point of their lives.

How could you get sucked into this vortex and then go back to leading a normal life?
Parish: You can do it, but it's not easy. A lot of people spin out. We're velocitized to this pace of life, too....

Their lives will never be the same.
Garcia: Whose lives?

People who experience this kind of thing and then have to go back and live—
Garcia: The going-back part is the bullshit. That's the main thing—it always seemed like bullshit, the thing of going back.

Lesh: Going back to what?

Parish: I was talking about people that used to be part of the crew and aren't anymore. To them, that was sort of their high point—they couldn't adjust to that. But other guys have.

It'll spoil you for other work.
Parish: There is something to it....

Lesh: There's more to it than we imagine.

Garcia: Right—that's the thing that makes it interesting, for god's sake.

Parish: I've got a great analogy: There's this weird "Twilight Zone"—I think it's Telly Savalas—a backwards hillbilly guy that buys a jar that's got "the secret," and it's just a doll with a ribbon—

Garcia: The magic thing in the jar—

Parish: They bust it open...He buys it from the carny guy...it's just all this plastic toy stuff—

Lesh: Right, and it don't have no mojo!
    What's your point, Steve?

Parish: There are certain things that if you take them apart, it's not as mystical—

Garcia: Nothing but wood and nails. "This human! I took him apart, and he's not even alive anymore—just bones and meat. What good is this shit?"

Mickey Hart

November 11, 1984
Novato, California

After I finished the manuscript of Playing in the Band, *I asked each band member to take a look at it and offer any corrections or additions they cared to make. Mickey Hart very generously went over the entire text with me, and I recorded the session so I could transcribe his stories and add them to the book. Here are some excerpts.*

I met Kreutzmann at the Fillmore. Count Basie was playing, and I was hangin' out with Sonny Payne [drummer in the Basie band]. We were good friends. I loved Basie, and I featured myself as a big-band drummer then. Somehow, Kreutzmann and I met that night. I think someone pointed him out to me....I knew about the Grateful Dead.

I had the drum store in San Carlos, and I had a band. I can't remember the name of it, but Joe Bennett was the lead guitarist—he was from Joe and the Sparkletones....

Kreutzmann and I met and started talking about drums. We went out that night with a bottle of scotch and went around playing on cars. We weren't beatin' up cars or anything—we were trying to make music.

I had seen Grace Slick, but I had never really seen Janis [Joplin]. Kreutzmann said, "You want to see fire and ice? That's Janis and Grace."

So we went to see Janis at the Matrix, and we took Sonny Payne with us. Sonny couldn't stand it, because it was too loud. I said, "I'm not going anywhere. This is great!" And James Gurley picked up his guitar and he raped it. I'd seen anything like it. It was the best solo I'd ever heard. That amplifier was just pulsing on the floor.

What was it like to be a musician and see the Grateful Dead? How did the music strike you as a musician?
The Straight Theatre was so big and the PA was so monstrous that everything was getting washed out. All you could hear was the bass and Jerry—you couldn't hear any vocals, really, and you couldn't hear Kreutzmann. It was magnificent, though. The feeling was incredible. I couldn't tell where they were going; it was so unusual. I thought I really would like to play with this band. I thought this would be an incredible challenge. I thought it had great spiritual content. Whatever hit me at that moment wasn't within the realm of logic or understanding....

We were talking about you being drawn into the Grateful Dead.
That's exactly what it felt like. It felt like some kind of force field from another planet, some incredible energy that was driving the band and pulling you in at the same time. This was what music should be like. I knew that it was very special—not your normal entertainment fare.
Show business was no consideration. When you see something good and you know it's good, you don't have to be told in any ways but the ways that you value things.
It was prayer-like music; it wasn't music that was going into the music business.
I wasn't part of the Haight before then....I wasn't part of the flower-power hippie scene.

Not everybody would have been attracted to that music.
Of course not! Nor would just anybody have wanted to *do* it. That's why I'm in the Grateful Dead and they're not. It's that simple: I think there's a calling for it.
...We've got transformation going here. We don't have a popular recording group. That's what the trappings may look like in some respects, but that ain't what we have.

Walks like a duck, looks like a duck...barks like a dog.
Exactly!

The music is everything; it is a musical organization. But we're not necessarily involved primarily in music. You can't look at it quite in the normal musical tradition, because we have not picked our roles. Our roles have been picked for us. And the thing that we do has something to do with archaic humanity. There's a leftover piece that we've picked up, somehow, and are able to transform again—that feeling or sense of music.

Do you know what a psychopomp is? This is an escort of the souls of the dead into the other world. The Grateful Dead have the ability to transform. We're playing music, but that's not all we're doing. We're doing something else besides entertaining. People come to be changed, and we change 'em.

Why is it that you can bring some people to it but you can't make 'em get it?

Some people aren't ready to change. They don't come into the environment with a sense of openness…if you come to it with a lot of prejudices, you'll walk away with twice as many. But if you come to it wanting to be moved, wanting to have fun, and you have a positive attitude—that's what the Grateful Dead demands. It makes you look inside and think of things you never thought of. It makes other realities seem common. I don't want to get into cosmic mumbo-jumbo. You don't have to have acid, you don't have to take drugs to appreciate what the Grateful Dead does, by the way. It alters the experience in certain respects, and each drug alters it in a different way….

● ● ●

We're constantly updating this music as we go along, at a very rapid rate—from beat to beat. The Grateful Dead listens to the Grateful Dead.…Jerry's listening to me; I'm listening to me; Bobby's listening…we're all listening to each other, and we're making this grand agreement as to where it should be. And it's changing every quarter beat, or two beats, or four beats. Sometimes it'll shift in a minor way—somebody will adjust a little bit…until we all adjust into the right place, and then we've got it.

These adjustments are very subtle; what you are hearing is a result of them.

● ● ●

When we were at the Potrero Theatre, on Potrero Street, we used to go in every day and play. Hunter lived there, I think. That's when he was drinking. We'd push the door open and he'd be there on the floor with wine bottles....He was taking speed and drinking wine, and writing all that beautiful stuff.

We would play, and Hunter would sit there and write. This was where we worked out "The Eleven," and all that odd-time stuff, I believe....

In the old days, we'd wake up every day and play. That's all the band was there for. We played a *lot*. Now we don't—we get together and we play from time to time.

To do what we did you have to be in shape—not only mentally, but physically. You have to practice it. You can't practice the Grateful Dead, but you've got to practice playing.

I don't play every day anymore, because my interests are in a lot of things.

It's not the absolute core of everybody's being anymore.

No. In order to keep it going we have to give it time to breathe. We couldn't keep at it that intensely. It's okay, man, because we're enjoying it....We couldn't have burned at that intensity for very long, or we would have been a crisp.

People have grown up, and things have changed. We're less willing, on some levels, to explore certain places now. It's risky out there...and sometimes it's not as rewarding as playing it straight. Sometimes playing it straight is more musically rewarding than going out and playing it weird, because a lot of times when you get weird you don't bring back that much results. The rate of success is not that high when you are improvising totally all the time.

Some people in the Grateful Dead want to fail less than others. I don't fear failing.

Succeeding in the Grateful Dead is creating a feeling. If we can't create the feeling, then we have not succeeded.

We're played this stuff a lot, and you can only twist the song so many ways. We've taken every song and twisted it more ways than you can imagine.

● ● ●

"Dark Star"

I played guiro a lot; a lot of scraper stuff.

We'd go back and forth, give and take on that stuff—one person laying on one part of the groove and the other laying on the other. It was very light. We tried to not have it broken up, stop and go. It was more of a flow.

I played the gongs, all kinds of stuff. We were moving all around. Maracas, gong, drum set.

"The Other One"

The thing about "The Other One" that was so thrilling was that it had all these climaxes at this incredible rate—and it was already at a very strong pace. Kreutzmann and I started to do this phasing trip, where we'd split the band in half—or two and four, and so on. We'd do threes against fives, against fours....We called it "going out."

It was totally spontaneous, but the idea was to *go out*. It was important to not go out too soon; we had a tendency to go out too fast. We had to find out where it was a little better before we went out, because when we threw the ones away—the basic beats...You have to really know where they are. That was our experiment in rhythm, in polyrhythm—"The Other One."

Brent Mydland

Brent was fighting it for a while....He's not quite as crazy as we are. He's getting there....He didn't believe in the structureless form, that our form was valid. I think he just came to this as a job.

How did it feel to you guys to have a "hired hand" in your midst while you were doing this thing?

He had the chance of becoming one of us. I wondered, for a while—I was the hardest critic, in a way. He didn't have the passion at first. Then his attitude and his playing changed, and he relaxed.

God, he must have been intimidated, playing with the Grateful Dead....He was seeing so many inconsistencies around him in the music. He was used to playing music that had a beginning, a middle, and an end—that repeated, and had bridges and stuff. And people wouldn't forget lyrics, and they'd play it the same way every time.

It killed him! He probably thought every bar was another mistake or two. Until he saw the beauty in it, I couldn't see the beauty in him. He knows now, and I really like him. I think his playing is really nice. He's a better player than when he started with the Grateful Dead, and he's doing more with what he has. But it was strange at first.

Phil doesn't play anybody's song the way they want him to play it—

So why should he expect them to play his songs the way he wants them?

Exactly. There it is. That friction, that tension…You can't really hire any of these guys and make them play anything.

Blues for Allah

We miked a box of crickets, and throughout the second side of *Blues for Allah* there are crickets on the basic track. We slowed them down, sped 'em up, played them backwards at half speed.…They sounded like whales, and they sounded like chirping birds.

We made this thing called "The Desert." Garcia was engineering, and I was in the studio. I played all my little percussion things—bells, metal, glass. We made about a twenty-minute track.…And he gated it with a vocal gate, a VCA [voltage-coltrolled amplifier]. He was saying "Allah"— the desert says "Allah." You don't hear a voice—you hear the desert saying the word in place of his voice.

[Grateful Dead Records chief Ron] Rakow was waiting for four or five days 'cause we were already late with the masters. Healy and Garcia and I, for a week—incredible!

We had to be really quiet, because I was playing this metal and wood stuff with a paintbrush!

It changes from wood to glass to crickets…mostly my percussion instruments.

After we were finished, we let the crickets go on Weir's mountain. We liberated them after the session. We'd kept them alive, fifty of them, and we miked the box. And for years after, Weir had exotic crickets outside his house.…

I'll do anything, pretty much. Garcia's patient enough to let me get it together, but then he'll give me one or two passes. Sometimes he just records me warming up on it and keeps that; "No, that's it!"

Robert Hunter's *Tiger Rose*

I was going through a catharsis here. Mickey Hart as Mickey Hart knew Mickey Hart could never play straight drums on Bob Hunter's record. He couldn't play bass drum, snare drum, high-hat and cymbals—Hart didn't play like that. Hart wasn't a straight drummer. Hart was a space drummer—up until that point.

I was faced with an inner decision here. So what I did was split my personality. "B. D. SHOT"—Bass Drum, Snare, High hat, Overhead, and Tom-tom—was the basic signature of the drums on the console.

Shot's consciousness wasn't anything like Hart. Shot could play the straight stuff all day, because he wasn't Hart and it was no threat to Hart.

Hart couldn't handle that then. Even the New Riders of the Purple Sage was a lot more spacey than Hunter's stuff. I didn't want to play Hunter's stuff for the rest of my life, and Hart wouldn't do *anything* he didn't want to do. Ain't nothing like that in this body.

I had to deal with it in my own space and time, so I thought schizophrenia was called for at this point. So I named myself B. D. Shot. And Hart played percussion.

We finally made peace, and Hart and Shot became one again after that.

Why was Hart credited as "Anti-Producer"?

It was my studio, and I was in it all the time, kibitzing.... Being called "Anti-Producer" is an honor, in this world.

Record Producers

Lowell George was mad. We wrote a great song one night, but we never recorded it. It was called "My Drum Is a Woman." We wrote this song about all my instruments and what I thought about them, how I address them. Lowell played good guitar, but he was no producer—certainly not the Grateful Dead. He did too much coke. There's no way for him to have any kind of rational judgment.

Keith Olsen was a good producer, and a good engineer. He was the most qualified. But he had a problem; he didn't know the Grateful Dead, and he wanted to mold the Grateful Dead in his own image.

He did something that was one of the most disrespectful things that has ever happened to me musically in my life. On the second side of *Terrapin,* "At a Siding" and "Terrapin Flyer" are mine. The "Flyer" was supposed to be a timbal solo with me and Garcia doing duets, timbal and guitar. Olsen erased one of the beautiful timbal tracks in Europe and replaced it with all these strings. He played it for me, and my mouth *dropped....*

He took a lot off, and then I put my timbal solo back on. But he didn't ask—he erased it off the master and replaced it all with strings.

He had this thing about gates...it was no way to really play, because you had to open the gates exactly perfectly each time. You had no real expression.

Mechanically enforced consistency—

Right. He turned us into another kind of...monster.

But somehow, there was something about him that I liked. He was good. He knew how to make good sounds, and he had good ideas. It's just that he was an egomaniac. He didn't know the Grateful Dead, he had no *simpatico.* He was in business—it was just bucks. He would have liked to make a great Grateful Dead record; it would have been a great feather in his cap.

No one's done it, you know?

I have a soft spot for him in my heart, and I'd also like to ram my foot up his ass.

Egypt

Phil and I said, "Let's go to Bill [Graham]. We'll get him to take us there." At that time we wanted better gigs, and we wanted Bill to buy us a PA. So I made placards that said, MORE GIGS, BETTER PA, EGYPT OR BUST, and we went to Masada [Graham's home] at around eleven o'clock at night and started shining flashlights in his windows.

Bill comes out—"What's happening! What's happening?!"

"OK, Graham! Back in the house! We're going to talk business!" We went in the house, and I took his phones off the hook and we started to talk. We told him we wanted to go to Egypt...we talked for hours, maybe all night.

The next day he called up Zippy [Richard Loren, the band's manager at the time] and said he loves us but he thinks we're irrational, because there's a war going on.... He said he was going to do it, but he really didn't want to do it because he didn't think we should go. There was a war on.

I said, "That's why we have to go over there. We have to be part of this, and this is a way we can do something." Bill didn't see it like that; he thought it was dangerous, and he thought it was just another Grateful Dead acid trip or something. So we said, "Fuck you—we'll do it ourselves." We practiced saying that different ways—"Fuck *you*, Bill— we'll do it ourselves." "*Fuck* you, Bill—we'll do it ourselves."...Which, of course, we eventually had to say to him.

So we did it ourselves. And after it was all together Bill said, "Wow, what a trip!" So he bought some tickets, and he and his boys came over and enjoyed it with us. They were pleasure crew. No producing—he was just a guest and a participant. I've never see Bill higher than this.

Pigpen

Pigpen was the *musician* in the Grateful Dead. When I first met the Grateful Dead, it was Pigpen and the boys. It was a blues band, and Pigpen played blues harp.

Pigpen was a kind man. He looked so hard, but he was a kind, soft man. That's why he had to look so tough, because he was so kind, he would get stepped on.

We roomed together.... He drank and I didn't....

If there was one black chick in the audience, he'd always go home with her. Somehow he'd always have her up by his organ...by the end of the evening, she'd be up sittin' on his stool. He just loved black women. That was his preference.

He'd get down on his knee, and he'd bring that audience right up. He'd talk right to ya, you know. He *played,* so hard. But he played the blues, shuffle stuff. That was his medium. He *was* the blues; he lived it, and he believed it, and he got caught in that web and he couldn't break out. And it killed him.

Was he an unhappy guy?

I don't think he was. He was just living the blues life, you know? Singin' the blues and drinkin' whiskey. That's what all blues guys did. That went along with the blues.

The first person my grandmother met when she saw the Grateful Dead was Pigpen. We came off the plane in New York and she was there to meet me. She had never seen long hair—she had just read about the hippies—and then she realized that we were *that.*

"Grandma, I want you to meet my friend Pigpen." And he goes, "Huh." He grunted. She loved Pigpen. He didn't scare her at all.

She sort of grandmothered us all. She was there at all the shows. She and my grandfather, Sam, were our first old fans.

• • •

Years ago a guy came to me with a skull. The story was that his brother was killed in an accident on the way to a Grateful Dead concert. This guy was the biggest Deadhead of all, and he was the one who'd turned his brother on.

He spent every minute of his life around Grateful Dead music, so his brother wanted his skull to be always around the Grateful Dead. His last wish would have been that, so his brother brought me the skull.

I kept it on my recording console all these years.

I thought, "This is *really* a dead head!"

I always give Bill Graham interesting gifts. I thought it had been here long enough, so when Marty Balin and the *Life* photographer and the others came here [to videotape Mickey for a Bill Graham tribute] I thought, "What can I give Bill?" It had been here long enough.... I gave it to Bill and said, "This guy didn't like the show. He wanted his money back."

The Africans say...a person's not dead unless all of his deeds are forgotten and there's nothing left of his physical remains—nothing to show that he once lived. But until that happens, he still is alive. So this guy—the Ultimate Deadhead—is still alive.

I knew Bill Graham would understand....

We have shared some experiences with him.

He always wondered what it was, and after that he understood a little more of what it was all about. He didn't want to get his feet wet, because...he was an observer, not a participant. He was like a tavern keeper.

Bill Graham cosigned a loan for me when we were making something like twenty-five dollars a week. Weir and I were hitchhiking to gigs with our guitars and drumsticks. Fifty dollars a month, I remember. I paid it back, and he has always come to my aid in one way or another.

He's made enemies, and he's made friends....We're one of them.

John Barlow

January 10, 1986
KFOG, San Francisco

This interview was conducted in the production studio at the radio station where I produced "The Grateful Dead Hour" (then known as "The Deadhead Hour") before I began producing it at home and distributing it nationally. Very little of this material made it onto the air.

Barlow: I don't like to say [what the songs are "about"], because when you start saying what it is, especially on the meaning level, then you've denied [the listeners] the opportunity to write their own song. They get locked into what you were thinking about.

Well, it's not like a term paper, you know—"The themes are man's inhumanity to man, and the acid rain."
    Listen, man, sometimes...We're not real polemical, but every once in a while I'll get on a crank and have to say something about it. But given the nature of the band, you can't say it too blatantly, you know.

What does that make "Throwing Stones," a pamphlet?
    Hey, you should have seen some of the orations I wrote before that. I mean, there was some pretty bald stuff.

259

What the Grateful Dead does is work on consciousness, which is the best way to approach politics anyway. You change consciousness, and politics will take care of itself. But it seemed like there was a pressing need for everybody to have an anthem all of a sudden, and there still is. We have to be thinking about these things, and I felt like we had to say something very direct and strong, but it took a while before we found something that had the right tone.

It really works. There's still one line that I know you haven't finished yet....[1]
There's several. I mean, we may throw the whole thing out and start from scratch. I don't know. [*Laughs*]

Don't throw out the two lines I kicked in, okay? I'm very proud of my little tiny contribution.
Which ones?

"Shipping powders back and forth / Black goes south and white comes north." I gave those to Bob a year and a half, two years ago.
Glad to have you aboard!

The other half-line I've contributed to a Weir song seemed to have pissed you off royally: I replaced "kissing the toe of your boot" with "sipping champagne from your boot" [in "Hell in a Bucket"].
That's right. And I may never forgive that.

Talk to Bob. I just suggested it. He's the one what plugged it in.
[*Sighs*] I know. I know. You were just doing your job.

No, I was trying desperately to get a piece of this important action, you know—"Hey, I helped Bob Weir write this song."
Ha! This important action! Well, I don't know. I have a substantial piece of this important action, and it is not necessarily a day at the beach. Maybe better to visit, occasionally throw in a line. You've probably got exactly the right system.

Yeah!
Nah, it's actually fun writing for the Grateful Dead. I'm glad I do. It's been a terrific ride.

---

[1]"Hist'ry's page, it is thusly carved in stone" was changed to "Hist'ry's page will be neatly carved in stone" in time for the recording of the 1987 album *In the Dark*.

I'm sure for you it's been frustrating, alternating with complete unabashed joy.

Yeah, to the extent that I've ever had complete unabashed joy without ever having a revelatory experience or engaging in drug abuse.

• • •

Grateful Dead music really has a complex emotional flavor to it. It's very dense, and it leaves you room to lurch around and attach your own meanings to it, but it strikes chords deep down inside me that no other music does. There's a particular bittersweetness to a lot of Garcia's work, a wistful kind of thing, a prettiness.

There's so much belief that's been brought to bear into the system. This is a very ill-defined religious phenomenon, I think. The belief that comes in creates a whole different kind of psychic or spiritual environment that has almost nothing to do with music. It has a lot to do with music on one level, but less and less the further up you go. And—well, I don't know how to put it. If I knew how to put it we wouldn't have to play this stuff.

[Laughs] Well, you'll know it when you hear it, though, America.

That's right. That's right. It's like Justice [Hugo] Black's definition of pornography—"I don't know how to describe it, but I know it when I see it."

Well, I think maybe that's cool for the Grateful Dead, because we wouldn't want anybody else telling us what we're thinking anyway.

That's right. Ignore alien orders.

• • •

One of the things that really made it possible for me to plow through the psychedelic wilderness around the Grateful Dead was your comment to me in 1982 about community. You said communities aren't based on geography any more, or on economic necessity, and what we Deadheads have is a community that transcends all those locality things, but it's a community nonetheless. "As much as any mining town," you said.

Well, that's a particular nut of mine, if for no other reason than because I come from a very small town in an isolated place. I come from *someplace*; after I went away to school and started looking around America, I found that most people *didn't* come from someplace, in my sense of the term. Most suburban areas, there's nothing to go back to, you don't even know the people next door.

And I came from a place where even my enemies would help me out if I were in certain kinds of trouble, because there's that bond that we all share. But America, for whatever reason—and corporate policy has a lot to do with it—is erasing the whole idea of community, and people need that desperately.

So the Deadheads, I think, have come up with something kind of wonderful. They have done a little conceptual blockbusting and realized that you don't have to do it in one place, it doesn't have to be out in the middle of the cornfield somewhere, it can be anywhere in America. And they take it on the road.

And it doesn't necessarily have to be at a Grateful Dead concert, either.
Oh, no. No, I don't think it is. I don't know very much about what it's like inside the Deadhead community, really. I always kind of wondered, but it doesn't seem like it has to be right there with them. It has its own independent reality. And people know each other, they help each other out, I think it's great. It's one of the things that makes it possible to do this, for all the frustrations that are involved, because you want to go on supporting that. We're doing some pioneering work on how to create communities and keep them together in the future. Rather, I should say the Deadheads are. I don't think we have much of anything to do with that....We have the same relationship to their community as corn does to a small town in Iowa. Probably. We're the focus, and that's it.

● ● ●

[*"Walk in the Sunshine" is played.*]

That song is called "Walk in the Sunshine," and you Deadheads haven't heard it much 'cause I don't think the Dead have ever played it live.
For good reason. That's the worst song we ever wrote.

[Laughs] But it could've been worse.
Well, that depends on how you look at it. Now I'm wondering. But at the time we were under duress, we were already in the studio, and Weir and I had been battling over this song, and my father died the night before that was written, and I had to write the song and get back, for obvious reasons. And I was feeling especially burnt out, and I wrote the first thing that came into my head, and it was *just terrible*. It was straight out of a greeting card. Sort of a hip cosmic greeting card.

"Go placidly amid the noise and haste...."

Well, yeah. *Desiderata* is a lot better. Painfully obvious. It was like [a] fourteen-year-old's very earnest poetry. But it was all I could come up with. I was just shell-shocked. So I figured that the only way that I could get Weir to do it so I could get out of the way, whatever the consequences, was to write something that was really twisted and perverse that would make the sunny sentiments of "Walk in the Sunshine" seem much more palatable, and then he'd agree to do it, and then I could leave.

So I wrote a song called "The Dwarf."

Based on the Lagerkvist novel.

Right, based on the Pär Lagerkvist novel about a very twisted little man able to manipulate everybody in power around him. It's kind of a great song, now I see, but I figured if I gave Weir this twisted song it would work.

The pity was that I didn't throw away "Walk in the Sunshine" and just give him "The Dwarf" and let the devil take the hindmost. That's what I should have done. [*Laughs*]

Well, I've seen the lyrics of "The Dwarf." It's definitely the obverse of this lyric we just heard.

Exactly. It's the Thanatos for the Eros here. But much more interesting.

Ace has, arguably, the best of your collaborations, or some of the best of your collaborations. And the best of Bob's collaboration with Hunter.

Yeah, I think so. It's also the first of our collaborations. We hadn't set up ideas about ourselves as collaborators—we were going at everything from a purely fresh standpoint. It was also written in the middle of nowhere in the middle of the winter. And I was just getting used to the idea of being back in Wyoming, and Weir was just getting used to the idea of being the kind of guy that could go out and make a record all by himself. So it had that nice freshness of a beginning.

Well, he didn't get too far away from home with his first record; he ended up using the Grateful Dead for almost all of it.

Yeah, it ended up being their studio album for that year, but that certainly wasn't the way it was approached in his mind. That was what made all the difference.

This album really sort of represents the emergence of Weir as a singer-songwriter, too. It was from this point on that [he and Jerry] started alternating songs [in concert]....

Yeah, he hadn't been writing songs before that. Neither had I. That's the deal. That record has aged very well, too. With the exception of the one song, I don't look back on those songs with the usual degree of remorse.

Oh. There are songs you regret deeply?

Most of them, in the sense that I don't think that we've ever done anything that's as good as we can do.

Now wait a minute. By the definition that we've been discussing here all night, no Grateful Dead song is ever really finished.

Well, yeah. Right, right. I'm just talking about recorded work, really. There are songs that have become, on their own, something that's as good as we can do, and that "we" is a much larger "we" than just Weir and me.

Any conjectures as to why it's so damn difficult for the Grateful Dead to make it work on an album?

Oh, well, I think it's one of those simple things. Remember in college there were these guys that had to write one paper to graduate? Just one paper. And you could've put a .357 magnum to their temple and they wouldn't have been able to punch one typewriter key. They're forty-five years old now, and they still lack that single credit that would get them a college diploma.

There's an element of that involved: there's one record left to do for Arista. But there's also the fact that it is such a symbiosis between the audience and the band, and the intensity of the involvement between the audience and the band has become such a major part of it, that I don't think they can really do it in the studio anymore. Whatever it is that the Grateful Dead does is not something that can be done under glass. It's got to be done out where things are visceral and human.

Why don't their live records work better, then?

Well, you know, I've often thought that maybe the whole thing is just mass hysteria. That I get sucked up into as well. A better way of putting it is that there are many agents at work in a Grateful Dead concert that you can't put on tape. Everybody's said that, and it is very true. I go to shows where I'm transformed by what I hear, and I come back to the hotel and listen to the tapes and it's abominable.

So I don't know what goes on there. It's magic, man.

In selecting tapes to play on the radio show I run into that a lot. It's like "I was there, it was great. Why is it so flat on this tape?"

No, there are other parties. There are other things going on that we dimly perceive and probably can't imagine in some cases.

Boy, that sounds like deep hippie talk. I'm glad KFOG doesn't get to Cora, Wyoming, is all I can tell you. I don't tell my neighbors this stuff. [*Laughs*] They're used to me talking about cattle prices and the weather. I don't have too many opportunities for this manner of speculation.

Well, we're proud to give you this forum, Professor Barlow....

Yeah. Well, and it's great to talk—I assume that what I'm talking to here, besides a large object with a soft end, are Deadheads, who I don't really know and understand very well, but I always have liked a lot. Deadheads mean no harm, which is a lot to be said these days.

You folks are trying to keep something alive that needs to be kept alive. You're not an artifact, and you aren't archaic, and you aren't taking refuge in the past, you're pursuing the revolution. And I really appreciate that about you.

Thanks, Deadheads.

Robert Hunter

February 25, 1988
San Rafael, California

Interview for "The Grateful Dead Hour" (then known as "The Deadhead Hour"), around the release of his album Liberty *(Relix Records RRCD-2029). When I arrived, Hunter had the microphone and tape recorder set up and was all set to co-opt the process.*

Hunter: Well, good evening, David Gans. It's very nice to have you on our program; we've been looking forward to this for a long time. And I'd like to ask you a few questions. To begin with, I hope I don't disarm you, but which came first, the words or the music?

It varies. Considerably.
　It does. Very good. The second question: How does it feel to be behind a nose such as yours? The whole world has been asking this question, David.

I really don't know how it would feel to not *be behind this nose, so I really can't differentiate.*
　That is a good answer. All right…

I solicited some questions from my friends out in the electronic world. I got a bunch of good stuff. Let's see.... Here's a great story. This guy writes, "I was living in Colorado and he played in this small club called the Blue Note. I was first in line to get a seat inside, and there was hardly anyone else in line when they let us in. Hunter was onstage when we walked inside, doing some last-minute setup before the gig. My friends and I walked up to a front table and sat down. Hunter looks up as we sit down and appears real surprised. He looks right at me and says, 'What are YOU doing here?' I don't know what to say, so I shrug and say, 'I'm here to see you.' As he finishes what he's doing, he keeps looking up and staring at me. Finally, he leaves the stage and walks right up to our table. He comes up to me and says, 'Boy, am I glad I got a better look at you. When you walked in I thought you were Bob Weir! [Laughter] It really freaked me out thinking that Weir had come to see me."

Weir did come to see me once. Freaked me out. Fact, the whole band came to see me, and I was not prepared for it. I was playing at the Cellar Door in Washington, DC, and in they came. They made me nervous [*laughs*], especially doing "Jack Straw." But I bravely did it.

"How many of your songs do you write for you, and how many for Jerry, or do you just write and divvy them up later?"

I've written 83 specifically for Jerry, and about 192 specifically for myself, of which I have recorded some 47.

Are you making up those numbers?
Sir?

Are you making up those numbers?
Are you calling me a liar?

No, I'm asking you whether you're making up those numbers. [Laughs] They sound a little too precise.
Next question, please.

[Laughs] "What fiction do you read?"
I've been making a crack at the Oz series lately [L. Frank Baum]. I've gotten about three of them down. I've been reading Walker Percy; read lately *The Thanatos Syndrome* and *The Last Gentleman* and *The Moviegoer*.

I just finished the funniest book which I have ever read. It's *A Confederacy of Dunces*, by John Kennedy Toole, who finished the book, could not get it published, and committed suicide. His mother got it to Walker Percy, a smudged carbon copy, and absolutely *drove* Percy until he read the book, which he did with great reluctance, and found himself totally, totally captured by it. It won the National Book Award, and I recommend it to everyone. The only book I can think that compares to it is *The Ginger Man*. Donleavy's amazing.

So do you generally read fiction, nonfiction—what sort of stuff?

I balance it. I tend to read serious work. I'm reading Noam Chomsky right now…*Language and Responsibility*. It's partly political and partly language. It's an interview, and gives a fairly good grounding in Chomsky.

I just finished Heidegger's *What Is Called Thinking?* and in and amongst that I was reading *Ozma of Oz*. I like to keep things balanced a bit.

Why do you suppose a guy like Chomsky doesn't get more attention for his views? He certainly has some controversial and powerful ideas that seem worthy of consideration.

Well, his linguistic ideas are very formative in philological circles. He's an intellectual; that's why his ideas don't get broader coinage. But within the circle of those who are moving and shaking in linguistics and philology, he's very, very important, formative.

…He's an entire iconoclast of the pressure system—you know, the unwritten agenda of American education and newspaper presentations and whatnot—and could certainly be viewed as a very disruptive leftist. But he looks at the system, and what is closing our minds up, and objects to it. This sort of thing, when it's put in very intellectual language, is never welcome. This sort of thing is frozen out. I'm not a Chomskyite, I'm simply reading it, and this is my feeling as to what the answer to your question would be.

"Do you listen to music for pleasure, ever, and if so, what sort of stuff do you listen to?"

Yes, I do listen for pleasure. Mostly I've been, for the last year, going through the history of string quartets. I read a book on it, and I'm trying to see who fit where, starting with Haydn and moving up to the present.

That's been my pleasure listening. I'm moving into Beethoven piano stuff now.

I just wanted to *know* that. It feels criminal to be a member of Western civilization and to not know Beethoven and Bach, Brahms—if you have the capacity for enjoying it. Life is a bit too rushed, perhaps, to sit down and learn all the sonatas at this point, but I have a great deal of leisure, and the sort of life I've picked out for myself, a certain amount of time at the typewriter and you're burned a little bit. What do you do to refresh yourself? I listen to music.

Any pop music tastes you'd care to discuss?

Just picked up the new Nina Hagen CD yesterday, the compilation disk. I'd say for the terminally weird, this is your piece of pie. [*Laughs*] She does "White Punks on Dope" in German....[*Laughs*]

I'm very fond of the Smiths' work, especially the album *Louder Than Bombs*. I think Morrissey really has a handle on something. I do admire his work. And the fellow who does the lyrics for The Call...I don't know his name—

Michael Been.

Michael Been. Yeah, he's a hell of a songwriter, too. I can listen to his stuff many times and find levels in it, which is something.

In the BAM interview with Jerry Garcia, he mentioned an additional verse of "Friend of the Devil" that he doesn't perform.

"You can borrow from the devil / You can borrow from a friend / But the devil'll give you twenty / When your friend got only ten."

Any good reason why he doesn't use that?

I may not have given him the verse at the time when he locked it into concrete in his head. I may have given it to him later and said, "Here's another verse." And he had the form—where it should begin, where it should end—formalized at that point. It might open the song up to being a different sort of ellipse than it is. Perhaps. Perhaps he doesn't like the verse, perhaps he's simply being perverse. Check one, check two, check three...[*Laughs*]

Are there any similar situations, other songs that you've updated, or done additional stuff to, that he's not incorporated?

Well, there's the "Terrapin" business, where there's a good deal more where that came from. But then again, that's another thing which is finished, as far as Garcia and the Grateful Dead are concerned, and so be it. I don't see, after all these years, kicking that dead horse anymore [*Laughs*]....That's another one of those projects that could've gone on and become a triple album, if I'd had my way. I had a lot to say about *Terrapin Station*.

So you were more closely involved in the musical process of that one?

No. No. That happened to me very fortunately. Jerry had written some changes and I had just written "Terrapin," and we met, and his changes and my lyrics went hand in glove. I think we were both approaching *Terrapin Station* from different directions and met in the center and there it was. There was something more than uncanny about the way that thing just happened.

That song is very meaningful to me. I wrote it in front of a picture window overlooking the storm-lashed bay. There was lightning in the sky. It was one of those moments when I just *knew* something was going to happen. I was sitting there in front of my typewriter, just very, very open to this, there was no furniture in the room, it was a bare room.

And I just wrote "Terrapin Station" at the top of the page, and said, "Well, hmm, what's *this* about?" And I said, "Let my inspiration flow," and so actually the beginning lines describe the invocation. A name occurred to me, and then the beginning is an invocation to the muse to deliver further information on this, and make it *something*. Give it sense and color. A magical moment, and the Dead carry it right on into what they do, and the performance of it. But for the record, I don't know. I'm amongst those who's not a fan of the record, but the live performance of it—*Mmmmm*!

You want to talk about your recent projects—your rather ambitious literary effort, translating into a language you don't regularly speak?

The Duino Elegies.[1] Last night I went into the studio with Tom Constanten and did, by my own estimation, one hell of a reading of those elegies. Boy, they just *roared* out of me, and Tom was playing Brahms and Chopin and a little bit of Scriabin as background music for it. I think we've got quite a little number here—I'm going to give it away free to public radio, and also make up cassettes and bundle them with the book, because

---

[1] Rainer Maria Rilke, *The Duino Elegies*, translated by Robert Hunter. Eugene, Oregon: Hulogos'i, 1987.

I feel that a lot more people will listen to it on their cassette machines than will ever read the book. Don't you? [*Laughs*] I think that's the appropriate place for poetry. It *should* be read [aloud]. It's only second-hand when it's on the page.

. . . . It's often said that poets shouldn't read their own stuff.
Well, this is only marginally my own stuff. It's my choice of words and phrasing. Out of all that's available. I took what I felt best supported the emotional tone of the elegies. And so it's easy for me to read it, because it's my word choice. But it's Rilke's ideas, not to forget, and those ideas still rock me when I read them. And reading them aloud, which I've done quite a bit of recently in order to prepare for this reading, I find that the meanings become more and more apparent to me, and the interlacing of the meanings throughout the elegies, the grand idea that this is moving towards—I can't read it enough or speak it enough to thoroughly know it, at least at this point. It's still surprising me.

How did you get to that place, though? How can you read poems in German and be so deeply affected by something in a language that's not in your own? Can you speak German?
Well, you can *read* the German, and get the cadence and flow of the German. And I tried to approximate the cadence and flow of the German language in it. My German is not strong, and I used other translations, for example, to show me when he moved into subjunctive tense, or some-thing, and for idiomatic expressions which I might not be familiar with. And I used Cassell's German Dictionary, you know, and broke every word I didn't know down and saw all the shades of meaning. It's very, very good—Cassell's Classical German Dictionary—because it gives you the meanings of a German word, say, in the 1800s. The shades of variation you'll find in Webster's complete dictionary or the complete Oxford, the *shades* of meaning. Which is very valuable, because I found that many of the words had been mistranslated, I felt, by previous translators, that they made Rilke sound more ambiguous than he was. And I felt very often that the wrong shade of meaning was insisted on in earlier translations, and just sort of bled on into further translations. So I think I stopped a lot if that with this. That I have offered alternatives to readings which are kind of tried and true at this point and moved on into further translations.

So the thing was that your first engagement with this stuff was through somebody else's translation?

Oh, yeah, the Spender-Leishman translation, which I find is a very worthy first effort of bringing Rilke into the English language. It's stiffer than hell. But I don't want to get into criticizing other people, because it's a great thing to break the lock on Rilke at that point, and parts of it are marvelously done. I didn't feel it flowed and sang well enough. But then, Spender didn't speak German and Leishman did, and Leishman would insist that maybe Spender was being a little too floral, or something, here, and so it was very much a collaborative effort. If Spender had had the German, and really cut loose on it by himself, I think we would've had a more musical translation of the elegies from the very beginning.

I have a translation of "Stella Blue" in French... and at the shows last week I thought it would be really interesting to hear "US Blues" in Russian.
In Russian?

In Russian, because Russian's so full of Americanisms already anyway that you could pretty much leave "back-to-back chicken shack" in there, for example... I just think it would be fun to try that song in Russian.
I'd like to hear that.

Well, Henry [Kaiser] says it's worked for him real well in other contexts, and as I say, anything to give me a new bite on certain tunes. It'll be fun to see what happens. But I know a lot of people who speak French, so I'm going to have several different people do "Stella Blue," and then try and compile them together into one.[2]
That's a very good idea. Somebody'll be inspired on one line, somebody'll be inspired on another.

Oh, exactly. And the people I'm asking are from different walks of life, too—my mother, for example, who doesn't really know much from the Grateful Dead but certainly knows her way around French. In fact, she's translating—she's working on a book compiling the stories, seven or eight different women's stories, of emigrating from the old country to America, and where they ended up and stuff. And she's interviewing her aunt and uncle, who fought in the Resistance in World War II, so she's translating these lengthy interviews from French into English.
What a lovely project. I wish her well on it, I really do. When people do things like that I'm just in awe. It's nice. I'm thinking of—I'm going to

---

[2] I did come up with a couple of good translations, but I chickened out because I didn't feel at all comfortable singing in a language I don't speak.—DG.

interview my father, who's about eighty-six now, no, eighty-seven, so he was born just about the beginning of this century, and I feel that his points of view should be written down. I'm going to interview him on tape and then get a secretary to type it up, and see what I can get out of this.

His father was a Presbyterian minister from Scotland, and so he was raised up in a strict Presbyterian Scottish environment. Very tough. Very tough. His father died at ninety-nine—almost made it to a hundred.

That should be interesting. I think it's a crime that people aren't out there with tape recorders, talking to everybody about things like that....
Well, if you have the ability to interview, and you have a very interesting historical specimen in your own family—excuse me, Dad [*Laughs*]—yes, I think it is a crime to not get the benefit of that wisdom down on tape, and if it's coherent enough as a complete piece, perhaps to try and publish it. And if not, at least I'll have that record.

What prompted you to write that letter to Rolling Stone *defining obscenity?[3]*
I was just sitting there one day, at my word processor, and this definition of obscenity suddenly came into my head and—"You know, this is a good way to look at things," I thought to myself. "I know! I'll write it down and send it to *Rolling Stone.*" I wrote it down, I put it in an envelope, I put a stamp on it, I put it out in my mailbox, and ten minutes later the mailman picked it up and it was gone.

Rolling Stone called me at the office, and asked, "Say, is this *coming from anywhere?* Uh, is this *relating* to anything?" And I said, "No, no, no, it just occurred to me as a correct thing, so I sent it to you." They said, "Oh, well, thank you very much!" [*Laughs*] There was nothing more to it than that.

Why Rolling Stone?
It occurred to me that it was a thought worthy of a large audience, and *Rolling Stone* has a large audience, and I had a stamp and an envelope,

[3]On the letters page of *Rolling Stone*, February 25, 1988:
Wisdom From The Dead
Suggested legal definition of *obscenity*: Actions directed toward the suppression of activities that do not palpably harm others. Suggested definition of *supreme obscenity*: Bending the definition of *palpable harm to others* in terms of one's own moral or ethical beliefs.
Robert Hunter
San Rafael, California
Hunter is one of the lyricists for the Grateful Dead—Ed.

and their address, and I didn't want to think too much more about it. [*Laughs*] I like to do things fast, like bam-bam-bam-bam-bam, that one hour later I have something in my past that I didn't have before, such as a very oddball letter to *Rolling Stone*.

Have you had any further thoughts about the definition itself?
No. No, it seemed sufficient. I think you could run a country on that precept.

"I have long thought that 'Scarlet Begonias' could've been included in Lyrical Ballads, with the proviso of course that you had accompanied Wordsworth and Coleridge on their walking tour of northern England in late 1797, and agreed to contribute the piece in order to help defray expenses. Do you feel any special affinity with either of these poets, or with the English Romantic poets in general? What are your thoughts on the nature of the imagination, its potential to transform objects in its grasp, break down customary perceptions and prejudices, and reorganize experience into a new organic truth? And, who do you pick in the National League West this year?"
No, no, yes, no, yes, no, and is that a baseball league? Yes, uh…

Sorry. I knew that question wasn't going to get anywhere…
If you want to talk football, on the other hand…I like football because they use a larger ball, and I can see it. See where it's going. But not very much.

"Collaborations with other than Garcia have been quite successful. Why don't you write with the other Gratefuls more often?"
Um, because Garcia makes it easy. You know, he makes himself available to do it, and when I give him a piece of material he'll either reject it or set it, and he gives me changes, which I *will* set, generally—he doesn't give me anything I don't like. He's been coming over lately and collaborating. And he makes himself available, he's a genius, he's got an amazing musical sense, and no one else makes themselves available or particularly easy to work with.

There's the "black hole" phenomenon where you hand a lyric over, and it disappears into the void somewhere. And Jerry is conscientious about keeping his communications together on it. I'd say it's almost as simple as that.

I'm willing and open to work with anybody who won't give me a rough time or try to rewrite what I'm doing.

This leads me to ask about the collaboration with Bob Dylan. How did that come up, how did it go, and what's happening with it?

You couldn't be easier to work with than Dylan. I brought the book—I think it had fifteen to seventeen songs—in to the Dead before we made *In the Dark*, of which "When Push Comes to Shove" and "Black Muddy River" were selected. I took about three of them for the *Liberty* album, and Dylan took two of them for his album, set 'em, and sent me a tape. That's what I call easy to work with! He just flipped through the songbook that was sitting there at Front Street, liked these tunes, put 'em in his pocket, went off, set 'em to music, recorded 'em, and...First time I met him he said [*Dylan voice*]: "Eh, I just recorded two of your tunes!" And I said, "Neat!" [*Laughs*]

He didn't even ask first?

Bob Dylan Doesn't have to *ask* a lyricist if he can do his tunes! Come *on*, man!

I gotta just say this for the record: you got your Grammies, you got your Bammies, you got your Rock 'n' Roll Hall of Fame—as far as I'm concerned, Bob Dylan has done two of my songs, and those other things sound far away, distant and not very interesting.

And you like what he did with the tunes?

Very, very much.

That's "The Ugliest Girl in the World" and—

"Silvio."[4]

Okay, that's settled. Back to the Garcia collaboration.

Jerry and I have five new tunes carved out right now. I don't want to give you titles because they're all tentative, and I don't really want to say much except that they're on the move. It seems to be a bit of a jinx to talk about things like that before they're actually done.

I was doing an interview on KQED the other day and a guy came out and said, "Hey! I heard on your interview there that you were writing some new tunes with Garcia. I sure hope you guys aren't making a record, because you're already popular enough, and I'm having enough trouble with the new fans." Oooooh. And that was a legitimate point of view he was putting forth, you know. And I said "Hey [*Laughs*], I dunno...."

[4]Bob Dylan, *Down in the Groove*. Columbia OC-40957, 1988.

Well, what about that? Things have apparently changed.... Selling out a stadium is some sort of success!

Toni Brown just called me from *Relix* and said that she can hear almost nothing but Grateful Dead on WNEW, which is the big station. And, you know, a year ago this simply was not the case. We've entered the mainstream, the radio consciousness now, and I think in certain respects we're turning into Johnny-come-lately media darlings.

The flip side of this coin is the bigger they are the harder they fall, and I'm worried about next year. I don't like what's happening this way. Unless it *is* organic, organic in the way that critical mass and nuclear reactions are natural. But—oooh, it's a long way down. I mean, we're going up in a balloon ride right now, and the atmosphere only supports a balloon weight up so far. This is really problematic.

Why do you suppose it happened?

I think "Touch of Grey" was a hell of a hot little tune. I think it was very, very well recorded, and released well, followed up with a hell of a video. I think we genuinely got ourselves a hit, and a hit does what a hit's supposed to do: propels a band to the top. I think it's as simple as that: we got a hit record.

What influence does that have on the next record—on how it's done and what they want to do with it?

Well, it was successful enough as a recording venture. Everybody in the band likes this record. Nobody faults the recording. The Grateful Dead for the first time did what they should have done all along: got themselves on a stage as though they were playing for an audience, and *played live*. Without an audience. The tape machine was the audience, and it's a live record. Took it in the studio, processed it a bit, and neated up the vocals, but the sound is live because it *is* live. We did what we should have done.

You can't get this with people yowling and carrying on and pressures of performance. You're going to get a *different* thing. This is an ideal way to record, you know, with real cleanliness and separation. And yet live playing.

Is it safe to say that you didn't set out to write a hit record, it just kind of happened?

Well, you know, I wrote "Touch of Grey" seven years ago. I've been performing it for years. Jerry saw the possibilities in it for being more than I was realizing, and reset it and made a monster out of it, I think.

No, we're not going to set out to make a hit record. We didn't set out to make one this time. It's just the coincidence—this tune seemed to click with some emergent factor in American consciousness, and blammo, there it was. The shoe fit this time.

So what has it meant for the Grateful Dead, do you suppose—and to you—this kind of success? You say it's problematical. . . .

Well, you know, I haven't seen any money from this yet. You see where I'm livin'. I *have*, however, contracted to buy something a little bit bigger than this crackerbox. I haven't closed on it yet, and the bank is willing to take a gamble that I'll be makin' some bucks this year. And so I get a house big enough to raise this new kid. But I have not actually laid hands on much in the way of money from this yet. I don't know when it comes or how it comes, but anyway, whatever comes, I've got it spent already. [*Laughs*]

So once again, I'm going to be—actually, for the first time gonna be able to really make this move from one economic level to another. But I'm not going to see the money. I never *do* seem to see a whole lot of the money. . . . You know, I've been struggling for the last bunch of years. I drive used cars, stuff like this. All of a sudden, I'm forty-six years old, I'll be able to buy a new car and a new house. And I'm real pleased about this. But as far as money goes, there's not a whole lot more I want. So I'm not really looking, personally, to make the big hits or anything. Because royalties and stuff over Grateful Dead albums, the way they've got it cataloged now, now that things have moved up a notch, should free me to go ahead and write without financial pressures for a while. That's all I'm *praying* from it—but then again I bought myself a new house and gave myself a *crushing* financial pressure, so I don't know. I might have a bigger box to live in. And the same worries, I don't know.

So what's the problem? You mentioned the fact that this big success, this balloon, is problematic.

What goes up comes down, and anything that the public suddenly embraces, they let go of that embrace just as soon, that's all. And it's going to be a long way down.

Well, the only problem with this is that if you embrace the business of being embraced too much, right? I would think that the Grateful Dead are sufficiently aware of the falseness of that sort of stuff. I mean. . .

Okay, say you wake up every morning and there's a ham sandwich and a chocolate shake beside your bed. And you have your ham sandwich, you have your chocolate shake, you get up and you live your day. You wake up the next day, there's a ham sandwich and a chocolate shake by your bed. And this happens for a year or two. One morning you wake up and there's just a ham sandwich. *Hey, where's my chocolate shake?* And then a little while later, you wake up, there's no ham sandwich, there's no chocolate shake. You feel deprived.

Maybe I'm afraid that we're going to get the whole stack of ham sandwiches and chocolate shakes and they're going to be taken away from us. And that's true hunger, to wake up in the morning without a ham sandwich and a chocolate shake beside your bed, once you're used to it.

I suppose…I thought you were going to say—
You think we're above being spoiled. [*Laughs*]

No, no, no. I don't think very many people in this world are.
Do you think we're corrupt?

That is the question. But I thought you were going to say you wake up with a ham sandwich and a chocolate shake every day, and suddenly you wake up with a ham sandwich, a chocolate shake, and a girl, and God knows what else, you know.
Or you wake up with a ham sandwich, a chocolate shake, and a *tapeworm.* And as long as the ham sandwich and the chocolate shake and the tapeworm are all there at the same time, fine. [*The interviewer collapses giggling.*] But you've got the tapeworm, no chocolate shake, no ham sandwich, then you're in real trouble, David. [*More giggles*] We should all have these troubles [*Laughs*]

So, uh, name that tapeworm. Get to know it. Make it your friend [Laughs]
Yeah, but you've got to feed it. A tapeworm by its nature *must* be fed.

"What did you think when you first saw the 'Touch of Grey' video?"
I was shocked. I thought, "What is the message of this thing?" These skeletons and this death imagery. And then the second time I thought it was delightful and very funny indeed. And I think that that little dog running through there, grabbing the leg bone, clued me to the joke. Well, even at the point where I was seeing it like first shot as a horror film, when they dissolve into the band itself playing, there's that joyous feel that happens. I caught that even the first time.

I will look at something like that for the first time *severely* critically. There's too many hopes, dreams, and expectations to go at it with an open mind....I've probably seen it half a dozen times. It continues to be an interesting video each time I've seen it, though.

As the author of some of that imagery, I don't know why it should shock you so much. Well, I don't know—actually, you're not responsible for all the bones. You're mostly the roses guy, aren't you?

Well, uh—well, er, uh—[*Laughs*] [*Dylan voice*] Whatever you sa-ay...[*Laughs*]

Would you like your songs to be performed by other singers? And if so, who?

I'd like "When a Man Loves a Woman" [from *Liberty*] to be performed by Frank Sinatra. And I even asked Annette [Flowers, the Grateful Dead's publishing person] if she would try and find out who his agent was and get it to him. I don't think she took me seriously. I *meant* it seriously. I think he could do that song a *lot* better than I do, and I think it's right up his alley.

Why don't you go see him when he plays at the Oakland Coliseum next month?

Me? [*Laughs*]

We can get you in backstage, man.

Oh, I wouldn't know what to say to Frank Sinatra, for crying out loud. And, I mean, I just think when you're talking top singers, top phrasers, people who can really handle a song, Sinatra's top. And he invented a genre. I don't care for much of his material.

Other singers than that—I wouldn't mind seeing Barbra Streisand do one of my tunes, and I'd love to hear Nina Hagen do "Scarlet Begonias" in German....

I've always wondered why more people don't do your tunes.

They're perceived as being Grateful Dead personal property. Or have been. Years ago I answered that question satisfactorily to myself. I said, "Well, why don't people do Grateful Dead tunes?" and I said, "Well, why don't they do Jefferson Airplane tunes? Oh, well, I *know* why they don't do Jefferson Airplane tunes: they're so tied in with that band and its image, it wouldn't occur to anyone to do it." And then I answered my question about the Grateful Dead songs, by answering that question.

I guess that can be safely said for a lot of the tunes, that they would be hard for somebody to make into their own. But some of them, I think, certainly stand up as songs.

I think it will begin happening now that we're not perceived as sociologically threatening. And we aren't, by the very fact that we're being played on AM radio now. By that very fact.

Yeah. That's the issue: sociologically threatening. What has happened—it can't just be merely a function of radio having no memory, that while they were laughing the Grateful Dead out of their offices, the program directors suddenly fell in love with the Grateful Dead. Of all the radio stations that I deal with—certainly "Touch of Grey" and the success of In the Dark *made selling my radio show an easier thing to do. But for example, Oedipus, the program director at WBCN [Boston], says he loves "Touch of Grey." His girlfriend is a big Deadhead, and turned him on to it....*

BCN used to be a real big Dead station, as I recall. I remember...I was going around promoting *Workingman's Dead*, just for the heck of it. I said, "I'd like to go out on the road and this'd be fun to do. Give me the record, I'll go on out and promote it." Did a lot of radio interviews, but they said, fine, but *don't play the record!*

I got into BCN, and I was doing an interview right around ten or eleven o'clock at night. They twisted my arm, and I said OK, I'll let you play *one tune.*

The first notes of "Uncle John's Band" began, and *lightning struck the station*, and we went off the air. So we got back on again, I said, "No way!" [*Laughs*] So BCN *almost* got a scoop on "Uncle John's Band."

The same guy at BCN took out a copy of—no, no, no, this must have been another time. I think it was several years later that I went into a station, I think it might have been BCN again, and he took out the record and showed me "Casey Jones," and there was a scratch, right—a· nail scratch across "Casey Jones." And he said, "The program director did this. He said we are *not* to play this, because the word *cocaine* is used in it, and the word's coming from the FCC that if any of this kind of stuff is going on, we stand in danger of losing our licenses." I went, "Oops, *that's* where my hits go...."

It's a shame, isn't it, that you can't use the word, no matter what context you use it in?

Well, it gives you a Chomskyish point of view suddenly about the way these things run. About how our programming really is being handled from somewhere. I mean, this is an *anti*drug song. You couldn't say the word back then; subsequently, you could.

Well, things are tightening up again, you know. The Pacifica radio network just recently ran into a problem with trying to air a reading of [Allen Ginsberg's epic beat poem] Howl.

Oh, speaking of *Howl*, when we were talking about my reading of *Elegies* earlier there, it occurred to me to say that Allen Ginsberg made a recording of *Howl* once.[5] Have you ever heard it? I think that is one of the finest things that has ever been put on a record. He starts in out in a totally flat New York Brooklyn voice, "I saw the best minds of my generation destroyed by madness and starving hysterical naked angel hipsters?" [sic] And I thought, "*God*, this is such an eloquent line—why is he throwing it away like this?"

Well, the fact is, he was just gettin' into it. And by the time you get halfway through that record, or close to the end of it, there are storm clouds raging around. There are lightning flashes. I mean, Allen Ginsberg and *Howl* had become one. And he just starts from nowhere, he builds and builds and builds through that thing. I *highly* recommend that record to anyone.

I wonder if that isn't the thing they were talking about broadcasting, because it was a program sort of on the history of censorship or of, you know, liberty in broadcasting and stuff. I don't know if it was a new reading, or...

There is a line in that poem which is ultimately objectionable to all Western cultural preconceptions *and* oedipal taboos and everything else. That line is supercharged. *I* won't say it over the air. As a matter of fact it was x-ed out in the written version. It was done with ellipses.

Interesting. In an interview segment with Jerry and Phil, just because the word shit *was audible in the flow of conversation, not in any scatological reference, but just as an interjection, you know, a color word, at least one of my stations found it necessary to excise it.... Not for fear of the FCC, necessarily, but indirectly. Mostly for fear of the owner of the station, and he did say that if it wasn't the first segment of the first program they were going to broadcast, he probably would've let it go. But still, I thought it was pretty absurd.*

[5]*Howl and Other Poems, read by Allen Ginsberg.* Fantasy F-7013, 1959.

Yes, it is absurd, the feeling that combinations of letters can be taboo. There are combinations of *words*, such as, you know, "Down with the republic!" you know, yelled under inciting conditions with Molotov cocktails, which, I suppose, could be considered…But individual words, no. I don't—I'm intending to use one in a song simply to make my statement about this. One of the songs I've been working [on] with Jerry—not to be shocking or any other reason than Thou Shalt Not Deny Us the Right to Use Words Just Because Children Might Hear Them. The fact that children might hear things is the bedrock stand that censors are taking, and you know, that's what censorship is all about: "My children might hear this."

Well, go ahead and use these words around your children, then! You use 'em in the army, you use 'em around your workplace, why be hypocrites? Go ahead, lay 'em on your kids. Just request that they keep their language clean around home, but—I always insisted to my son that we don't use these words at school, because you're gonna get in trouble with the teacher. There's nothing wrong in these words themselves. But I don't want you to use them, because I don't want you to get in the *habit* of using them. I want you to have control over your language. I said, "I know you talk this way around your friends, and I talk that way around my friends, too. Home is where we will learn how to speak the kind of English that you can go out and speak in public."

On the other hand, other of my friends don't feel this way at all, and they use the same language at home that they would use in talking to me, and I find it refreshing, and I'm not sure that's not the right way, either.

Well, I certainly think that the whole business of protecting your kids from a word is kind of a strange practice. Once again, you know, we could always get into the question of what's the real obscenity, you know, a four-letter word beginning with f, or a four-letter word beginning with k, for example. You know. Or actually, the act of— Maybe that's it. When you act these words out, which ones are really obscene, fucking or killing? Well, you know, that's a whole 'nother debate for a whole 'nother arena, I suspect.

Yes, yes.

But you, for example, use the "F" word in "Wharf Rat," to perfectly marvelous effect, and so far nobody's dropped dead over that.…

And you know what, that's the first time that the "F" word actually ever was used on a recording. But—the legend is that the Jefferson Airplane used it in "Up Against the Wall" ['We Can Be Together," on *Volunteers*] and it's printed in the lyrics, I believe, but you go ahead and play that record, and see if you can hear that word. You can't hear that word....

But they covered for us. The perception was that they had said it, and although as I said you can't hear it, so we were covered in a way. We could go right ahead and *say* it then. And there we go. We did, as I said, the first sixteen-track record, and we're the first ones to use the "F" word. [*Laughs*] What a claim to fame!

I mean, it's Lenny Bruce's legacy and we can't let him down entirely. But as you know, it's not the salt—my obscenities are not the salt of—oh, I can't call them obscenities now, after what I wrote in *Rolling Stone*. What can we call these words? loaded words. Words which are taboo in this society because they refer to reproductive or excretory functions.

Well, think of the hugeness of this mechanism designed to deny the existence of an everyday reality in our lives. It gives me a headache sometimes.

Don't think too much. It is there. You certainly acknowledge that it is there, and you work around it. And if you have the need to say the "F" word in public, and it's a strong enough need, I say go ahead and do it.

...I think it's a safe assumption that "The Deadhead Hour" reaches a lot of people that may never have seen the Grateful Dead live. Surely a lot of people whose arrival at the Grateful Dead is fairly recent. I don't really want to ask you what it all means, but I think it is a valid question to ask how it's all changed in the last couple of years, because of all these numbers and the new popularity and stuff. What do you suppose—

The first thought that I'm trying to run down here that just went zip in my head is I can't ever recall a time when it hasn't been changing, and changing, and changing. It seems every year we're into some new phase, and it's just another new phase. The phases tend to be bigger and bigger, is all....What is different about this phase and another phase—I don't think we'll know until this phase is over. We can look back on it and say— you know, there was a phase when you could say that what was happening was that kids were turning on to Quaaludes, and you were starting to get these dumb-outs at the show. There've been various drug phases that have altered the nature of the audience. There's a dry conservatism in the country now, which is—and I think one reason that the Deadheads are growing and jumping aboard right now is we look like an alternative to a grave parentalism which is overtaking the nation. We're *not* parental. The Grateful Dead do not attempt to be parental. We say, do what you want to do. Like we don't take stands for or against drugs. There are individual stands, some people in this band have been through a few things like that, and they're sharing the wisdom of their information that this leads nowhere. Fine. But we're not taking a group stance. And there's a group of Deadheads who have an orange umbrella[6] off somewhere, and they're the Drug Free Deadheads, and they invite people to come gather around there. I like that. That's nice. I don't think that you need to be stoned out of your mind to enjoy the Grateful Dead experience. If you *are* stoned out of your mind, well, then you're experiencing that, too, in your own way— I'm not—so long as you're not degenerating, ruining your body, you know, ruining your brain and bashing your head against the wall. I don't want to tell people what to do and not to do, personally. I may personally view it with alarm, but it's not my province to tell other people what to do, except by example.

Well, even leaving aside the issue of drugs, the liberty that's represented by the Grateful Dead—I mean, whether it's intentional or not, I think you're absolutely right that our scene is viewed as a nice escape place where you can be free of that kind of authority.

Now I think in some stadium situations—we haven't quite understood all this yet, and we've let forces *be* more authoritarian, the cop in the parking lot business, which are beyond our control. You *have* to hire police for those situations or you can't play them in the first place. It's a question of are we going to play or not.

And if you hire him, they *are* going to get out of line. Boy, "If you ever to go Houston, you better walk right, you better not gamble, and you better not fight. Sheriff'll arrest you, boys'll take you down, next thing you know, you're Nashville bound."[7] Walk right, kids. And we can keep this thing going a *long* time.

Well, let's talk about the possible directions it could take. It seems to me that it would be very desirable to allow this scene to thrive by encouraging

---

[6] Actually, it's a yellow balloon. They're the Wharf Rats, a twelve-step support group of Deadheads in recovery. They have meetings during the break at Grateful Dead shows.

[7] Hunter is quoting Huddie Ledbetter (a.k.a. Leadbelly) in "The Midnight Special."

responsibility. That's what the community that I belong to, the Well,[8] is discussing now. There seems to be, concomitant with the rise in the size of the crowd, a rise in the frequency of unwelcome dosing, for example, people who have no intention of going to the show who just come to sell their goods outside, you know, things like that. We're hoping to maybe develop an idea among our own community—which is to say the Deadhead community at large—to maybe become a little more self-governing. Not to depend on the band to do it. but to get the rest of us out there in the parking lot encouraging people to behave in a more responsible...

Maybe towards an end that when there is no more Grateful Dead that there is a community formed that needn't wither simply because they don't have their band anymore. Because it will come, that time. And if there can be a strong liberty-loving community at that point, which has evolved its own ethics, I think that community can hold together.

Well, it remains to be seen whether the community would survive beyond the demise of the band. Nobody's in a hurry to have that particular test, you know, thrown in our faces. It's been my contention for a long time that I don't stop being a Deadhead when I leave the Henry J. Kaiser [Auditorium]. Along with that—see, I'm not willing to lay a huge amount of it at your feet or at Jerry's feet or at the Grateful Dead's feet. What I've learned from the stuff in your songs is very valuable. There's a huge number of phrases and words and ideas that I've gotten from that stuff that aren't even necessarily what you intended to put across, right, but whatever it is, an outgrowth of the Grateful Dead experience has been a philosophy that is quite sound and quite valid, of thinking for ourselves and taking responsibility in our lives and doing right things without—

Well, if all the songs seem to somehow or other come to that conclusion, or they're coming from that place, I think it's reasonable to expect that *is*

[8]The Well (Whole Earth 'Lectronic Link) is a teleconferencing system through which people with computers "talk" to other people in public discussions and private communications. Subject matter ranges from broad and global concerns such as politics and sexuality and computers and culture to specialized niches, including a burgeoning community of Grateful Dead fans who use the computer facilities to talk about the many facets of their fandom—tapers trade tapes; tourheads plan their trips and arrange meetings on the road; ticket ordering information is shared and extras offered for sale or trade, etc. As John Barlow has pointed out, the Deadheads are a community without a physical location—and the Well and other computer systems around the country make it possible for that community to stay in touch in between the times when we're meeting at shows.

my philosophy. And the question is, do *I* live that philosophy, at that point. And I try to. I try to be a good messenger of what I'm writing, because it's not going to come to me to write. I have to write what I feel, and how I feel about things, no matter how far out the situations that I take, I think you'll always find that they're relating back to a central philosophy which is growing in me. And as I get more feedback from the people that it affects, I begin to understand that I do have a philosophy. If you'd asked me a couple of years ago, "Do you have a philosophy?" I'd just say, "Live and let live." I think it's getting a bit more detailed than that at this point.

Not to lead you astray from your question there, but it's my interview and it occurred to me that I'd like to say that.

Well, if you're willing to take credit for it, go for it. The philosophy, I mean. I always thought that it wasn't fair to impute too much to the band. Because whatever I'm getting out of it—you've always taken great pains, I think, to avoid being pinned down on literal meanings and stuff, which is to your credit. And you and Barlow both have consistently said, well, you know, the listener is entitled to write his own, or interpret his own version. But at the same time, I don't think it is a coincidence that I feel the way I do, and that I can cite so many things in your songs about it.

No, it's not a coincidence. I am coming from somewhere. I'm a bit of an alarmist—I'm one of the vanguard of the first to react to a perceived social malaise. I pick up on these things very quickly—it's my talent to see these things and to address them and to kind of generalize them and to get down on it. And to write a—hopefully, an amusing song, that may illustrate something without, maybe, coming right out and saying it. I mean, there are songs that just come right out and say it, like "Loser," or something. Or "Deal," that just come right out with the line, say this *is* the way it is. Or "The Wheel." There was a point, I think really high on that *Garcia* album, where all those songs occur, where the message was being laid out in no uncertain terms. I tend to do that, I think, a wee bit less these days, and go more for the illustration without the proverb. I may be wrong. I know I tend to...

No, I hear "watch each card you play, and play it slow." And "every time that wheel turn round, it's bound to cover just a little more ground." What's the opposite number in, say, "Touch of Grey" or "Black Muddy River" or something?

It's hard to say that there is such a thing in "Black Muddy River," which is just an examination of what it's like to be forty-five years old. It's just a good look into the deep dark well, and the heart resonances in that area. And a statement of individual freedom, that no matter what happens, I have this black muddy river to walk by.

I hesitate to define for you—I could talk for hours about what I mean by "black muddy river," and I don't mean a literal river running around. It's a deeply meaningful symbol to me, and I think just a little thought into like archetypal subconscious resonances gives you all you need to know about what we're talking about here. And past that you're setting it in concrete, and just as soon as that's done, that's not what it meant at all.

OK, well, back to the philosophy stuff instead then. Because I don't really feel that it's my place to interpret or instruct. But I have the opportunity, with my radio program, to illustrate, demonstrate. And as these things become real issues out there, you know, how are we gong to survive in a world of cops, civic upheaval, ticket scalping, T-shirt piracy, etc., etc.

Walk right and keep your nose clean.

Says who? I mean, in this world, I'm here to tell ya...

That's the common knowledge. It's been passed down for the last ten thousand years. The solution to everything. Walk right. Keep your nose clean. Don't meddle too much. And when you see something that's yours to be done, and there's nobody else doing it, that's your legitimate territory. Take it. As Woody Guthrie said, "Take it easy, but take it."

Well, what does that say to young people who are not particularly happy with the options laid out in front of them, who find that a Grateful Dead concert is the perfect place to get completely nuts. And leave shit all over the place, and maybe even do something dangerous to somebody else, like dosing 'em. See, that's where freedom and liberty become a conflict. You know, taking liberties.

All right. Along with these other things about keeping your nose clean and walking right, there's the age-old wisdom that's passed down through all Deaddom—which is, don't ever drink anything out of a cup that you don't know where it came from at a Grateful Dead concert, and avoid suspicious white powders. Never take a white powder that you don't know [*Laughs*] the source of. I mean, this is just little bits of common sense.

But as for solving this other problem—oh no, I can't solve this, this is the biggest one—this is our big, big problem now. What to do with the unruly factor now that's causing a large group situation to become aggravated and exhibit mob behavior. I don't know, I don't now that anybody's ever known, short of imposing absolute authoritarian control, and that is, of course, the opposite of what the Grateful Dead stand for. Will we be forced to become our own opposites. Interesting philosophical question. Perhaps everyone is. Because we're dealing in large amounts of money, profit-making here. Crowds, and like that. I mean, if you want to be spared all these hassles you go out in the desert and become a saint and really go for the real true values. See what's to be seen. Commune with your spirit and be, become a saint. Fine. We are in the marketplace. We have to deal with these things.

Well, I suppose even the saints have to deal with the paradox, like Saint Anthony had to lacerate himself. He was so horny he had to beat himself all the time. So who knows. Who knows. I think it's the human condition. I don't think there's an easy way out, and I do not see the millennium and the jubilee right around the corner here on earth. And Grateful Dead have become, by their very size, a microcosmic example of what's happened in the world at large. Some of you are going to get killed. Some are going to get run over, some of you are going to get your arms broken, and some of you are going to fry your heads out from being dosed, and short of authoritarian control, lack of Grateful Dead, and lack of any freedom-inducing organization, what you gonna do? You can pay your money, you can take your chances. But be aware, you know. Be aware. Don't come to a Grateful Dead concert feeling that you're just going to melt into the mix and providence is all going to take care of you. Like that. You must be a responsible human being. I mean, back we come to this— we're responsible, and all of a sudden I sound parental when I'm saying this. I don't see any solution. I mean, each individual has to be straight. Perhaps group pressures can be applied. Once that happens, the turn to factionalism and the holier-than-thou attitudes. I don't know, it's a murky mess and the bigger we get the murkier the mess is gonna be. But still, a good thing can be had. And generally is.

Well, yeah, that's the thing that keeps people coming back. I mean, currently what's going on are two things. The band seems to be a little bit stale, for lack of new material, which seems imminently to be solved, and the other thing is the crowd seems to be larger and a lot of people are running into this problem of people who don't know how to walk like an Egyptian yet, or—

[*Laughs*] Yeah. Sideways. That's the answer, David: sideways. It just had never occurred to me before. I really needed you to come over and tell me this. Yessir! [*Laughs*] This word has taken on a whole new meaning for me now....I have been using it a lot, over the years, and I'm wondering if that's what I mean by it. [*Laughs*]

Bear

January 13, 1991
Oakland, California

I'm not at all sure why Bear (Owsley Stanley) chose to break his years of media silence with me, but I'm not one to question such a gift. His name has been legend since the dawn of the counterculture—when I was paying five dollars for sacchharin tablets on the San Francisco Peninsula, better-connected kids on my block had genuine Purple Owsley. I have no idea whether I ever had any real Owsley acid; for that matter, I'm not sure whether I ever had any real acid in the sixties

But LSD was just one of Owsley's specialties; sound was another, and the combination of the two made him an essential player in the Grateful Dead saga. When my career as a journalist got rolling, I covered the technical beat for consumer music magazines and eventually for Mix: The Recording Industry Magazine. *I interviewed Grateful Dead sound designer Dan Healy for* Recording Engineer/Producer *and speaker designer John Meyer for* BAM *and later* Mix, *and both men cited Owsley as a driving force in the development of high-quality audio systems for rock 'n' roll.   In one of the very few published profiles of Owsley extant, Charles Perry wrote about his ex-housemate in the November 25, 1982,* Rolling Stone, *which memoir Bear hotly dismissed as excessively creative."[1] "Perry was a dweller on the outskirts," Bear fumed. "When he sent me a copy of [the* Rolling Stone *piece], I went to [housemates] Willie Spires and Bob Thomas and let them read it, and I let Melissa*

---

[1] Bear has complained about his treatment in several books (e.g., *Storming Heaven* and *Acid Dreams*) and magazine articles on LSD, the Dead, and other counterculture matters. The story he told me jibed pretty well with what I've read, though, and I felt he was candid enough to satisfy my shit detector.

[Bear's chemist girlfriend] read it. Bob said, 'Hey, that ain't the way it happened'; Willie said, 'That ain't the way it happened'; Melissa said, 'I don't know anything about that.' So Bob and I went to Charles and said, 'This is an interesting work of fiction, but it didn't happen that way. you were not privy to this thing. The Brown Shoe...may have been a commune to you, but it wasn't a commune to me. Everybody paid their rent to the landlord; we shared a kitchen; the fact is that we were all friends and none of us had much money and whoever happened to have some money would buy a bunch of food and we'd all eat." Perry's observations, however, are unarguable: *"Once when we smoked some hashish and developed a case of the munchies,"* Perry wrote, *"he accused me of trying to poison him with apple pie. 'I haven't had any plant food in my system for years' he groused between mouthfuls. 'My digestion will be fucked up for a month.'"*

Bear *"could be overbearing, but it wasn't ill-inspired,"* Perry also wrote. *"He wasn't a bully. There was something disinterested and nobly intentioned in his relentless enthusiasms. His ideas were never boring."*

I think *"relentless enthusiasms"* is a hell of a phrase.

"When he found out about the Acid Test and he found out that there were musicians getting together and playing stoned on acid, he had to find out what was going on," Phil Lesh told me in November 1984. *"He came to meet us, but I knew him already: I'd been eating his acid for a year already."*

In Storming Heaven: LSD and the American Dream, *author Jay Stevens titled the chapter on Owsley "The Alchemist"*[2] *and states that "without Owsley the Acid Tests probably would never have taken place, for the simple reason that LSD was too difficult to obtain. The dream of handing out thousands of doses was just that, a fantasy, or had been until that cocky little boho materialized out of the crowd of teenyboppers and said, 'I'm Owsley.'"*

"This was the second bar in the Owsley legend," wrote Stevens. *"He was the Pranksters' chemist."* Stevens also states that it was Owsley's contention that *"the Divine Force had given mankind LSD to counteract the discovery of nuclear fission."*

Acid was not illegal when Bear started making it. *"By the time the Acid Tests ended,"* Lesh continued, *"we had struck up a bargain: 'You build a sound system for us and we'll play the music.' Everything we do today is an offshoot of his ideas, which he developed through*

---

[2]Alchemy is a favorite theme of Bear's. Alembic, the audio and instruments and recording company founded by Ron Wickersham, Rick Turner, and others and heavily patronized by the Grateful Dead and other world-class musicians, was named by Owsley. An alembic is a vessel of distillation, both alchemical and philosophical.

conversations with us. He knew enough about acoustics, but he had to understand what musicians wanted."

For a few months in 1966, Owsley supported the Grateful Dead. "He was our patron, in the ultimate sense of the word," Lesh recalled. "He didn't send us a check—we lived together. He paid the bills…Bear bought us time, and space—well, he didn't buy it for us, we all bought it together. Bear will be the first one to tell you that. It was patronage in the finest sense: he never once thought about the money. We were able to be the Grateful Dead, and if they hired us, great. But we could at least eat."

I first met Bear in 1982, backstage at the Greek Theatre, when he kibitzed on my interview with Dan Healy. My next encounter with him was at Phil Lesh's house a couple of years later, when he arrived with a map of the world showing the mean temperatures at the height of the last Ice Age and delivered a ninety-minute lecture on a thermal cataclysm that he said would begin with a six-week rainstorm and leave the entire Northern Hemisphere uninhabitable. Where would we go to survive this? To north-central Australia, where he and nouveau survivalist George Harrison, among others, had already begun to colonize.

It all sounded eminently logical, although neither I nor any of the others in the room had any way of validating or refuting his predictions. Still, when Bear passed around the Australian visa applications, we all accepted them politely but noncommittally. Lesh said something to the effect that when the storm hit he'd probably just take a walk up the ridge and watch the world end; I quoted George Harrison: "When your number's oop, it's oop."

It was an interesting encounter, though. It gave me a glimpse of the power of this man, who is widely regarded as a genius and a crank and who is admired and respected even by many of the same people who roll their eyes in resignation when he approaches.

In the last few years I've encountered Bear backstage at Grateful Dead gigs, brandishing his jewelry cases and showing his exquisite works to people he meets there. They are beautiful indeed. One popular item is a belt buckle with the "Steal Your Face" logo, a schematic skull with a lightning bolt creasing its immense forehead. It's a design Bear created with Bob Thomas, about whom I know little except that he did time with Bear and turned Robert Hunter on to bagpipes.

I suspect the reason I got this interview with Bear is that whenever I ran into him I wanted to talk about sound, not LSD. I don't know, but at a Dead show in Sacramento in June of 1990 I asked him again for an interview and he agreed. I wasn't sure what I was going to do with it until I signed the contract to compile this book—and, of course, as soon as I had a good reason to conduct the interview the actual getting of it became problematic. Bear spends his time between tours creating new art pieces, and his concentration is exclusively on that process. Many dates were tentatively made and then canceled, until finally in January 1991 he arrived at my door with his girlfriend and a small bag of coffee beans, inspected my sound system, bitched about my speakers, offered a few suggestions for improving the acoustics of the room, turned a plain condenser mike into a pressure-zone microphone by placing its nose against a large piece of glass (don't ask), and then sat down for a six-hour interview that yielded the following transcript plus a couple of major digressions into politics, the inappropriateness of vegetable matter in the diet of human beings, and some fine points of speaker design and manufacture.

Were you already into audio when you first encountered the Grateful Dead?

Not really. A few months before I met the Grateful Dead, I had bought a hi-fi. I went around and tried to figure out what was the best hi-fi. I had a pretty good-sized place [in Berkeley]—must've been a fifty-five-foot-long room, about maybe thirty-five feet wide, just a big single room. I wound up going around and listening to a lot of stuff, and I decided to buy a Voice of the Theatre system, which was about the ugliest hi-fi system you could possibly conceive of. It had a cabinet on the bottom with a fifteen-inch speaker in it, and it was in a large box about the size of a small fridge. It had a little horn mounted up on top. The driver was maybe four inches in diameter; it was a relatively small horn. It looked like something that someone had rescued out from behind a screen at the local small movie theater.

It had a nice, tight sound— to me it sounded tight. Of course, later I learned it wasn't; we learned things to make it tighter. But compared to the average run-of-the mill speaker, it sounded OK. And it would get loud, and I wanted something that would get loud.

As it turned out, it wouldn't get loud enough, but when I started out with the Grateful Dead that became the Grateful Dead's PA system. [*Laughs*] My stereo became the Grateful Dead PA. It had a McIntosh amp, two channels, forty watts per channel.

What was your first encounter with the Dead?

Well, I had this pal. His name was Gaylord. He was a black dude. He lived in Berkeley. He kept wanting me to go down to Kesey's. He said, "All these Hell's Angels," and I thought, this has got to be the most violent bunch of guys I'd ever heard about. The idea of going down and hanging out with them didn't sound like it was going to be safe, and certainly not fun. Oh no, he says, you're really mistaken about these guys. You should really do this. I said, OK, Gaylord, one of these days. And he kept after me for months, and finally one day he came by in his car and I got in the car and went down there with him.

It was a big scene. It was totally different than anything I had expected. I thought I understood psychedelics, and Kesey and his bunch proved to me that I didn't understand psychedelics, or at least all the ramifications of it.

What had you been doing with psychedelics?

It was something that I was doing. It seemed to give me access to my head in some way. I can't exactly explain it. It's not something I've ever been able to put into words. I got involved with it because the first time I did it I realized it opened a door. And it was a place I wanted to explore.

I got involved maybe more deeply than I should've, because I didn't like poisoning myself with unknown things.

You just wanted to make sure you could control what you were taking?

I wanted to know what I was doing. And I guess I'm a good cook, is all I can say.

But the thing is that you only need very tiny amounts. And so even a fairly small amount of it is a lot.

What was different about what Kesey was doing with it?

Well, it was magic. It took you into a place that was like the descriptions in the books by the Rosicrucians and the Freemasons. It made sense of all the different occult things that I'd read. It was the introduction to magic. It was a pathway to another place, and it seemed to give you access to mental powers that were written about and talked about, amongst the Hindus and amongst the ancient alchemists and magicians. And direct: it seemed to go direct and give you access to those things. It was like a tool, like a tool to work on the consciousness.

The material always gave me great visions, incredible visions. I'm sure that it's the root source of the art that I do, even today. I'm sure it was the root source of my ability to manipulate sound—which I looked at as an art form.

I never looked at myself as an engineer, any more than I looked at myself as a chemist or anything else. Not a scientist. I have a scientific background, because I'm interested in everything, and science is just a way of describing the physical universe. And alchemy and the occult is just a way of describing the nonphysical universe. And I was interested in both aspects. Art is a way of creating something yourself, as a man, which can say something about either the physical, the nonphysical, or both.

One of the earliest things that happened to me with regard to psychedelics was that the universe became even more three-dimensional. It seemed to have more dimension and depth and space to it. Colors and things seemed very intense. At one of the Acid Tests—I don't know which one it was, it might have been Watts—it was a very strange experience where all of a sudden I was *looking* at sound coming out of the speakers. This happened on several occasions. It also happened at the house we were staying in in Watts, where I actually saw sound coming out of the speakers....What's that called? Synesthesia.

I've never talked to anyone else who's actually had that experience, but I actually had that experience. And it was funny because I'm looking at this sound, I'm really out there, and all kinds of other things are going on, and I was thinking, you know, that doesn't look the way I thought sound...

The lady I was with in those days was quite direct about everything. Her name was Melissa. This was long before I met the Dead. Whenever we would get high, and things would start getting really weird, she would insist on dealing with them as though they were real—not a hallucination, not something that the drug was doing, "this is reality"—and force me to deal with it. So I never got into that space that a lot of people get into where they say, "Oh, it's the drug that's doing this. This is a hallucination. This is a nonreal effect which is being produced by a chemical which is in my brain." I had to deal with it as though this was the absolute concrete everyday reality *now*—deal with it, right? And that was interesting, because it's different that way, see? You have a whole different set. It's like the difference between driving a car in a video game or getting in a car, and she wouldn't let me drive the video-game car. Deal with it! On the street! Now!

And so when I got to this is point in the Acid Test when I saw sound coming out of the speakers, I was totally programmed to accept whatever I saw as being real—more real, perhaps, than my everyday life, which I'd come to believe was restricted consciousness, where I actually saw less, or felt less, or perceived less.

And so the telepathy and the almost telekinetic kind of things that go on, that you experience when you're on acid, I accepted as real, that they were actually there. There are probably people, I thought, that can do this. So the idea of Uri Geller bending the spoon or doing things like that, that never amazed me. That just seemed like, "Oh, he's figured out how to do it without having to have an amplifier in his system. He's got it straight. People who are telekinetic, people who read minds, people who have precognitive visions—oh, well, they've just learned how to do it without having to think."

And you read all throughout the Hindu stuff about the fakirs, who are capable of doing things, translating stuff, levitating their bodies, manifesting things in the physical world and stuff like that, and people think it's sleight of hand, or it's hokum. I don't think it is. I think it is that through their meditative states, they've managed to kick whatever storehouse of whatever it is in the brain that the acid kicks, only they've learned to do it without acid. Which is probably better, but sometimes it takes a lifetime, and not all of them make it. Out of maybe ten thousand people who follow the yogic practices, maybe three or four get to the state of becoming that kind of a high master.

I would imagine that it would have some relevance that you came from a culture that doesn't really honor that kind of stuff very much, or pay much attention to it at all.

You mean the physical orientation?

Well, what passes for spiritualism among the white Anglo-Saxon Protestant types is pretty anti-mystical.

Judeo-Christian-Islamic. It's the soldier's religion. From ancient days.

We're finding that out in a major way right now, aren't we?

Hey, the Romans had so much trouble with the Jews that they had to run 'em out, had to disperse 'em. They never stopped fighting them. That was 70 A.D.

When Constantine wanted to have better control over his troops and subjects, he produced Christianity. Which is maybe an odd way of looking at it, but he called a whole bunch of Christian representatives together and said, "Agree upon something." And he may have done even more than that, I don't know, because what we hear about it now is what the church preserved to tell people. All we know is that there were about seven thousand written documents at that point, which was in the fourth century, and most of them were destroyed. Most of the writings that became canonized were primarily the writings of a soldier, Saul of Tarsus [a.k.a. Saint Paul].

Certainly everybody recognizes the warlike nature of Islam. So we have the three major religions that are connected with the materialistic culture in the Western world, and science, which was the remaining investigating urge remaining from alchemy—which was a philosophy about the world, life, universe, God, what it is. Because of the belief that the practitioners of alchemy had that they could understand the universe by manipulating the physical things, which then became chemistry and physics and so forth; that, by understanding the rules by which the universe was put together, they could extrapolate these rules into the unseen universe and into other things.

Alchemy teaches that "as above, so below." If you understand something that works on one level, you can understand it on another. A common example of this is the similarity in the structure of the solar system and the structure of an atom. Which can be represented or thought about in a similar fashion.

We seem to be coming back to that now, as this chaos theory emerges, and fractals as a way of explaining—
I always thought like alchemy itself was like a seed, because it embodied very basic concepts, usually described as the Seven Principles. And that from that seed, when it was planted, grew basically two— actually it was several, but basically two plants. One plant we call chemistry, the other plant we call physics. There was also biology, etc., etc., etc.—all the different disciplines. But two basic disciplines, which are physics and chemistry, two distinct ways of looking at the physical interactions of objects in the universe. One the mechanical interactions, one the chemical interactions, the reactive interactions.

But as these sciences developed, and as they began to dig deeper and deeper and deeper into the structure of matter, all of a sudden it wasn't solid anymore. It became vibrational. It became energetic. It became fields. And things like the Heisenberg uncertainty principle, which says you can't describe everything about something, appeared. All kinds of different things all start—it starts to get very strange, and turns back into just vibration, you deal with it as vibration. So you might say that the plants grew up and they flowered, the flowering being modern technology. And then they set seed, and the seed is alchemy. Comes right back again, the same thing. That's the way I look at it. The individual plants are highly specialized, but when they come back together they produce a unified concept once again.

So it's more cyclical than linear—and we like that.
Yeah, well, everything is cyclical. We go back to alchemy. The whole concept of the universe as a conscious entity which is dreaming it all up makes it easy to understand such things as telepathy. Why astrology? Well, astrology is a description of how the cyclical things that you can see in the recurring angles and relationships of the planets can be used to connect or to relate to the nature of events on the earth. And after hundreds of thousands of years of watching it, people evolved this "Oh, yeah, well, when this happens, things are likely to do this." Over a long period of time, a lot of observation, we have come up with this thing. But you can't scientifically measure it. There's no direct connection. The only connection is that everything's being thought up in the mind of the being that's thinking everything up at the same time, according to the rules, the rules being what we describe as the laws of nature. We know some of them, we don't know all of them. Mostly they're simple.

Were you already thinking about this stuff when you started taking acid?
It's hard for me to say, because I'm not a meticulously scientific kind of guy who kept journals or anything else about the way in which I thought about stuff. And so as my viewpoint and my philosophy evolves, it replaces the philosophy that was there. In some cases I can remember what I thought before, but mostly I've found out that I can hold an idea or a concept, and then suddenly I'll discover that it's wrong, that it's fallacious, that I'm mistaken. I immediately discard that and replace it with the new information. It's like taping over a tape. I don't necessarily want to go back and remember what a fool I was. [*Laughs*]

So you went to Kesey's acid scene—
Went down to Kesey's house, and I found it very interesting. Interesting enough that I went down several more times, and one of the times—I had heard about this band, which the first time I went down there they were calling the Warlocks, and I didn't pay that much attention to it, except [the Pranksters] were obviously all excited about it.
Next time I went down someone came in and said they'd just picked the name "Grateful Dead." I think it was Mountain Girl, came in and said that—"Oh, they've got a new name, they've named themselves. They couldn't be the Warlocks, because some band in Florida had that name."

Which band I never heard of after that. [*Laughs*] I don't know if they really existed or not.

I didn't actually see them play until I went to the Muir Beach Acid Test [December, 1965]. That's when I saw them play. Whether or not I ran into Garcia or someone else at Kesey's during those visits, I don't really recall. The only person other than Mountain Girl and George Walker, maybe Page [Browning] and Kesey himself, was maybe Terry the Tramp, one of the Angels, I remember him. But I don't remember whether Kesey was there. There were several times, there was a big party of people all going in every direction at once. Very difficult to make a whole lot of sense out of it, because it was totally different from the scene I was in, which was relatively quiet up to that point.

Kesey was the kind of guy that reached out, took your knobs, and tweaked them all the way to ten. All of them. And the whole scene was running at ten all the time. It was almost as sudden, and as different, as discovering psychedelics themselves for the first time, at another level.

I would venture to say, then, that the social aspect of it—the collective acid experience—probably was part of the eye-opener there, right? I mean, everybody was tripping together, and in on the joke together, or in on the multiple jokes?

I think it was more than that. They did specific things. They made specific sounds. They did specific stuff. They'd loop tape machines together and do delays and get reverberation, the sound reinforcing itself. There's a certain persistence—like when you're really high and move your hand, you get a smear. Well, there's also other kinds of persistence, and they reinforced all these things.

It seemed as though they had rediscovered something from ancient ways and ancient times. A lot of the music that's used in shamanic rituals does the same thing, which we discovered later, but this totally came up in isolation. None of these people in Kesey's scene had any roots in the shamanistic rituals at all. That was the other group of people that I'd run into every so often, that were more into those things. The Millbrook guys, Janiger,[3] all those guys. They were more into that. [I don't know] whether they actually got into the rituals or not, because I just had some contacts with them—you know, take a few trips with them, and that sort of thing— but I didn't follow that line, didn't go down, never went to an Indian peyote meeting, although I've always had the desire to do so. And I never

---

[3] Oscar Janiger, now head of the Albert Hofmann Foundation.

went to a *curandero* in Mexico with the mushrooms or any of those things. So I've never actually seen it. But from the best that I can figure out, all those rituals contained a lot of the elements which the Pranksters discovered, or rediscovered, or invented, or something.

That's probably not that much of a surprise, though. I'm certainly of the belief that a lot of that stuff is in our genetic—a lot of this stuff, the reason we get that recognition from it is that some of it emanates from our own neurology and DNA.

One of the more interesting plants on this planet is cannabis. As far as I can see, all the talking about *cannabis sativa* and *cannabis indica* and *cannabis ruderalis* is rubbish. I think there's one plant, cannabis whatever-you-want-to-call-it, and that all of these interbreed completely, and that there's a lot of different cultivars. Just as if you looked at a Great Dane and a Chihuahua, you might think they were totally different kinds of animals, right? But obviously they're not, they're just cultivars.

And so there's a lot of different variants and variations amongst cannabis, but it's a single plant. And it seems to produce a substance which has an effect on meat-eaters. It does not seem to have much of any effect on herbivores.

People are carnivores. People are almost, but not quite, obligate carnivores.... If you eat vegetables, you're called a vegetarian. If you're an animal that's adapted to a diet of plants, you're a herbivore. It's a better term.

Herbivores do not seem to get intoxicated by cannabis.

So it's our chemistry, not our choice of food, that calls us meat-eaters.

Yeah, yeah, yeah. Our bodies are highly adapted to a diet of meat, but we've retained some of our monkey roots so that we can survive between periods of no game. Most predatory animals are totally controlled by accessibility of game. If a cat cannot find prey, the cat will die. The cat, of course, will eat anything from bugs on up—anything that'll move, it'll eat. But sometimes men have occupied areas in the planet where there isn't any other kind of food, and if there's no game there's nothing to eat, and he dies. Eskimos are that way.

But he seems to have retained a lot of that vegetable processing machinery left over from the time when he was swinging from branch to branch. But that's so far back, maybe five million years or so, so far back that we only have the most rudimentary systems remaining from that. The result is when we eat a lot of vegetable matter we don't live very long, die at about sixty or seventy. Your body becomes heavy rather rapidly. Your teeth rot away. Things like that. All kinds of problems occur.

If you eat a mixed diet, foods all taken in at one meal, you're more likely to suffer more extensively more rapidly than if you eat them at separate meals. But basically our bodies are capable of digesting vegetation, which is very useful. It gives us a survival edge, which is why we have it, and why we're lucky we have it.

You can take a pot plant, might be forty pounds wet weight. And you take an ounce of that and feed it to the dog, and the dog gets so stoned he can't stand up. On the other hand, a deer can walk up to the plant and eat half the plant. Nothing. He can eat the equivalent of about a pound, the tops off that plant, one ounce of which would incapacitate the dog, and the deer will walk over to the next plant and eat some.

So the deer just doesn't have the chemistry to process it and get what we would call the benefit of it.

Right. There was a doctor, I don't remember his name —if it's important to you it could be looked up. He did extensive research around 1860 in India on the effects of cannabis, because it was a big thing, it was a traditional herb used in large quantities in India and he found that when he fed experimental amounts of it to various animals, he determined that there was virtually no effect observable in herbivorous animals. I think he tried goats and rabbits and sheep and some kind of deer or antelope, it was a series of them. And yet carnivorous animals, like cats and dogs and people, seemed to get a strong effect from it. Insects that eat plants don't seem to be repelled by it. It doesn't seem to bother them. Cabbage worms will eat it up like crazy.

Another thing is that the plant growing out in the wild is usually very weak. As they say, wild grass is no good. It's trash. But when people grow it, it keeps getting stronger and stronger.

I feel very strongly about the telepathic nature of plants, which has been demonstrated by various people. There was a lot of publicity about fifteen or twenty years ago by a guy named Jim Backster, who put electrodes, like lie-detector electrodes, galvanic response meter, onto plants, and found that you could threaten them with fire, or even *think* about threatening them with fire, and they'd react. He found this reaction on every plant he tried it on.

My own experiences with psychedelics led me to believe that plants are highly conscious entities. Very conscious. And they're not troubled by having an ego, because they don't have to make a decision. The ego is a restricted kind of consciousness that an animal has to have in order to be able to sort out and just accept some input so as to make a decision to do something. Because if you have all inputs all the time, you're almost unable to make a decision. It's too much data. Too much stuff. You're swamped. A plant doesn't have to make much in the way of decisions; it roots where its seed fell. That's it.

But it does express itself in various ways. One example is the orchid that resembles a certain bee. So completely does it resemble a female bee that the males try to mate with it. It smells like the bee, and it looks like the bee, and it's shaped in such a way that when the male grabs it, his head pushes up against the pollinia, which are the pollen balls that stick to him. And he attempts to mate. And he leaves that flower and goes to another one and tries again. He leaves the pollinia that he picked up from the first one and picks up a pair from that one. And he might actually hump a dozen flowers in turn, right? This may reduce his ability to mate with the proper female of his species, but it does the flower's thing.

And yet flowers have no eyes. Orchids have no eyes. To imitate the female, the plant has to know what it looks like. So the plant knows what it looks like. Not only does it know what it looks like, it has to understand the practices that that animal undergoes in order to put itself in there to take advantage of that.

I think you're construing "consciousness" rather broadly here, aren't you?
Of course. Why should you restrict the definition of consciousness? My experiences of plants through psychedelics led me to believe that—it's an extension of my alchemical belief. The basic tenet of alchemy is that the universe is mental, that there's a being which is nothing but mind, pure mind, and that all that we experience is the creation of this mind. According to the rules, which are the laws of nature, the rules of physics, the rules of chemistry, and so forth. Attraction, repulsion, polarity—all these things are still mental. And since everything in the universe is mental because it is the mentation of the being which is mental, everything has to use the same kind of mentality. In other words, all consciousness relates and is the same. So there shouldn't be any trouble being able to communicate mentally with any other living thing, whether it be another man, a dog, a plant, or anything else, because all thought has to be of the same nature, because it's all manifested by it. The way in which we manipulate sound waves in our language, the way in which we put this language together, is more expressive of us and of our culture. As

we're beginning to understand, other animals use sound to communicate in much more complicated fashions than we had previously thought. Dolphins, for instance, and even monkeys, and perhaps even other animals. There's always been people like Indians who would say that they could talk to the animals and that they knew what the animal was saying when it made a certain noise. Certainly they've been very successful in teaching American Sign Language to chimpanzees. So I see no reason why one should doubt that behind that all is a common modality of thought.

So you regard it all as a continuum then, from rocks to, uh, gods.

Yeah. Which is why I think people are attracted to crystals, because a crystalline substance has a highly ordered electronic behavior, and the behavior of thought and mentation has electronic nature to it. There's a flow of electrons. And in fact one of the very interesting things, as a little aside...we found that some of the psychedelics seemed to affect our ability to interact with inanimate equipment. Specifically, when someone at a show or in a room where someone was playing music was to take some DMT, which is a rather powerful psychedelic, the music would immediately become louder and more strident. It has a certain tonality to it, a certain quality to it, which is very distinctive.

Generally we'd all do it, right [*laughs*], and we thought, "Oh, well, it's just one of those things." But then I got back to that thing that I'd learned from Melissa: Don't assume that this is an illusion caused by the substance. Believe it's real. So I said, "Hey! I believe this is real."

One thing we noticed was that the tubes would get red hot and burn out half the time and it would tear the voice coils out of the speakers. And yet we couldn't make it do that ordinarily. So I actually started making some measurements. We'd measure the amplifier at its maximum output, with a musician doing everything he could to get the max out of it. Then somebody would smoke the DMT—but not everybody, just one person. And we'd measure it. And it would go up six dB.

That's quadruple power, right?

Right. It would go up more than that sometimes. And yet we were absolutely sure we were at the limit. It would be something like 127 max. Somebody would smoke it, it'd go to 132. And it would literally melt the voice coils. Where did the power come from? The tubes couldn't handle it. They would often burn up. They would often get hot, and the internal structures in the tubes would melt. Where'd it come from? What was going on?

I evolved a little theory—I don't know, because obviously this is something that you could do some scientific research on, it would be well worthy of it. The idea being, if there was some type of circuit that was more sensitive to it than others, you could measure different circuit sensitivity. Then you could optimize that, and perhaps you might even be able to develop a circuit that had that property to such an extent that a person could affect it without having to take the psychedelic. And it wouldn't matter what—any interaction of any kind that you could initiate with your mind would enable you to build something that would directly control a machine. Because a computer could interpret anything, once you could get into it that way, you see. Which is what we need—we need a way of controlling machines directly.

It's like an example of many of the opportunities that psychedelics present to man, which are being completely thrown away because of the irrational approach that people are taking to them. This is real. The amplifier changes. The sound changes. The music also changes, so whether that's a psychic effect on the amplifier or on the musician, I don't know. But no matter what effect Person A's taking of the psychedelic could have on Person B who's playing the guitar, there's no way that Person B could make that guitar get louder by himself. The guitar, everything, got louder, got stronger, became more strident. It changed in quality, but it also became much louder. That came from a direct effect on maybe the electrons flowing in the equipment—which is the thing about the organization of electrons and the similarity, or the very close association, of the quality of consciousness or of thought to electronic motion and matter. Because certainly the most elaborately constrained electron would be the one that's associated with DNA, which is billions of atoms, sometimes, an enormous number of atoms, all of which, arranged in a very precise way, would order the motion of electrons in a very, very precise and specific and special way.

Which would have frequency and resonances and stuff... if you take your "as above, so below," then we can assume that there would be ripples and harmonics of that all the way up into perceivable realms.

Probably, yeah.

Did you like the music when you first heard the Grateful Dead at Muir Beach?

It scared me. They seemed to have—all that seemed to have a connection to a very scary, possibly dangerous aspect of reality to me....

I read about you pushing a chair around that building, which made a lot of noise....[4]

I remember pushing that chair around. I remember all kinds of different things. I remember all kinds of noises and sounds and things. The Pranksters would make these noises, and the noises would seem to get inside your nervous system, as if there was some type of a plug or something in your head. It would...make the connection available to be plugged into something. A psychic cable.

Ah. Strip away the insulation.

Yeah, you might say. Like a hymen, perhaps [*laughs*]. A mental hymen. And then the connection would be made, and all the people would be linked up and start sharing thoughts and images and ideas. It was not just thoughts, but you saw like a patchwork of images, and you felt a patchwork of body sensations and everything else. It was very definitely a gestalt, multiple-mind kind of phenomenon.

Polymorphous synesthesia.

Could be. Yeah, that might be a good term. That would certainly describe it.

Obviously other people felt this, too.

But that was the first time anything like that had actually happened to me. It was very weird, and scary.

---

[4]In *Garcia: A Signpost to New Space* by Garcia, Reich, and Wenner (page 52).
MOUNTAIN GIRL: One of the highlights of that one was—dare I, shall I breathe his name?— Owsley pushing a chair along this wooden floor, this old wooden chair, running it along the floor making this noise, the most horrible screeching and scraping. It went on for hours, I'm not exaggerating, it just drove everybody completely up the wall. That was really an incredible exhibition of making yourself...uncomfortable...making other people uncomfortable.
JERRY GARCIA: No, man, it was just the guy completely freaked out with his body, running around...that's what that was, I mean he was completely freaked out.
MG: He was scraping that chair and listening to the noise and lovin' it, I guess that was what was happening.
JG: How do you know?
MG: Oh, I watched him for a really long time
JG: That wasn't it. I talked to him about that a lot and he just...his mind was completely shot, he thought that they'd come and taken it from him.

Nobody would talk about it. You didn't talk about it, you just did it. Whatever you had done, whatever was going on in that scene for what, a year or two before I ran into it, they had slowly but surely built this up, and it may very well have been instinctive.

I thought, "These guys are fantastic." But it was scary. The music was scary. Pushing me to the edge. The sound of Garcia's guitar was like the claws of a tiger. It was like dangerously scary. Very, very to the point. You can't talk about this stuff. I thought to myself, "These guys are going to be greater than the Beatles someday." It wasn't as though I just thought that, it was almost like a revelation, like looking into the future. I just instinctively knew that there was something like that....I did think that these guys are going to be greater than the Beatles. That was the way I recognized the thought I was having about it. It was the terms in which I subvocalized that to myself.

And in a way, they are, because the Beatles were a phenomenon of the universal attractiveness of their music, and the intense teenage involvement. We find that intense teenage involvement in dozens of different bands, we find excellent musical output in dozens of different bands, and they create a lot of fans—but they have not created the kind of thing that's associated with the Dead.

They played for a while and then they played again and all these other things were going on, and then there was this one paranoid little sucker in there, and he thought something, and I picked up his thought—because we were all linked together, it was this total telepathic loop, which meant that it was like being at a very noisy cocktail party inside your head. This guy saw somebody come into the place that he thought was a narc. He thought, "Narcs!" I thought, "Narcs!" I went right out the side door. I was gone.

Acid wasn't illegal yet, was it?
There were all kinds of drugs going on there. It didn't matter. This guy's paranoia came in on my party line and out I went.

The thing about me pushing the chair around was maybe ten or fifteen minutes.

It was just somebody else's salient memory of that night.
And I saw one set of the Grateful Dead, and some other stuff, and I was gone. I was running up the road.

But you went to see them again.

Oh, yeah, but it was a while. That was so freaky, that whole trip was so freaky, that I thought they [the Pranksters] were messing with something that was probably very dangerous. It was not so good.

The next day, or a few days later, I told Kesey, "Hey, you're messing with ancient stuff. And without any maps! You may need to be careful about this—it was kind of scary." And he kind of laughed at me—well, it's sort of like the guy who gets on the roller coaster for the first time. Supposing some guy was a Yanomami Indian or something and he comes out of the forest and the first thing he does is somebody puts him on a roller coaster. He's never even seen civilization, and somebody puts him on a roller coaster. He'll get off that thing and say, "That's very dangerous. That's scary." And yet other people go around and around, again and again and again.

You had taken acid a lot before, so it wasn't the acid that was the scary part—it was the Grateful Dead that was the scary part?

No, it wasn't the Grateful Dead. It was nothing to do with the Grateful Dead.

The linkage was the scary part.

Yeah. The Prankster thing.

The group-mind.

Yeah. Which the Grateful Dead were part of. Grateful Dead were Pranksters. They were musicians, but they were also Pranksters.

The next time I saw them was at the Fillmore Acid Test, and I met Phil [Lesh]. I walked over to him and I said, "I'd like to work for you guys." Because I had decided that this was the most amazing thing I'd ever run into. And he says, "We don't have a manager..."

I said, "I don't think I want to be the manager."

He said, "Well, we don't have a sound man," and I said, "Well, I don't know anything about that, either, but I guess I could probably learn. Sounds like more fun." [*Laughs*]

That's how that happened.

For a long time, it was like no matter whatever else we were doing, we *had* to be at the Acid Test every week. That was it. No matter what other shows we did, or anything else, Saturday night we were there. Other than that, I don't know how many of those I would have gone to. I didn't actually think of myself as a Prankster per se. I found it all kind of scary, and every time, it provided days and days and days of sorting it out and putting it together, trying to get it together. It was sort of like a crash course in how to become a jet pilot when you had never seen a jet before. The way they did it was they dropped you in there, took you up, and said, "The *controls are yours!*" [*Maniacal laugh*] Whoa! Barrel rolls! Immelmanns! Tailspins! Right into the ground, some times. But psychically you recover from all this, I guess, if you're tough. I guess most of us were. Occasionally some people weren't; it's unfortunate. But because of the way in which it was undertaken in those days, and the fact that we used to take huge amounts of acid—we used to take 250, 300 mikes or more; Kesey preferred 400 or more. Albert Hofmann[5] told me that was a substantial overdose, and I said, "Yes, in retrospect, I realize it was, but…"

What do you consider an optimum dose?

Oh, I don't know. People nowadays seem to take around 100, 150, something like that. They call 'em disco hits, I think.…All I know is that the result is that people—it's like first you have training wheels on your bike before you get the 1,000-cc Yamaha. It's a little different effect, and the result is that people don't get so crazy, I guess. But in those days everybody got kind of crazy, and some people crash-landed and other people managed to make it further down the road, but the whole scene became very, very, very loud and very weird, and it attracted a lot of attention. It attracted a lot of social concern, because a lot of people were experimenting with radically different social matrices which were frightening to our cultural leaders and societal leaders. The police and the legislatures and the business community—basically the people who were concerned with maintaining a stable society—saw this as a very threatening and frightening phenomenon. A lot of people acting very weird and doing things that just didn't fit. They passed a lot of laws against it and tried to suppress it in various ways.

Whether or not the psychedelics would have been included in the basic matrix of antidrug laws or not without the heavy influence of some people like Art Linkletter, I doubt.

---

[5]Discoverer of LSD. See his memoir, *LSD: My Problem Child—Reflections on Sacred Drugs, Mysticism, and Science*. Los Angeles: J.P. Tarcher, Inc., 1983. Distributed by St. Martin's Press.

That story about his daughter's suicide—

I heard that she was not on [LSD], but just the fact that she had been taking it was enough. Somewhere in the past, she had taken it.

There were a lot of bogus stories like that. "People went blind staring at the sun!"

Chromosome damage!

There were scientists ready to cough up all this crap to suit the political agenda. We still see that.

Sure, we were taking large doses, because that's what we thought was the right amount. Some people were psychically crashing into walls. Nobody knew about it. We didn't come with a shaman, with a thousand years or ten thousand years or a hundred thousands years of traditions and a ring of people holding your hand to show you the right way to go. It's not something that you started at puberty with. It's something, all of a sudden, bang! you're shot from a cannon. And some people had a little problem with it, and so some people did themselves in when they weren't on it, some people accidentally died when they were on it—hey, I can't justify that stuff. I didn't know any more than anyone else, right? All I knew was that it was better to take a known substance in a known quantity than an unknown mixture of who-knows-what at god-knows-what quantity. That was the only difference.

I didn't advocate it; I never told anybody to go out and take it, or anything else, but I knew I wanted to take it. I knew it was important to me. And I didn't want to poison myself, I didn't like Russian roulette with chemicals. I didn't think it was appropriate.

I would say, then, that what you were doing was essentially taking responsibility for it, for yourself and for your partners.

You might say. It's one way of looking at it. It was all a matter of consent at that point. But the fact is that out in the culture as a whole, all kinds of bizarre things were happening.

In fact, it bothered me. I didn't know for a long time whether it was a good thing or a bad thing. Eventually I realized that the psychedelic itself was neither good nor bad, any more than a very sharp knife is good or bad. You can use a knife to whittle a sculpture, you can use it to trim your nails, you can use it to cut up your food, or you can use it to stab somebody. The knife itself is not the operative thing there, but it took me a long time, because of the fact that it's so powerful and it changes consciousness so much.

So you thought it was an intrinsically good thing at first.
I didn't know. And that was the reason why I cycled in and out of it for a long time. Eventually I decided it was just getting too weird to handle.

Well, then, I would say acid upset your moral constructs—
It made me think about it very seriously.

It did for a lot of people.
Because of the fact that things happened that weren't positive. Nonpositive things were happening as well as positive ones, things like the example about the girl that jumped out the window. And Charles Manson. And the fact that one person would take acid and become like Gandhi. And another person would take acid, like some of the Hell's Angels, and say, "Oh, man, I love to get in a fight when I'm on acid." Why? "Cause everybody else is in slow motion." Right. Well…[*Laughs*].
Kesey said, "All this does is turn up your volume. It don't change who you are, it just turns up the volume." The basic nature of the person is simply amplified. Well, in a social context you could understand how those who feel responsible for the social matrix itself don't want something that may produce these kinds of effects.
The reason is suppression.

But you don't outlaw automobiles because they can be used to run people over intentionally. Any tool can be a weapon.
That's true. And they lump everything together. I do not consider psychedelics a drug: you don't take it as an escape; you don't take it to cure something; it doesn't suppress you. It's a different thing. It came out of a religious matrix, it was always in a religious matrix, it affected me in a religious kind of way. It's part of the Native American church, where they specify it as a religious thing. In all the ethnobotanical matrices, in the cultures of Central and South America, and even in Africa, it's always used in a social matrix, in a religious or a quasi-religious way. Sometimes we can't, from our viewpoint, always recognize religiosity in things that people do.

You were asking me how you thought the Grateful Dead scene relates to psychedelics. I don't know how it relates to psychedelics. All I know is that at one point I joined up with a band that were Pranksters; they were part of the scene that was doing something that was right out on the edge, the edge of consciousness, the edge of social, the edge of magic, the edge of music, that was very dynamic, a band composed of five guys that were among the smartest people I'd ever run across. To find that many really smart people, people whose minds operated in the same function zone that mine did, [who] could carry on the most tenuous and stratospheric of conversations with nobody gettin' lost, that blew my mind, number one. It's unusual to find that kind of a bunch.

I've worked for a lot of bands: I've been on the road; I've worked in halls where they come through, a different band every day; in festival situations. I've worked situations where I've had a lot of contact with a lot of musicians, and by and large I find that there's a great many really bright guys involved in the music, but to find that many all in one group is truly unique.

That Prankster scene didn't sustain too much longer.

It was sort of like, if you set fire to a skyrocket it's going to be brilliant as hell, but it doesn't go very far and it doesn't last very long. It attracted so much social pressure on the individuals that had it not been for Kesey getting busted and all these other things happening, and the intense amount of social and police pressure on it, who knows how far or where it would've gone? But as it was, it did its thing ultraspectacularly, but by necessity it had to follow that old Prankster saying: "Nothing lasts." It lasted as long as it did, and that was it.

Everybody describes the Acid Test as being—"We were not performers in the Acid Test," that anybody who walked in and paid his buck—

Everybody could get stoned and freak out and flip out, do anything they wanted to because *it wasn't like a gig*. Nobody was being paid to be at the Acid Test. The band was playing but they weren't being paid. When we went and worked at the Trooper's Hall or the Longshoremen's Hall, we were doing a show, we were being paid. It was different. Even in the beginning, there was a great reluctance to get weird at regular shows. There was no reluctance to get weird at the Acid Test because they said if they can't play it doesn't matter. If they don't play well it doesn't matter, because nobody is paying to see them, it's not a matter of having an audience that you're performing for, it's just a big party. But they had to be at the party, they were an essential part of the party. In their minds that was the essential thing that had to be done every Saturday night, which I found not to my liking at first.

What do you mean?
It was a little too weird, a little too heavy, and it was hard to control and it looked like too much exposure and made too much heat. All those things. I was not a real loud thing at that point, and I didn't want to be a loud thing or attract a lot of attention for any reason. And here was this scene that was so loud that if you put it on the moon it would attract attention. And here was this band of incredible musicians making this magic music, which I thought was more important to do than to do this other crazy thing.

So you were sort of an impetus toward professionalism?
I've always been that.

What was your goal then? Distillation of the musical thing? Were they not dosing for the gigs that were gigs?
Not often, and not like at the Acid Test. There was always a reluctance to do that because things tended to fall apart, they tended not to work. They have always had a sense of responsibility to a paying audience.

That is professionalism.
Always, right from the beginning. There was never a time that it wasn't there.

But at the same time they retained a huge amount of the nonprofessional ambiance of that. They always had that in appropriate proportions.
In the old days you went to a show and there were no spotlights on the band. There was a light show and there was a lot of other stuff going on. It was like a huge party anyway. And the band never were flashy dressers or anything, and they never sought being in the floodlights. It wasn't like that, it was the music. I don't believe that there was ever a time that the band wasn't more concerned about playing music.

People who say this, that, and the other about the Grateful Dead show are people that can't hear the music. The music sounds to them like it's meandering, or it sounds like it doesn't have a center or focus or anything else. Well, true, from time to time it doesn't, but on many levels it always has something happening. There's always a level at which it *is* happening. The thing is that some more straight people that go and sit down at the show, if the show isn't one of those dynamic, tight events, which maybe one out of four or five is *totally*, if it has any moments of musical misshapenness or elaborate bridges or just heavy sections that are jazzlike but never quite jell and focus—which sometimes happens, because any improvisational music will have that. I've even heard Keith Jarrett get into those kind of bags, where he'll go meandering off somewhere, and just doesn't come back to where you might like to see it come....I think that that influence in the music tends to make it that way, and if you've got somebody going to see something like that [who's] not jazz-oriented or who cannot really hear the kind of musical ideas that are going on, won't know and they'll say, "They're all over the place...no focus and no direction." You hear that all the time.

And that, of course, dilutes the gestalt energy in the building.
I don't think so. Gestalts are not always composed of everyone.

The more unanimity the better, I would tend to think. Wouldn't you?
No. I think, in fact, that the presence of every kind of person, every different level of engagement and disengagement, is more important. It's like a reaction vessel that has all the pieces of whatever can be made, and it makes something but it doesn't use all of the pieces all of the time.

But one of the things about it is the idea that the most distracted person can suddenly snap to, right? Isn't that one of the things that you would want to see happen in that realm? All of a sudden the music finds its focus and all of the sudden the wandering minds find their focus as well. I mean, that's one of those fun things about Grateful Dead, hauling in somebody who is unsuspecting and watching them get it.
It's like a sculpture. When you look at a sculpture, what you're looking at is the surface. You don't know what's inside, but there's more inside than there is surface, so most of what a sculpture is when you look at it is indeterminate. It could be nothing, or it could be something, or it could

be another sculpture or dozens of sculptures, or just random noise. 'Cause all you perceive in the sculpture is the form itself, not the substance within. The thing that you're talking about, the gestalt consciousness, is also like that.

I have strong tendency to use sculptural viewpoints in most things. For instance, when I'm working with sound, I work with sound in three-dimensional fashion which to me is palpably three-dimensional. I do that in the way in which I set up stages for a live show, in which I orient speakers, the kinds of electrical things that I do to the sound. To me it is physical, and you can walk through the hall and feel its shape and change, For instance, you experience a certain spatial form, dimensionality, if you listen to *Old and In the Way* with headphones or something—even with speakers. Move around the room: you seem to be moving around the stage, it changes as you move around. It's all valid but at one time you'll be on one side and at another time you'll be on another side, and sometimes you'll be in the middle of it. It's always coherent, it's always three-dimensional. But the spatial image changes, your perception of it changes, and it seems palpable. It seems real, like a sculpture. It's the way I look at sound. It flashes back to the time that I saw the sound coming out of the speakers.

You've only got two ears. The shape of the ear colors the sound, but you can detect all kinds of different things, the information from two auditory sensing units, one on each side of your head. Those two units create a totally three-dimensional space in your mind, and that three-dimensional space which is created from your sense is as illusory as the reality of the sound. But what your ears do is they tap into the total matrix of what is in the room. All the energy that's in the room, whether it's bouncing off a wall or coming from the speaker or whatever, enters your ears—and inside, your brain sorts it out. Because of the fact that humans use language as the single most important survival tool they have—our mouths are modified for it, our ears, our brains are modified for it; our brain does a tremendous amount. I watched a TV program where they were talking about the ability of the cat to localize sound, and I've read things about the dolphins and their use of sound and bats and their use of sound, and owls—most owls hunt as much with their ears as they do with their eyes. In fact, the facial disk of the barn owl is extremely important. Owls' ears have two different sizes and shapes; the feathers on one side of the head are different than the feathers on the other side.

I have something like that. When I was nineteen I had a diving accident, I jumped off a high board when I was learning some clown dives from a bunch of Hawaiians that were in the military station and were coming to that pool where I was working as a lifeguard. They were teaching me these clown dives, and in one of the clown dives you go off and you go in on your side with your hand over your ear, but you put that up at the last minute, and I missed. The water went in and almost shattered my eardrum. It didn't, but it caused a heavy hemorrhage which filled the entire inner ear with blood, and there was no way to get it out. The doctor didn't want to cut the eardrum and take it out. Maybe he should have, I don't know, but anyway…antibiotics in those days were pretty primitive. The result is that by the time my body had absorbed that blood clot some bacteria and mold together had established a culture in there. And the result of the culture was that it produced something sort of like arthritis in the three little bones that articulate together. There's nothing wrong with the eardrum, there's nothing wrong with the nerves, but the linkage between the eardrum and the nerves has to go through this bridge of bones, the articulation of which was interfered with by the scar tissue caused by that infection. The result is that the two ears have slightly different response. So as far as my brain is concerned, there's absolutely no confusion about which ear is which, just like the owls, with the two different-shaped feather things, the different-shaped ear holes [that] give them a totally different signal from the two sides of their head, which allows them to pinpoint the mouse, or whatever it is they're after, very precisely. And if you look at most animals that need a highly developed stereoscopic sense in their hearing, they have this imbalance between the two sides. Man's ears are not normally that different, but due to this injury—it's a funny thing where a handicap becomes an advantage—due to this injury, and the psychedelics which amplify everything, I was able to sort it all out, so I produce a sound picture where all of the high-frequency stuff is actually coming from my left ear because my right ear, above like six thousand cycles, isn't very sharp.

And the difference in the shape and sound of the two ears means that all the low-frequency stuff, which is the stuff that gives you direction because it's the phase-different stuff, the signal arrives at your head, there is only about six inches' difference between the two ears, which means that it's one two-thousandth-of-a-second difference if it's coming straight from one side. That's a very small difference.

Did you learn all of this stuff on the job?
Yeah. I knew nothing when I started. I just said, "Hey, yeah, I'll be the sound man, and we can use my hi-fi." I didn't know anything about it, but

I did notice one thing straight away, and that was that the instruments that they were using looked like somebody built them in their garage. When you opened them up they had parts that came out of a 1932 radio. And, in fact, that was about right. It was Les Paul who took apart a radio and put the parts in his guitar…put a magnet with a coil of wire wound around it in a guitar and plugged it into an amplifier. And that's where it all started. Basically the guitars in 1966 were identical. They still had a magnet with a coil of wire around it, six screws in the top of the magnet—and sometimes not even the screws—and a wax capacitor and a cheap potentiometer. That was it. Crude, very crude. The wiring looked like the wiring I used to take out of old radios from World War II and from old wooden house radios.

And the bodies themselves didn't seem to be all that well constructed. I thought, Here we are with the technology that is putting things in orbit around the earth, and what has changed? In the days of Bach, the highest technology that man could produce built the organs that he played, and here the musicians, the equivalent of Bach, modern musicians that are writing and playing music, are forced to play on something that looks like it belongs to the World War I and World War II period. This is wrong.

But I'm not an engineer, and never was, so I thought we gotta do something about this, and so I started looking around for someone that could help. I ran into this kid Tim Scully, and he seemed to know about electronics. I thought, "Hey, I need somebody," "Do you want to do it?" and he said "OK."

Is he any relation to the Scully tape recorder people?

No, no relation to them and no relation to Rock, who was the manager in those days, but he was a bright kid and he knew enough about electronics, how to wire two or three parts together.

All I knew, basically, was what I had learned to be an electronic technician in my Air Force period. I was a ham radio operator and I knew something about the theory of the operation of radios, and I had worked as a broadcast technician, but I wasn't a design engineer. I more or less understood how things worked and I knew how to solder stuff together so I could build things, but I didn't consider myself a design engineer in any way, shape, or form.

I knew we had to do something, because the technology was so primitive that it seemed like it was holding the music back, that we could go to another level if we had better instruments. Half the time they'd crackle and pop and hum and there would be distortion out of the speakers, it wouldn't be controllable and the guys would make a sound not what they wanted. So we went wholly the other way and we tried using hi-fi stuff. Hi-fi stuff wasn't heavy-duty enough, and the Voice of the Theatre speakers weren't strong enough. I went down with Tim and talked with the engineers at Altec Lansing, and they weren't interested. They said, "Well, you want power here, use this driver"—and that driver rolled off at three thousand hertz. "Oh, you want it to go higher? Well we have this one, it goes to nine thousand," but it would only take two and a half watts.

I said, "No, we want one that's this powerful that will go twice as far out as that; we want to go to fifteen thousand."

"Well, you can't do that. We don't want to, we're not interested. Besides, we sell all the speakers we make anyway. Get lost."

We went as far as we could and we tried and tried and tried, made all kinds of stuff, and even tried centralized, and eventually got to the point where in the fall of '66 it'd grown like Topsy into this thing which required a separate pilot over there controlling things while the band was playing, which was unsatisfactory. It didn't always produce just the kind of sounds that it was supposed to, which was a problem. All of their amplifiers, everything, the guitars all plugged into this box that Tim had. Everything went into this box. And then out of the box it went into the amplifiers and then it went into the speakers.

The thing was that nobody could define what it was that it had to do. The musicians themselves couldn't—they'd say, "Well, I play the guitar and I want to hear a sound." "What kind of a sound?" "Well, you know, the right sound." The musicians couldn't talk about it. And I hadn't a clue. I just knew that what was was too primitive and Tim, he didn't have a clue as to what to do. So we were constantly changing things, wiring stuff, trying to find out how to make it do whatever it was that everybody in their own way knew but nobody could communicate about. It was not something that could be defined. So this was just like one of those dead ends that you go off along.

It finally got to a point where it was just not working and everybody sat down and said, "Hey, it's not working," and I said, "I agree with you, I don't think it's working." And they said, "Well, we want to do something different." I said, "Fine, go to the music store and pick out what you want. I'll buy all the stuff you have now, for the amount of money it takes to buy all this stuff you need." So they went and got all of the stuff that they wanted, and I took all of the stuff and sold it off. I sold some to the Straight Theatre, some to Bill Graham, some to this, some to that—it all got sold. A lot of it I gave away. Actually I traded it back in to one of the music stores, and they sold it to Graham. And a few weeks later I walked into the Fillmore, and there's my old hi-fi on the stage!

By that time we'd learned how to improve some of the other kinds of amps. We improved the physical instruments by putting high-quality components in them: instead of $2.50 worth of parts we put $25.00 worth of parts—that alone improved a lot of things. We learned how to make better cords and stuff, and lots of things had improved. At that point I went off because there was something else I had to do; they went all off with this stuff and started playing.

One of the people that joined up with them at that point was [Dan] Healy. And Healy is a very pragmatic kind of a guy who liked to tinker with stuff and fix stuff. Not that he was a design engineer—he wasn't—but he was a consummate troubleshooter. He could go into something that wasn't working and find out what wasn't working and fix it.

His very pragmatic approach led him to go and just rent a whole bunch of speakers. He'd rent three times, four times as many drivers as he needed. So they's blow everything up in the first set, and he'd pull off the blown parts, put on another set, and halfway through the second set he'd be up there taking them down and fixing them and putting them back. And the rental companies would get all this stuff back and it'd be just blown to bits. So *they* went down to Altec, and they were big enough, right?

So when Harry McCune [San Francisco's leading sound contractor] went down there—

Right! When they went down to Altec and said, "Hey, this is no good," Altec started working on the stuff. We couldn't do it! We went down two years before and begged them to do it, nobody would do it. As soon as it started meaning dollars and cents, "Oh, well, we can rent this stuff, rent it, blow it up, take it back, because we don't have to worry about buying it." They'd raise the rental price a little bit, but they can't because they gotta rent to all these guys that *aren't* blowing it up, they can't make a special price to you because you'll go to their competitor, which was what happened—there were two or three different rental companies—and so all of a sudden Altec and JBL were getting all this blown-up stuff, so they had to fix it. It was no longer a point of why improve it, people are buying as much as we make. We put a financial twist on it, right? We started tweaking their ass real hard, because it was expensive to replace these, and so suddenly the big manufacturing concerns that had a monopoly on the sound market were forced into doing these things.

In 1968 the Carousel Ballroom thing came together and I was sound man at that, along with Bob Matthews. I started tinkering with the little amplifiers. Specifically, a musician named Elvin Bishop asked me if I couldn't improve the sound in his little [Fender] Princeton amp that he liked to play, which wasn't very loud and had to be miked in the PA. One time he played in there and he said, "Well, you know, I wish it were louder, but I don't want a Twin Reverb 'cause it's too much." So I started taking it all apart and applying some rule-of-thumb principles and changing a few things. I put in a different power supply, did a little hot-rod trick on the output stage that I'd learned working for a cheapo hi-fi company once back in the past, and did a few things to it, and it came out a screamer. I even put in a twelve-inch speaker but left the ten-inch hole in the front board—I made a heavy-duty front board and bolted it in there so it choked it a little bit, and it turned it into a real screamer.

It sounded good. Elvin liked the way it sounded and that was that. Then I built one for Jorma [Kaukonen] and Garcia and a bunch of other people, a lot of people did it. I wound up for a while having a sort of production shop at the Carousel hot-rodding these speakers. I'd drill an extra hole in the front and put in a middle control so it had treble, middle, and bass.

The whole idea was to try to bring the equipment, which is basically prewar design, up to date. We'd open up one of those things and it'd be full of wax capacitors. We'd pull all of those things out and put in modern Mylars.

So I started installing these things into the amps that the musicians were using, trying to improve them. We'd change the grounding systems; we put shielding in the guitars; we found wire that was foil shielded, and it had a couple of wires inside and we only used one of them, to drop the capacitances, because the longer the cord—especially the rubber cords— it's like taking the tone knob on the guitar and turning it down. If you took the guitar and used this little short wire about one foot long and plugged it into the amp, you could hear what the guitar was capable of putting out. So then you could compare that to a regular rubber cord, and it was amazing. It was just like turning the knob down.

I learned that from the radio stations, 'cause in a radio station if you have a ground loop you got a problem because the signal from the transmitter is getting back into the audio wiring in the studio. I chased down and pulled ground loops out of every radio station I worked for. Every single one had ground loops in it. If you can get rid of radio-frequency ground loops, audio is a cinch. So right from the git-go with the Dead, we got rid of all that stuff. It was very rare.

The only time we had a serious problem was at Woodstock. And the reason we had a problem with Woodstock was that the transmitter that they were using for the radio signal for their helicopters was grounded in one place, and the stage was grounded in another place. There were two ground rods driven into the ground, and they were separate. The result was that the ground system on the stage was not at the same ground potential as the transmitter. So all of the equipment on the stage was acting as a supplemental antenna, receiving the signal from the transmitter. And it was in everything! But worst of all was Phil's bass, for some reason. It really focused in on Phil's bass, and we were going nuts trying to figure it out, because it had been going on all of the time—every band that played was having this problem.

Well, I got the house electrician and we started searching. We found the two ground rods and I said, "That's it." We pulled the ground connection from the stage off that rod, ran over to the other side of the stage, and clipped it on to the same rod that the transmitter was going into. That was it.

How long did it take you to find that out?
Um, about ten or fifteen minutes.

Then what was the interminable delay at Woodstock?
The guys who set this thing up had this idea—they had these half-cookies, big half-cookies, a big circle, twenty-five feet in diameter, made out of plywood with two-by-fours underneath that were split down the middle into two half-cookies, with casters underneath them. They'd set a band up on a half-cookie, and then they'd set another band up back-to-back on a half-cookie. Then for the set changes, they'd rotate this thing around like a wheel, and then pull one off and slide another half-cookie over it with another band. That way they could set them up over on the side. They had like three or four of these cookies.

So one was performing and one was loading out.
Exactly. But! Ram Rod and I took one look at that and we said to the guy, "That ain't gonna work."
"Yes, it is."
"No, you don't understand: Our gear is so heavy that that will break. You can't put the Grateful Dead on one of those cookies."
"You've got to go on the cookie!"

"But we're telling you it's going to be a mistake! It's gonna be much simpler to let us set up behind these guys, take 'em off and then the other one can come in, we'll take it off, we'll move it as fast as we can, we'll get a couple of other crews, we got plenty of people—"

"No, you gotta go on the cookie!"

"Okay." So we set up on the cookie, and sure enough the thing hadn't rotated ten degrees when all the casters went "Wham!" [*Laughter*] Ten degrees! So now we had to do all of this while people were waiting. We tried to tell 'em, it might be a little longer but not a lot longer, because they could've shoved the other cookie out of the way, we could have set up, the whole thing would've worked, but they wouldn't go for it.

Now, go back to the Carousel when you were doing all of these mods for all of these guys. This was collectively run Airplane–Grateful Dead Carousel?

Yeah. [Ron] Rakow was managing it.

Were you connected to the Grateful Dead specifically?

Not at that point. I had a little problem in December [1967], and in January or February I was really itching to do something.

What had happened was they passed a law. The law said it's no longer legal to make [LSD]…It's a misdemeanor to make it or possess it or sell or anything else, it's a misdemeanor, mustn't do it. So we finished it all up, and I had a stash of material that was crystalline and couldn't be sold or anything. It couldn't be given away—I couldn't do anything with it because it was in a form that you couldn't handle. So I was thinking, I gotta put it into tabs, but I didn't want to do it because it was illegal.

Then the whole scene would run out. Nobody had any, so I thought, "Well, I've got to put it up" and when I did, an associate of mine was giving it to the wrong people.

It was an unfortunate event, and unfortunate circumstances, but I always looked at it this way: what I was doing wasn't for personal gain. And, in fact, I wound up with nothing in the end. We gave away probably more than was sold. We sold what we had to to keep the thing going. And it provided a fund for the inevitable, which was in case we got into trouble. And the lawyers ate it all and everybody else ate it all and it was all gone.

The powers that be don't believe that.

They think you're sitting on a few million?

The powers that be are sure I made millions. Millions.

Nowadays, of course, you couldn't pay your lawyer with that money, because they'd have seized it already. But let's not get into that.

Well, there wasn't anything to seize.

Remember I told you I wasn't quite sure whether it was a good thing or a bad thing? In order to have something to take, I'd make some. And then it would all go, and then eventually I'd run out of stash. So I had to go and do it again. But every time I did it, I was concerned about whether it was a good thing or not, so I'd watch. I'd watch when it came in, I'd watch as it went out....I had personal worries and doubts about it. When a guy who was a close friend of mine, when a girl walked out the window at his house on the second floor, and broke herself up—didn't kill her or anything, but broke her up—I was really upset for weeks trying to figure out whether that was my fault or not. What was my role in this and in all of these other things, and all the different things at every level of effect that was in my hands, so to speak, it made me very conscious of that.

When you went to trial, was any of this stuff brought in...or was it just a straight crime?

Nobody wanted to hear anything about it. The lawyers told me not to talk about it.

So the fact that you were being conscientious about it never entered the formula either.

It had nothing to do with it.

For a long time, they were never convinced that it was an underground person that was doing it. Because the dosages were so perfect and so uniform. They thought it was coming out of some company somewhere.

All I know is that I made it in small amounts, and it was very broken up. The total amount was so small that you would die if you knew how little I ever actually produced.

At one time?

Total. I mean, probably more than that gets made every week now.

Yeah, right. By less responsible people.

Who knows? All I knew is that I put my hand on the reaction vessel during the procedures, to put my energy in, to focus it, so that it could be the best it could be, and then I would work very, very carefully to purify it to the point where I'd throw away twenty percent, because to get the cleanest out some of it couldn't be recovered.

Anyway. So you got busted in December '67, and the Carousel was—
The Carousel started in February of '68. And I was looking for something. I needed to do something.

You were awaiting trial? Out on bail?
Yeah.

So you were hot-rodding amplifiers and hanging with the musicians and...
I was running the sound system. I was the sound mixer. Which was something I knew how to do.

So you didn't work with the Dead when they played the Fillmore, but you worked with them when they played at the Carousel at that point?
Well, when the Dead came in and played the Carousel I was the house sound man. When they played there Healy mixed for them because he was their sound man. I mixed for a lot of bands that were there.

The Carousel closed in June, and in July or August, somewhere along in there, Healy suddenly decided to go back to work with Quicksilver, whom he worked with when they first started. I don't know exactly why, all I know is that one day over at the Carousel, right about near the last shows in June or July, the Dead asked me if I would be their sound man again. And I said sure.

They were rehearsing in this gutted theater up in the Potrero, and everything was primitive, so I went to work for them again and started improving the gear. They were in the studio doing *Aoxomoxoa* all during that period. And I started working on the gear, trying to add the stuff I'd learned and bring it up to snuff. I was steady on with them from I guess mid-'68 till mid-'70, when they carted me off to the joint.

If I'd done the time that was appropriate for a misdemeanor—it was really only one offense, they made three charges out of it and strung 'em out—I would have gotten out in nine months. It wouldn't have been a problem. The Grateful Dead history would be different. Whether it would be better or worse, I don't know.

What do you mean by that?

Well, the scene had gotten bigger, more people had been hired, different kind of management, different kind of gig scenes. The whole thing had grown until it was quite large. When I left there were four guys working for the Dead: there was myself, Ram Rod, Rex Jackson, and one other guy that alternated between Johhny Hagen and Sonny Heard. They'd switch off, one would work for a while and then the other. So basically Ram Rod and Rex and I did everything. And we had the idea that every person should be able to do every job, basically, except that none of the other guys felt confident to sit in the front and mix the sound. But as far as any setting up, tearing down, we all shared the work and the responsibility, and if something had to be done, we did it. When I left [in July 1970], [Bob] Matthews became sound man. Matthews took over being the house guy when they stopped me going on the road, which was in February. They stopped me going on the road because we got busted in New Orleans. I had already been convicted and been sentenced and was awaiting my appeals. The Dead got busted and I was busted with them, and that sent a bad message to the judge, and he revoked my permission to travel. Matthews then became the sound man on the road, and I only worked when they were playing in the Bay Area, when they didn't have to travel.

Was Alembic an entity at that point?

Oh, yeah.

And it was formed by Wickersham and you and who?

In 1968, after I came back with the band, I still had the problem of primitive gear, primitive instruments, primitive gear—in particular the bass. Phil was playing a regular bass. Even though we hot-rodded it, it still seemed as though the technology could be pushed a little further. For a long time it'd be a problem to get...the guitars would be plenty loud, Garcia and Weir would be plenty loud, but you couldn't hear the bass.

Back in the Acid Test days I had discovered this cabinet that stood about three and a half feet tall and was about maybe twenty-four inches square and it had a big eighteen-inch speaker mounted in the bottom, face down. And it had flexible sides that were made out of Styrofoam with a rubberlike plastic around the outside, so when the speaker would move upwards, it would push the sides out; when the speaker would move down, it would bring the sides in. And it was built by a black dude in

Berkeley. It was called a Super Bass. And they used an Electro-Voice speaker with two voice coils in it. One voice coil was designed to go to the left channel of your stereo, and the other voice coil to the right channel. It was designed in such a way that it sort of filtered everything out except maybe one frequency, that must have been about sixty or seventy or eighty hertz, or something like that. Well, whatever it was, it was a large complement of an appropriate frequency, or subharmonic, that was in the bass. The result was that when Phil would play, this thing would provide just enough energy at the bottom so that you could feel it in your gut. I don't know that it was musically toneful. It gave him the power of the bass drum. You know how when you're standing right in front of the bass drum and you get that feeling, right? Well, you set this off to the side of the stage and hook it up to the bass with a big power amp on it and it gave that pump just like the bass drum to the bass. Phil loved it! All of us loved it! The dancers loved it! But it was really a pretty shitty piece of gear. But it did work, and I've never seen anything quite like it, before or since. But it was another one of our attempts to bring the bass up so that it could musically stand on its own with the other instruments, because it was always weaker. And so the bass was the focus of attention, right from the Acid Test days. Try to improve the bass, because the bass guitar didn't have the same standing or power, no matter what kind of gear you used, it just didn't have the ability to reach out and grab—it's much harder to get that much power at lower frequencies. The amps aren't as efficient, the speakers aren't as efficient; lots of problems with that.

So, shortly after I joined back up with the Dead, they found a warehouse out near Hamilton Air Force Base in Novato and moved out there. During this period of time I had met Wickersham because he was working with the recording scene on *Aoxomoxoa*. So I knew he was an electronic whiz, and a tape recorder whiz, and an audio expert and all that kind of thing. And along the way, through connections with the folk music scene—Bob Thomas and others—I'd met this fellow whose name is Rick Turner, who I knew was an absolutely beautiful maker of acoustic instruments. And he knew how to do the wood and all that sort of thing. I didn't realize that these guys are, like Chinese astrology, not what you would call totally compatible signs. One's a dragon and one's a sheep. The dragon and sheep are kind of on different paths. But Ron is a super sort of nice guy, a flexible guy. He's the guy, you could tell him something that's such utter total bullshit, that anybody else would say, "No, man, you stupid idiot, that's absolute bullshit," and Ron would start saying, "Yes,

yes," and he would very gently tell you and bring you to the point where you understood that what you said was utter total bullshit—without dumping on you. He has that ability to do it. And he's real smart, real smart.

Neither one of them really wanted to do it, and I sort of took them and stuck them together in the same pot, and said, "We gotta build better instruments and we gotta get the electronics together." I thought it should be called the Alembic, because the Alembic was the vessel in which chemical verification takes place. First everything breaks down and then it's built back up. It's distilled into the right thing. That's what we were trying to do, we were trying to take all of the technology and all of the experience and put it into a vessel. It was also the concept of the vessel, the concept of a place of where it could be done, which was the original, the warehouse was sort of thought of as the Alembic.

They wanted to give me a part of it, and I said, "No, I don't want a part of it, I just want it to be, I want it to exist, I want it to do this thing with this idea: that we're going to make the kind of tool, so that a musician can go and get the finest."

If you want to win a race and you go to someone like Ferrari and you want to get a Ferrari, they don't give you a Ferrari. You buy the Ferrari; Ferrari doesn't have to give you a Ferrari to publicize Ferraris. I thought the Alembic instrument should be like the Ferrari, it should have a name, it should be sought after. I'd see this thing…whereas Gibson would make, say a five-hundred-dollar guitar, and the kid in the young band he can't afford a five-hundred dollar guitar, he can't afford a one-hundred-dollar guitar, but he really needs that five-hundred-dollar guitar, because he can really play it. Instead, the guy that makes three-thousand dollars in twenty minutes at a gig, they give it to him, because he gets up onstage and plays it and everybody says, "Oh, that's the kind of guitar he plays." So the guy who can most afford it is given it for nothing, and the poor kid who would like to have it can't afford it, and he has to see this dichotomy. It's bullshit, in a way. So I said I don't like that idea. If the thing's that good, then the guy who really should have it, the top musician, shouldn't be given it for free. He's the guy who can most afford it, he should pay for it. And the other kid, he will aspire to getting that, because that's the pinnacle, like the Ferrari, you're inspired by the Ferrari. With that totally different consciousness, totally different idea, approached in a different way, make it the best, use the highest technology and constantly try to push the envelope, make it beautiful and so forth, that was the idea. That is, I think, to this day what Alembic is all about.

But it wasn't a compatible situation. Fortunately, through it all I managed to maintain good friendships with all of the people that were involved. They were all my friends to start with. And I'm very tolerant of people anyway. I like people; I find them interesting. I think it's one of the things you have to have to be a broadly based artist. If you don't have an interest in everything and in everyone, it's difficult. All of your stuff will look alike.

In those days, we rehearsed. In those days, we had sound checks. I insisted on it. I didn't like to go cold into a show. For one thing, the stuff was kind of primitive, and I wanted to make sure if it worked. And there had been a lot of times when it didn't work, and it was really embarrassing. As we were trying to pull it all together, the equipment was becoming better and better and we were starting to get rid of some of that bullshit that was going on, things like the radios in the guitars and noises and stuff. I always felt that in every hall, and every hall had a different problem, different grounding…wanted to do sound checks. The band always did sound checks.

And we rehearsed. We rehearsed not only to get the music together, but also to check on the band's gear—to check on the guitars and the wires and to do maintenance on the stuff, and to get together and to throw ideas at each other. After every show, we'd gather in the hotel and play back the night's gigs. That's why I was recording all the time. That's how *Bear's Choice*[6] got made. It got made because we were always taping. There was always a tape. If it wasn't a reel-to-reel it was a cassette. There was always a tape being made. Something that could be played back. Something that could be listened to. That was how I was learning. They were telling me when the balance was right, when the balance was wrong, when this didn't sound right, when that didn't sound right. They were critiquing their own performances, and so forth and so on. We would find a weakness and we would try to correct it, on and on and on and on. They taught me, I taught them, they taught themselves. We all learned. It was a learning matrix in which everything was a constant flow of ideas and so forth. And there was no isolation. Everybody was involved. That was the scene that I left.

When I came back in 1972, Matthews had taken over, and Matthews didn't look at it that way. Matthews saw things in compartments, like a union organizer. Everybody had a job and a responsibility and that was

---

[6]*History of the Grateful Dead, vol. 1 (Bear's Choice).* Warner Brothers 2721, originally released in 1973. "Recorded 'live' at Bill Graham's Fillmore East February 13 and 14, 1970," says the cover. The album was mastered directly from Bear's stereo recordings.

his, and this was his, and this was his, and this was mine. All isolated. And this went on for two years. I come back, and there's this scene that's totally different, where nobody is going and helping the other guy—"Oh no, that's my job, that's your job, well, that's this job, that's that job." And all of a sudden I found that the three things that I did—recording, stage monitors, house mixing; I tried to sit up close to the stage so I could see and hear what was onstage, run the mix onstage from the board—there were three guys doing that job! Each one fiercely defending his little territory. There was no "I can do this, you can do this, you can do that, and we can switch around" kind of thing. No, it was "This is mine, this is yours, this is mine." And every one of those guys that had taken one of those positions, although they said, "Oh, yeah, yeah, come back"— suddenly there wasn't a place. I was still smoking a lot of pot—I smoked a lot of pot in the joint; I was really stoned all of the time—I was still smoking a lot of pot, so I was being everybody's fool. You know how with kids somebody would get down behind you and the next guy would push you over, stick you in the aisle and trip you? It seemed like that, psychically; that kind of thing was happening, so I was flopping down here, flopping down there, and being a real nuisance. Plus, you know, you go and get locked up for two years, see where your head is at. I come out of that, bang, right into this high-speed scene, which was not what I expected, and which nobody would admit to me. Nobody explained to me. I had to figure it out. Why is this different? Why are these guys not being nice to each other? Why is there this heavy jockeying going on, all of this stuff?

So what was it?
   Power trips. Lots of power trips.

Any idea why?
   Well, I don't know. I didn't try to analyze it, I just couldn't deal with it very well. I tried, but going from something which I considered as being an almost tribal thing of everybody sharing in all of the work and all of the obligations, and helping each other like a bunch of brothers, all of a sudden I came back and it was like the union and the management. It reminded me a little bit of working in industry, where the guy comes over to you and says, "Slow down—Joe ever there can't make that many parts, do you want to make him look bad?" That kind of thing.

A tribal thing, it's like as many hands as can help to lift a weight is fine, but when it's compartmentalized out there is no place for your hand. "There are enough hands to lift it. We don't need you. But we can't say we don't need you because we're supposed to." So it was very uncomfortable.

So I got into working on the systems a lot and then they started saying, "Well, we want to be bigger, we want to go bigger." We had some gear that was the Dead's, and then there was gear that we'd rent. But the rental systems—our stuff was starting to be different. I was starting to experiment with stuff again, trying to improve, to go to another level.

I was mixing. Matthews and I were sharing the work. It was like, Why are there two guys out there? Nowadays, today, there's three guys in the booth out there, or maybe four, right? One guy worked...two guys work for the PA company and then there's the mixer, right? Okay, well in those days there was no PA company, it was all the Dead's stuff. Similar gear, but Matthews and I were doing it. And so we divided the work. It wasn't compartmentalized. My head didn't work that way. His head worked that way, mine didn't.

One day he went AWOL. Didn't show up for the show. So I had to recruit some of the kids from this college that were playing that gig to carry the stuff back. Two of them took half of our PA and split. At the next show, there's no PA. I said, "I sent it to the truck." [A crew member] picked me up and threw me into a water cooler. I said, "Hey, these are my tools, and it's my job, and you're accusing me of messing everything up? I didn't steal it."

I said, "The problem now is to make this show happen, not try to blame me, physically." But it was that edge—there was a lot of coke in the scene—and this idea that everybody had their own job and compartments...you see the compartments, you see remnants to this day. You go on the Grateful Dead stage and every musician has a compartmented-off cubicle with this little guy, and they don't help each other. Each one does his own job.

There was a lot of cocaine and they were bitching at each other and using abusive language, and a lot of beer and everything else. I was feeling very uncomfortable with the whole thing.

So when the Dead said, "Well, we want to go to bigger shows," I said look, from my conversations with Wickersham and Rick and John Curl, John Meyer, and others, I believe that based on what the speaker makers tell us now, I believe that we can build an integrated system where every instrument has its own amplification, all set up behind the band without any separate onstage monitors. It's a single, big system, like a band playing in a club only large, and the musicians can all adjust everything, including their vocal level, by having a single source, by using this point-source thing. Because I knew from the way in which I experience sound, that if you could concentrate the source so that all of the sound had a common point source, it would all be coherent. All the wavefronts would be like a single person speaking. And that, no matter what it did in the room, it would be coherent—it would make sense.

If you go to hear a symphony orchestra playing in a hall, there's a hundred violins and fifty of this and timpani back there, two or three flutes over here, bassoons over there—they're all scattered around over a huge stage. The trumpet, when he's playing, it's going up this way. Other things are going up that way, and yet everywhere in the hall you hear the orchestra. And yet, if you walk around that hall, every place in the hall sounds a little different but it's all the orchestra. It's all a valid mix. The balance is a little bit different, but it all has a texture. And in a really good hall it doesn't matter. You go way up under the balcony, even, and you hear everything.

And then there's the example given by this guy Bose, who makes a speaker set so nine-tenths of the energy bangs against the back wall and yet it sounds great, some people love it, it's their kind of sound, right? I coupled that with my memory of seeing the sound coming out, and I knew that this inherently should be the correct way to do it. That by assembling the speakers to that the bass speakers would have a significant fraction of a wavelength long, they'd start to couple like a radio antenna. And, therefore, they would multiply their coupling effect far beyond any simple dB of loudness—it wouldn't have anything to do with loudness. In fact, I figured, you could walk right up to the stack and it wouldn't be any louder, and that you walk away from it and it wouldn't get less loud for a long way. In fact, it threw farther than any common system today does, with the exception of a unitary Meyer. Well, you won't see a unitary Meyer.

Center field at the Oakland Stadium.
Yeah, that's a unitary Meyer. Just a single MSL-10. All that's needed is the unitary. But the system the way the Grateful Dead use it today is the old-fashioned split system, which was—remember, the first Grateful Dead PA was my hi-fi, so I set it up like the home hi-fi because I was in

love with stereo. I still am. And I put one speaker on each side of the stage—of course, in those days it was only twenty or thirty feet across. I started the speakers on each side of the stage, because before that it was whatever was in the hall, or plug your mike into the Twin Reverb. There was no musical PA in existence in 1966—zero, there was no such thing.

What did the Beatles do when they came?

When they played in Candlestick they used the thing that they announced the baseball scores on. There was no hi-fi, there's nothing onstage, just a couple of speakers running to the mike. They always sang that way anyway, nobody had monitors. We were the first to institute monitors. That was something that appeared. We didn't know how to do it, we just figured if they couldn't hear, nobody could hear. We had to work on it.

What was John Meyer doing at the time?

He was working for McCune and had developed the JM monitor system that they used. This is in 1972 or 1973. Then, very shortly after that, he got a grant of some sort and went over to Switzerland. So he was gone during the middle part of this period when we were working on this system. Wickersham had a lot of interaction with him during that period of time, and so did John Curl, who had originally been working at Ampex with Wickersham at the time we started recording *Live Dead* in 1969. So he goes way back in his connection with Meyer. All of these people were inputting right from the beginning into the scene, with me and later with Healy, and with Wickersham, so that we've got a matrix of idea people. Well, the big system was a concept which I had carried right from the time I saw sound coming out of the speakers. I just instinctively knew that this would do it, and I pushed for it even though it looked like it was going to be an incredible amount of work.

I pushed for it because I was getting pissed off at the way in which every time I tried to do something, somebody would interfere. I'm not going to lay any blame, it was a group-consciousness thing, and they didn't even think of it that way, but that's the way I thought about it and that's the way it affected me, getting me pissed off that I wasn't doing what I was doing before.

The scene had changed; it didn't seem to have a place for me. It took two or three years after I got out of the joint for me to get back to more or less normal—and during this period of time...I finally thought, "Well, shit, if I build this thing and it works, then it does a better thing," because I always felt that I was only an aid to the musicians.

My idea about the sound man is that he has to become transparent. The recordist is different—and I was always a recordist. But a sound man running the house sound system, he's only an assistant to the musicians. If he's a total contributing musician and a member of the band, that's fine. If he's not, he should make himself so transparent as to not be there. My way of doing that was by constantly playing the tapes back, making the tapes exactly like the house....I'd listen to the house, listen to the tape, listen to the house, listen to the tape...and get the earphone to sound just like the house—walk around the house, walk all over, walk up onstage—make the sound in the headphones as close as possible to what I was experiencing in the hall. I played the tapes back to the band and they could tell you whether you're right or not, whether that's what they would do. So I'd become as transparent as possible.

Bear's Choice is an example of the tapes where I was trying to make myself as transparent as possible. And it's very interesting, there's only like sixteen mikes on the stage. Period. I just moved the mikes around until the sound coming to the hall was like the sound on the stage. And if it meant one mic here and one mic sort of halfway between there and there, and only two mikes on each drum set, or if I moved them all around, I got coherent, lifelike sound that was out in the hall like if I was standing onstage, that was on the tape like it was in the hall. And then tried to make myself as little as possible, so it was mostly just the band.

So then, an extension of that is, why not have it in such a way that the musicians have control of everything? Why not? They should be able to. If everything is coming from behind them, and it's designed in an array so it couples to go out to the far audience, but onstage they're able to intercept just enough of it so that it's not too loud, not out of control, and they can adjust themselves, their own vocals, they're listening to the mix of their vocals and they can adjust the level so that it's just right. Then you don't need a sound man! He's out in front, maybe with a walkie-talkie, saying, "Tell Phil to turn up," or whatever.

But the thing was such a monster. It required so many people, so much bureaucracy, so much logistics, so many trucks, so many stages, so many boxes, so much wire, so many amps, it became this huge thing! Because it was very inefficient. It was capable of producing a sound, but we produced a sound with three truckloads of stuff that you could do today with one half of the stuff the Dead carry, normally, as a PA. Just one half of that, or less than one half of that would produce the same kind of sound—as effective as that if it was configured correctly.

But they wouldn't do that? If you could do it with half as much gear...

Why don't they? Because Healy likes the conventional arrangement of sound. He likes to move things from speaker column to speaker column and do other things with it. His conception of the way in which a performance goes on, like this, a musical performance, is at least partly the concept of the guy who's operating the sound system. He's specifying the sound system, he's arranging the show, he's inserting the speakers, in conjunction with the lighting. Mostly the lighting guys work around the sound. And the band onstage, all they know is their own little matrix of sound. We call that microcosm. The greater hall is the macrocosm. My concept is to make the microcosm equal the macrocosm. Healy's concept is that the macrocosm is his—it is separate from the microcosm onstage, and he produces his macrocosm by moving things from speaker to speaker...he does a lot of it with the drums and stuff. In order to do that, from his standpoint way out in the audience, he wants it set up this way. So that has to do with his conceptualization of the musical performance that's going on, which he's contributing heavily to.

What you experienced in a hall when I was doing it was the Grateful Dead. Hopefully, very little of it was me, because in the big system I was not even there—I was out in the hall listening to it or walking around, or tweaking something onstage, or taking care of something. For a while I was doing the piano.

So there was no mixer?

That big system did not have a sound mixer. That sound mixer was the musicians themselves. To the extent that they could properly hear what was going on and to the extent that they were communicating with each other and with the sound technicians who were wandering around in the hall, was to the extent that the mix was perfect and the sound was perfect.

But it was a logistical nightmare. There were a lot of problems.

It sounded gorgeous. The clarity of that system was stupendous, and the space between the instruments was awesome. I remember that stuff so fondly....

You could walk two thousand feet from it and it still sounded like you were listening to—

Well, I literally did that at the Oakland Stadium [June 8, 1974], I started in the third tier and during the second set we walked all the way down in front. I was right under Phil's feet when he hit this gigantic note in "Wharf Rat" that blew our minds. The clarity of that thing clear up there where the wind was blowing and right down front.
It was a coherent system.

Each person had his own single-point-source system?
Right.
... This thing was out of control. And I was in a position where I was only controlling it like a puppeteer controlling a lot of puppets at once. I couldn't make my influence felt directly.

You mean the PA itself was balkanized in terms of who was running what?
It was very slippery. The only reason that it happened the way it did was that I figured ways of feeding my ideas and things in through people without directly confronting them.

So each guy had his compartment, his stack that he operated?
At one point, Healy was doing piano. at another point I was doing piano, Healy was doing something else, somebody doing something else. It was like, there were three of us that were basically sound men. Wickersham, Dan, and I. It was very difficult to say who was doing what, because there was no sound mixer, because there was no mixing board. And so we were all working with it ... there was no mixer, so we were all involved in it. And, because of the way it worked out, it happened because of the ideas that I had—which I had because I had an image, I was working from an image. This image was fed in through a lot of different people, through Wickersham, through Healy, through Curl. And I assembled the thing, but it was like remote control. It was very difficult to get it all together, and the result was that I couldn't concentrate on anything.

So, this '74 system, which was spectacular in its effect and in its cost—
It was too fucking much. There was a lot of coke and a lot of beer and a lot of booze and a lot of roughness and there were too many people

working, there was too much weird shit going on and there were too many power struggles at the top—management against management against the record company. The whole thing was just this weird energy going, always this maneuvering. The brotherhood was gone. There was a lot of talk of brotherhood, but from my viewpoint there wasn't any brotherhood. It was like a lot of guys protecting their territory, this is mine and this is yours and this is the other. And I was in there with this concept of cooperative, tribal, brothers all working together where everybody could do everything and so everybody does what they do the best. It wasn't working. I was very uncomfortable. And every time I turned around, I was pushed a little bit closer to the perimeter. Or that was my feeling.

Eventually it just became too much, and it collapsed on itself and the band just backed away from it suddenly, just like with the system that Tim Scully and I built back in '66: finally one day they came out and said, "Hey, we can't handle it anymore," so it changed. In this case they couldn't fire anybody—they always felt like *that* kind of family. They didn't know what to do, so they just stopped playing, hoping that the people would go off because they had to make a living, that they'd go off and somehow do something.

What did you do?

I got involved with some agricultural experiments. So when the band was sort of getting back together, I wasn't around. When they started back up, they started back up with the guys who hung in the tightest. Parish was working with the Garcia Band and Ram Rod was involved in something or other, taking care of the place. The core guys were the guys who had clung to the Dead and made something to do, or somehow were there, and those were the guys that were there when they started back up. And the others had gone off in different directions. I didn't have the leisure or the money or ability to hang around, because I didn't have it. The "millions" that I made were vaporware. Didn't exist.

So, it started doing its number again. Somewhere around 1978 Phil asked me to be his roadie, and I went and I worked for a couple of tours as Phil's roadie. But there again, I organized his systems so completely that I was up in ten minutes, I was down in ten minutes. All of my stuff worked all of the time. And so I'd set my stuff up and I'd go to help somebody else, and all of a sudden, "What are you doing? This is mine, you can't, this is no good." And I'd have all of my stuff put away and I'd go and help somebody else pack up. "What are you doing?" Here, again, I'm still thinking in the old mode, I'm still back in the sixties thinking everybody's a pal, help out, give a hand here, give a hand there.

All of a sudden they said to me, "Well, we're going to go to Europe, but we don't need you in Europe. But we're going to give you a ticket to go to Egypt."

I said, "You don't need me in Europe, you don't need me in Egypt." Somebody gave me a ticket—it wasn't connected with the band. Gave me a free tour ticket to the thing, and I went there.

I said, "You're going to the highest temple of alchemy on this planet. You're going to the ancient place, the place that all of the writings are about, the place that all the books speak about, the magic place. You're going there to make music, that music's got to be right. What I think you should do is practice and rehearse and practice and rehearse, then go and do a tour of Europe and play the best you've ever played and get better and better and better and *then* play at the pyramids, at the peak!"

"No, we gotta make a record."

I said, "In six weeks you're not gonna make a record. We're not talking *Workingman's Dead* anymore. I know how you guys work in the studio. You're wasting your time. If you do lay down any tracks, and you do a good show in Egypt, you're going to come back and you're going to start all over again. You're wasting your time, you've got to prepare for this."

"No, we're going to make a record."

I went to Egypt, and I started very carefully with the third pyramid and worked every day a little closer. And the longer I was there, the higher I was. I couldn't smoke pot, couldn't smoke hash, after the third day I couldn't even drink wine. It would make me weird, and I got higher and higher off of the place, very carefully exploring it, and looking and feeling. Finally, I went into one and then went around to the second one, and finally went into the second. I'd been there almost a week before I actually got into the Great Pyramid. I was feeling the place out, you know, exploring and sensing it, touching it, thinking. And I hadn't read any stuff before, just the odds and ends. I purposely avoided reading the books and stuff all about it. I didn't want to go there with an idea. I didn't want to go there with a concept. I just knew it was the magic place. I wanted to sense what it was. So I steeped myself into it.

I, and four or five others, were like a team, we were just together all of the time, exploring all of the time. And we discovered all kinds of interesting things about the way sounds propagated inside the passageways and how they coupled. One of us would go to one place in the pyramid and one of us would go to another place, and finally I worked out what it was. It had very interesting properties. The king's chamber was terrible, it was an acoustic nightmare. It was all the wrong dimensions and all the modes were all out of sync, they were not harmonically related in any way at all. But a sound that was created in there would couple into the passages and then the passages would couple into the other chambers with their own resonances, and finally, like if you'd put a sound in the king's chamber, it would go down into the subterranean chamber and it had incredible qualities. And a sound from the subterranean chamber would couple on up to the top and there were certain sounds in the queen's chamber that would couple through all of these systems of passages. It wasn't like a thing with echo chambers in it, it was like an instrument.

Over the days, over the om-ing and the humming and talking and the listening to people in various parts of the pyramid as the tours went through it and whatnot, I began to realize that it was like a gigantic organ, or it was like the cavities in your head. If you could feed it at the appropriate spots and pick up sound in other spots, like having a speaker and certain microphones in each of these three cavities and you were able to choose which one was being driven and which one was listening, you could excite modes inside the pyramid that were beautiful, they were incredible. It was like this gigantic instrument, it was on a cosmic scale. It had certain frequencies that were almost imperceivable to the ear, but you could feel them and stuff like that. And I was thinking about, I was testing all of this, because I knew the band was coming.

So when they came down, they're all like this [*drooping posture*] after six weeks in the studio. And they come in two days before they're supposed to play or something like that. I'm as stoned as if I'd just been dropping a hundred mikes every day—which you can't do, but as if I had—and I walked up and I said, "You know, I think I know how to wire the pyramid."

"We got it all figured out. We're going to use the king's chamber as an echo chamber."

I said, "I've been around the pyramid a lot, and I really don't—"

"We're going to do it that way, and that's the way we're going to do it. Fuck you." So I said, "OK, all right." And I just went off. And I'm thinking that here's this place that's so full of magic and so full of energy that you have to let go of ego to just even perceive it. Here's somebody marching in with a head full of coke—or an attitude full of coke, if not physically; I don't know whether they were or not; most of them were smoking hash every day, and powerful hash it is down there—and they're trying to deal with this thing with arrogance and determination and will instead of trying to find out what it is! I don't think a single solitary one of those people went into the subterranean chamber. They were too busy riding on camels and smoking pot to go into the pyramid or to go into the second or third pyramid or any of that. Well, they climbed on top of it, but we're talking about the first thing that was built. They drilled this hole down and hollowed out this weird cavity, which is as big as this apartment of yours, with the strangest cutouts on the bottom, like some of those old factories where they have these weird big nineteenth-century machinery embedded in concrete and you take them out and you see all of these strange posts and cavities and weird things everywhere and you know there was something in there, you don't know what it was. This thing is not like somebody would ever carve this for any purpose except maybe there was a machine that fit it, or something as weird as that, as otherworldly as that. Totally strange place. Totally strange place. And, so all of this went on and I went on with my thing and did my studies and went to Cairo and bought a few items and walked the desert and looked at the scarabs, and did all of the things that you do in Egypt if you didn't have all of this other stuff, and they built the stage and assembled the stuff.

The first day of the first show came and it was so bad I left at the break, I couldn't stand it. I went back to the hotel, I said, "This is so pathetic, I can't stand to be a part of it." And then the next day came and it was a whole lot more together and it was doing a little bit better. I stayed for the whole show, but it still wasn't even up to working level.

The last night, the eclipse, the big thing, I thought, "I'm gonna get high, I don't care how weird this pyramid is, it's time." So, about an hour or so before the show [*mimes popping a pill into his mouth*], I take a little. I was feeling pretty good, feeling pretty weird, I'm down on stage. Here comes Healy. "Oh, Bear, gee, I'm really glad to see you. Hey could you go up to the pyramid and help [John] Cutler? He's having a little trouble in the king's chamber."

I said, "Gee, I'd love to help you, but you know I just dropped about two hundred mikes of acid and I don't think I want to go anywhere right now." He looked at me and my eyes were all like this and he said, "Oh, OK" [*Laughter*]

If they had done it the way I thought they should do it, it would've been dynamite and everything would've worked. Because everybody would've been there two weeks ahead, they would've had two weeks. They could have listened, they could have looked, they could have played, they would have had plenty of time, they could try something, if it didn't work they could try something else, and the whole thing would've been totally different because the Egyptians gave them carte blanche, they could've done anything they wanted. For just a few Egyptian pounds, they'd open all doors and we could go anywhere we wanted. No problem.

Remember I said the macrocosm and the microcosm are now separated? The macrocosm/microcosm of brotherhood and community, which was the Grateful Dead family, propagated out into the audience and took hold. When I went away, it was macrocosm/microcosm, the Grateful Dead and crew were the same as the people that were out there. Well, the band/ crew thing, as the stages got higher, and got higher, and got higher, it produced a separation, a gulf. And the microcosm turned into something else, but the macrocosm continued to be what it was. It has its weirdness, like the five-dollar nitrous balloons and stuff like that, but somehow it manages to compensate for those—

There is more community feel in the community than there is...

Our stage was sometimes two feet off the floor. I was *in* the audience. I didn't have a dais, I didn't have ropes around it, it was all...all it was was a couple of chairs and a table, with people all there, you know. I could walk away from my thing, go to the back of the hall, walk all around, nobody'd touch anything. Come back, no problem. If I left a chair there, the chair was there when I came back. Nobody touched anything. When I came back, out of jail, it had changed to the extent that somebody stole my tapes out of the booth, '72, at one show. Somebody stole my oscilloscope out of the booth at another show. The stage was big, it was high.

When I'm walking in the crowd, when I'm out in the zoo—which is what I call that tribal thing out in [the parking lot]—I feel the sixties, I feel the way it all was. In the old days, there was no separation. The Grateful Dead, the Deadheads, the crew, the band, everybody, was the same, it was all the same. That's what we were, it was like a family. The fact is, in the very beginning, we all lived in one house, and it was very tough. Totally different people trying to get along on a minimum amount of money is difficult. But it was a beginning, but the concept of tribalism, of brotherhood, has propagated out and maintained itself as the band removed from, as they got to the point where they come off the stage into the limos and are gone, from the days when they walked through the hall, through the people, hung around. Have a gig that would go to dawn, sometimes.

Well, I imagine it was changing steadily while you were around, but you disappeared for two years and things changed and you notice the skip as you were gone.

Of course. And it wasn't like I had just gone to Europe and come back. I had gone and I had been inserted into a matrix of stasis. I was inserted into something that I went into with a great deal of fear, knowing that a misstep could kill me. I didn't know what I was going to deal with, I didn't know how it worked, I didn't know what the rules were, I had no idea what kind of a game I was going to play and it was, like, "Oh, you want to learn to swim?" and they threw you off the fantail of a boat in the middle of the ocean. That is what it was like to me to get thrown into jail.

So, what was Lompoc and what was Terminal Island?

Terminal Island was the first place that I went, first Federal place that I went, which was at the medium-security lockup, which is a walled prison with a yard in the middle. San Pedro, Los Angeles Harbor.

And then I worked my way into a position in the mess hall so I could eat the way I've always wanted to eat. Then I got released from a hold that they had on me from the bogus charge in Oakland and I was able to transfer to the prison camp at Lompoc, which is a place without walls. I was only there for about seven months, something like that, or eight months. And it was during those eight months in 1972 that I discovered I could make things with my hands. That's where I discovered that I was an artist, and I would not have otherwise. I got into the maintenance shop there because there was no advantage to being in food service because they cooked everything inside the walled prison, Lompoc main prison, and brought it out on trucks, and so I wound up taking care of the floor in the place. I was responsible for the appearance of the dining room.

Having done a lot of time in the Navy, I knew how to produce a super wax surface that required minimum maintenance. Most guys would spend about four or five hours a day working on that floor, trying to make it look right. And I figured out that I could spend four hours one day a week and half an hour every day, keeping it that way. And it always looked absolutely like a mirror, the whole floor always just looked like it was ready for inspection, every day, because of a technique that I used on it: I got it very, very clean and I put a nice coating of wax and I kept changing the rinse buckets. I'd rinse a little area and change the rinse water, rinse a little area and change the rinse water. Kept it absolutely clean. And any kind of spill I cleaned up immediately during the meal, so there was never anything, it was always shiny, buffed out. I didn't have to buff it but once a week because I had treated it with a clean dry mop and kept everything off the floor so it didn't get tracked into it.

After a month or two, this big black guy came and they assigned him to be my assistant, and he immediately told me that I was *his* assistant and we were going to do it his way, and this was his way. I said, "Look, it's this way, we don't have to do any work, we can switch off, different days."

"No, we do it my way, I've been doing this for X number of years, and we're gonna do it my way. I'm in charge here, I've been doing this for a long time, and I know how and what you're telling me is bullshit."

Did he prevail?

Oh, boy. Are you kidding? I took one look at that guy and I went to the steward and said, "I'm scared of this guy. I'm not going to explicitly say that he's threatened me"—which he did: he told me he'd push my face in if I gave him any trouble. I gave him some kind of story that they accepted, and I got transferred to the maintenance shop where Bob Thomas was working. Eleven guys were assigned to this shop, and we'd figured out that it only took around four or five man-days a week to keep everything working properly in the prison. There was a constant amount of work that had to be done, certain things had to be done every day. So we figured it out that each one of us only had to work two half-days a week in the total time to get all of the work done, and so we switched it off, so there was always three or four of us out doing something and the other six or seven of us were doing things like—hobby shop! All of the tools! Welding, woodworking!

So you acquired some skills?

Yes. All the raw materials you'd want and all of the tools you needed to work it with...and all of that time on your hands. And all of that smoke that was being smuggled in, all those ideas that that would make you do. And you had to look busy, so whenever somebody came into the shop, there was always a whole bunch of guys doing something. There was a whole bunch of things being sawed and ground and welded and this, that, and the other, all this bustling activity, and there were guys out painting, so something was happening all the time. And the guard that ran it said, "Look, I don't want anybody sitting around."

"Oh, no problem, nobody's going to sit around." He was happy, he didn't care what we did.

Do they know what a successful incarceration you had?

I doubt it, I doubt it. I had a hard time in the beginning because I kept telling them that I didn't do it for money, I was just doing it because of service to the community. As long as I maintained that, my time was hard. I got shit from everybody. As soon as I stopped saying that, they assumed I did it for money and I acquiesced, no problem then. That was the only reason that you were allowed to be in prison, was because you did it for the money. If you did it for any other reason, you were lying.